Domesticity and Dirt

*Housewives and Domestic Servants in
the United States, 1920–1945*

In the series Women in the Political Economy,
Edited by Ronnie J. Steinberg

Domesticity and Dirt

*Housewives
and Domestic Servants
in the United States, 1920–1945*

PHYLLIS PALMER

Temple University Press

PHILADELPHIA

The epigraph to Chapter One is from "Contexts," *Different Enclosures: The Poetry and Prose of Irena Klepfisz* (London: Onlywomen Press, 1985; distributed by Inland), and is used here with the kind permission of the author.

Excerpt from lyrics of "The Girl That I Marry" by Irving Berlin at page 137: © Copyright 1946 Irving Berlin. © Copyright renewed 1974 Irving Berlin. Reprinted by permission of Irving Berlin Music Corporation.

Temple University Press, Philadelphia 19122
Copyright © 1989 by Temple University. All rights reserved
Published 1989
Printed in the United States of America

The paper used in this publication meets the minimum requirements of American National Standard for Information Sciences—Permanence of Paper for Printed Library Materials, ANSI Z39.48–1984

Library of Congress Cataloging-in-Publication Data

Palmer, Phyllis M.
  Domesticity and dirt: housewives and domestic servants in the United States, 1920–1945 / Phyllis Palmer.
       p.   cm.—(Women in the political economy)

  Bibliography: p.
  Includes index.
  ISBN 0-87722-585-0 (alk. paper)
  1. Domestics—United States—History—20th century. 2. Home economics—United States—History—20th century. 3. Housewives—United States—History—20th century. 4. Sexual division of labor—United States—History—20th century. 5. Social conflict—United States—History—20th century. I. Title. II. Series.
HD6072.2.U5P35   1989
331.7'6164046'09730904—dc20   89–4442
                                                                 CIP

For the Women of My Family,
May, Laurissa, Maurine, Ruth,
Sharon, and Ashley

Contents

Preface

Housework is a persistent reality in my middle-class life. No matter what else I or other women in my family have done, we were always responsible for a high standard of home maintenance. It has also been a persistent political issue. From the beginning of my life, housework has divided women along race and class lines, at the same time that they were joined in their commitment to tending for people and doing the job well.

This is a book about housework and about arguments as to which groups of women will do such, and how. The book grew from three large questions. First, how did women come to feel they had to take care of people in private homes? Second, how did this work come to have a low social value? Third, how did housework divide women's lives along race and class lines?

These questions had emotional salience for me. As a white woman born at the end of World War II and growing up in Texas during the 1950s, I learned southern racial mores and female identity in a women's household. Raised by a formidable grandmother, with the income brought in by my mother and her sister, I saw white women as self-reliant and independent in many ways unusual for the 1950s. In our home, women went to the office every day, drove the family automobile, mowed the lawn, tended huge vegetable and flower gardens, and managed the family budget. They were physically strong and intellectually competent. Nevertheless, they relied on and benefited from the labor of black women, whose services we could afford because black women had few job options in the still-segregated southern economy.

From childhood I recall languorous, long days that began with mornings outdoors before the sun's heat forced us indoors for reading, punctuated with baths and changes of clean, starched clothing that culminated in some pleasant dress put on to welcome my mother home from work at the end of the day. We could attain this respectability because we always had a black woman to do the weekly ironing. A "daily" who came once a week, the woman did other chores during the winter—vacuuming, dusting, light ironing. During the summer, though, the load of clothes was so heavy that she stayed on her feet over the board for most of the day's labor that my family could afford, turning out beautifully crisp white and pastel sundresses, blouses, skirts, and handkerchiefs.

Not until I was a college student who had fled the South and joined civil rights work in the 1960s did I understand how my family had been able to afford the work of these black women. My undergraduate reaction was that we were white oppressors who had exploited the cheap labor of black people. Not until the consciousness-raising groups of the early 1970s did I realize that the independent women of my family had felt they must have domestic labor in order to achieve genteel propriety. They needed help so they could go to work themselves every day (and earn one "man's" salary from two full-time "women's" clerical jobs). And they wished to maintain standards of middle-class respectability while protecting the men of my extended family from bother. They had not wanted to be strong; they had been forced to be. And they expected and could count on the hard work of black women to help them.

I vowed, of course, that I would never put the burden of my housework on another woman, even as I assumed that this work was "mine." Participation in the women's movement augmented this commitment. I would not exploit the labor of black or any other women. And so I labored through graduate school and my first teaching job, working full time at school and study and then grocery shopping, cleaning house, going to the laundromat, ironing, cooking meals, sewing, and giving dinner parties. As I moved to professional stature, however, and came to the mecca of professional womanhood—Washington, D.C.—my responsibilities grew.

Nearly all my women friends in Washington hire another woman to do some of "our" work. I have a one-day-a-week housecleaner, and several friends with young children have full-time housekeepers. Almost no one I know cleans her own house, and many do not do their own laundry or prepare most of their childrens' meals. A feminist and former civil rights worker, I find that I have, like my mother before me, turned over some of the most tedious housework to another woman.

Like my friends, I am a "good" employer. I pay a high hourly wage, give paid vacations, buy holiday, wedding, and baby presents, and treat the Guatemalan-born woman who cleans my house with the respect her cheerful competence deserves. Yet I am still responsible for getting the work of the house done, and I am able to do so by buying the labor of a woman who does not earn nearly so much as I and who lacks the automatic Social Security and health insurance protections of my job.

This book is fueled by my personal dilemmas: my feeling that I should keep an orderly, pleasant house and will be judged as a woman by my house-wifely skills *and* recognition of the low social value of this work; my commit-ment to racial and gender equality and acceptance of the difficulties of paying another worker the same job benefits that I receive; my belief in a multi-racial, multicultural women's movement, yet my own reliance on women workers to clean my house without all the work benefits I enjoy. The book explores the creation of these cultural attitudes in the era just before I was born and the ways government and social systems acted to exacerbate these contradictions.

Housework is the quintessential "woman's" work—regularly identified with women of all groups and social classes. No matter what other jobs women may have, they are expected, in addition, to see that houses are cleaned, meals are cooked, and children are cared for. No matter what else married women may become, they are evaluated on their performances as wives and mothers as much as on professional and work achievements. (Many men now launder, shop for groceries, vacuum, and care for children, but I do not know a household in which they take primary responsibility for these tasks.)

Even though it is central to the definition of womanhood, housework does not stand high in men's—or even women's—esteem. Few women now or in the recent past view an adult life measured by dishes washed, meals cooked, and rooms cleaned with satisfaction. The number of children raised is often announced with pride. The number of diapers changed, school lunches packed, or clothes folded is not. (Enjoying these activities on occa-sion—cooking a special dinner or cleaning the house after a long project is completed—is not the same as accomplishing these tasks every day.) Women with the means to hire another woman to take over the regular performance of this work have done so since the nineteenth century. Women without such resources seek to contain these tasks within a limited portion of their days. And the poorest women in this society must not only carry out these tasks for their own households but also do them for a living, in private homes during the period covered by this book, and in public spaces—child care centers, nursing homes, hospitals, office buildings, and restaurants—during the 1980s.

Humans need the services assigned to homes. Bourgeois ideals devel-oped in the nineteenth century (and refined in the twentieth century) of wholesome meals, cleaned and furbished clothes, pleasant surroundings, and children paid attention to are valuable increments in human life. Their attractiveness may be seen in the popular imagery of World War II, when war's end for soldiers was symbolized by visions of clean beds, fresh clothes, and home-cooked meals. Popular appeals to "home" in the late twentieth century, seen in movies as disparate as *E.T.* and *Tootsie*, have psychological undertones of emotional acceptance, but home is physically represented by country cottage furnishings, big dinners, and closets of attractive clothes.

But the development of comfort as a bourgeois ideal was confined to the private home and did not become a public responsibility. Women became the caretakers of daily human life, while men presumably organized the larger social and economic framework that enabled this specialization. Men's world of business and politics provided income, but men foreswore responsibility for the effects of business and politics on everyday domestic existence. And women's caretaking work diminished in public esteem as it grew in sentiment.

Marxists and feminists have given numerous explanations for the devaluation of the labor and material required to care for human life. Marxists point to the obvious fact that housework does not produce commodities for exchange and remains outside the evaluative field of capitalist exchange. Feminists point out the universal denigration of female-identified work, which includes child care, cooking, and laundry.

These explanations stress women's victimization and not their complicity. They do not take account of the differential experiences of various groups of women. In this study I seek to determine by what concrete historical processes women learned to do housework in certain ways and learned their places as mistresses and servants, and how these concepts fit into general social and legal attitudes toward women's work and women workers. How did women come to accept arrangements that sustained the low value of the essential human work assigned to homes?

Why have we put up with the low value accorded to our central work role? Why have some women (op)pressed other women into service instead of protesting our exclusive responsibility and challenging men to work with us to reorganize how, where, and by whom housework is done?

My theoretical interest in housework and in the relation among women of different races and classes, coupled with training as a historian, led me to the topic of household work in the period from 1920 to 1945. In this book I am concerned with public debates in that quarter-century on the subject of paid household labor. The book examines the cultural perpetuation of romantic images of housewifery while social institutions simultaneously maintained a low value for housework and the personal services traditionally carried on where people live: cleaning, food preparation, and dishwashing, caring for children and the ill and aged, laundry, and the washing and cleaning of human bodies. This dichotomy is echoed in the division in household labor between women employers (primarily white and middle class) and the laboring-class women (black, Hispanic, Indian, Asian, sometimes white) who worked for them, which is a major subtheme of the book.

The interwar years in the United States attracted me for three reasons. First, sharp racial and class distinctions existed between women hiring and women being hired to do housework in this period. As of the 1920 decennial census, women of color assumed central importance as household workers. The waves of white immigrants from eastern, southern, and northern Europe that had supplied the majority of domestic servants in previous decades had been halted by war; immigration restrictions adopted in 1921 and 1924 drastically curtailed any postwar resumption of immigration.

As early as 1920, at least two out of five of the 15.9 percent of American women workers employed in laundry and domestic work were black. Throughout the two decades before World War II, the racial balance in the occupation hovered at 50:50 (despite counting the numerous Mexican-American domestics in the Southwest as white). Within the black population, the occupation defined norms for adult working women. By 1920, 46 percent of black women workers were domestics and launderers, compared to 22 percent of employed foreign-born white women and eight percent of employed native-born white women, including Hispanics.

The second attraction of this period is the existence of abundant data about what women did in private households (which is usually outside public scrutiny and difficult to document in historical records). Middle-class women's reform groups, continuing the Progressive tradition, focused on the improvement of conditions in domestic work: the largest and worst off of female occupations and the only one, to the reformers' embarrassment, controlled by women employers. Dozens of reports, surveys, articles, and letters documented conditions as reformers, housewives, and domestics struggled to standardize the job, to win government regulation of its hours and wages, and to adopt voluntary contracts. The rich holdings in the National Archives, the Library of Congress, the Arthur and Elizabeth Bancroft Schlesinger and Sophia Smith Women's History collections, and the National Board offices of the Young Women's Christian Association yield a remarkably detailed record of work life in private homes.

The third reason for examining the subject in this period is the historiographical foundation laid in studies of nineteenth and twentieth-century housework and household technology. Thanks preeminently to the work of Elizabeth Clark-Lewis, Ruth Schwartz Cowan, Faye Dudden, Evelyn Nakano Glenn, David Katzman, Vicki Ruiz, Mary Romero, Susan Strasser, and Daniel Sutherland, housewifery and domestic work are beginning to have a history. Pre-1920 employment trends and work relationships set the stage for studying the final era in which domestic work was a major job for women. Nineteenth- and twentieth-century trends in household technology and municipal services are the backdrop against which work in the home is done.

After 1945, live-in servants virtually disappeared and day work became the norm for domestic service that remained. Much of the work was taken over by the commercial service sector, where it continues to be done by low-wage workers who are usually women and often women of color, deprived of many labor protections and job benefits. I hope that this book provides a historical base for a better understanding of these contemporary relationships.

Finally, I hope this book illuminates why and how middle-class women have accepted the current design of housework, including its reliance on the labor of other women—often women of color, nearly always poorly paid, and usually relatively powerless because of age, immigrant status, race, and, in many cities in the late twentieth century, sexual preference. It is time for us to accept more responsibility for how housework took its current form and to work to change its design and raise the status of the valuable jobs required to care for human life.

Acknowledgments

Librarians guide historians to the nuggets hidden within massive collections. Those important for this book were numerous: at the Arthur M. and Elizabeth Bancroft Schlesinger Library and Archives for Women's History, Radcliffe College, manuscript director Kathy Kraft, library director Barbara Haber, and general director Pat King; at Cornell University's Labor Documentation Center in the School of Industrial and Labor Relations, historian–director Richard Strassberg; at the Archives of the National Board of the Young Women's Christian Association in New York City, librarian and YWCA historian Elizabeth Norris; at the Sophia Smith Collection, Smith College, archivist Dorothy Green; at the National Archives, most important because most difficult to penetrate, archivists Ken Heger, Jerry Hess, Jimmy Rush, and Aloha South; and at the Manuscripts Division, Library of Congress, Jacqueline Goggin.

A Schlesinger Research Support grant in 1983–1984 and grants from the George Washington University's University Research Committee in 1984 and 1986 provided the travel and copy funds necessary for a historical project and for the coding and analysis of 1934 household expenditure data. More important, they provided me superb assistance from the Schlesinger Library and Archives student aides and from four stellar George Washington University graduate students: Barbara Steffens, Mindy Chateauvert, and Jennifer Watson from Women's Studies and Lorna Forster from Sociology. Graduate Dean Henry Solomon facilitated university grants and eased my teaching load at key points.

Editors and readers clarified the book's direction and enabled me to see it to fruition. Sonya Michel's comments, Ronnie Steinberg's editorial savvy, and Michael Ames's efficient management helped me bring this book into existence.

During a 1986 sabbatical, I was provided with congenial writing space by Susan and Asa Briggs and Lisa Spry-Leverton. Rosemary Foot and Tim Kennedy helped out with a computer. My health was maintained by AA, Alexander Technique teachers Ulla Simmons and Michael Gelb, and acupuncturist Dianne Shelton.

Thinking of the myriad discussions, books, articles, and conference presentations that stimulated and nurtured this book is to recount my life of the past seven years. Among the most significant stimuli were the women in the Washington Women Historians, the Chesapeake Area Group of Women Historians, and the Washington area Marxist–Feminist Study Group. A group of scholars dedicated to making domestic work visible has been a constant resource: Shellee Colen, Bonnie Thornton Dill, Faye Dudden, Evelyn Nakano Glenn, Janet Golden, Elaine Bell Kaplan, Elizabeth Clark-Lewis, Mary Romero, and especially Judith Rollins, who generously read chapters and gave thoughtful criticisms. George Washington University colleagues who gave expert assistance or encouragement from their own research were Ed Berkowitz, Joe Gastwirth, Sheldon Haber, James Oliver Horton, Ann Romines, and Roberta Spalter-Roth.

Women friends, many with scholarship in divergent or related fields, asked good questions throughout the process and helped me believe in this book. I give thanks to Elaine Beilin, Eileen Boris, Jann Warren-Findley, Dee Hahn-Rollins, Vivien Hart, Mervat Hatem, Rubye Johnson, Terry Odendahl, Sharon Parker, Carol Rose, Michele Slung, and especially Jane Flax, friend and sister book-writer through the entire process.

Family always stand last in acknowledgments, sources of emotional though not necessarily professional support. I feel fortunate that my friends and family so often give me both. I thank the women of my family in the dedication, and here I recognize the affection and happiness I draw from my brother Sam and my nephews Laird and Mark. "Jason," woman's best friend, curled himself comfortingly at my feet during many days of reading and writing. My goddaughter Elizabeth shared weekend jaunts that re-created me. My family by marriage, Toni and Chris, Shay and Toby, Jason and Arlene, gave friendship, apartment space, and good design advice. And my true companion and husband, Marcus Cunliffe, helped me to believe in myself as creator and as book-writer.

Domesticity and Dirt

*Housewives and Domestic Servants in
the United States, 1920–1945*

One

Domestic Work Between the Wars

The building across the street
has an ordinary facade, a view of the park
and rows of symmetrical spotless windows.
Each morning, the working women come to perform
their duties. They are in starched white,
could pass for vigilant nurses keeping
order and quiet around those about to die.
And each morning, idle women
in pale blue housecoats, frilled and fluffed
at the edges, stare out of double windows,
waiting for something to begin.

With whom would you change places, I ask
myself, the maid or the mistress?
—Irena Klepfisz, "Contexts,"
    in *Different Enclosures*, 1985

This book describes housework in middle-class homes, and especially relations between housewives and servants, from 1920 until the end of

World War II—the final moment when housewives in large numbers could hope to hire another woman to do part of the work designated as "theirs." In contrast to most accounts of women's lives in the 1930s, mine stresses that a large group of women continued to employ domestic servants and to define themselves as mistresses, while large numbers of working-class women, especially women of color, saw domestic work as their most likely paid job.

A conservative era so far as women's roles were concerned,[1] this twenty-five-year span witnessed the perpetuation and heightening of household standards designed for a servant-aided home. Though household technology changed, and though women sought to modernize their homes through better management and equipment, ideals of domestic graciousness and service persisted in popular ideology and were sustained by the chance of hiring at least some servant labor. A majority of households, including those of the women working as domestics, could not afford to buy another woman's labor; nevertheless, middle-class housewives were considered the norm for all American women. Well-tended domestic space was upheld as the ideal center for social life.

At the end of World War I, feminists, educated middle-class women, and many working-class women had anticipated a liberation from work in the private home. Some had experimented with alternative housekeeping plans during 1917–1918 and expected the war and its aftermath to end access to domestic labor that the private home could afford.[2] Though Charlotte Perkins Gilman's demand that the major tasks of the private home be turned over to commercial agencies remained utopian, as did the architectural plans for cooperative apartments, most educated women did not foresee spending most of their adult lives doing housework with house care as their primary concern.

By the mid-1920s, however, alternative possibilities had faded, weakened by the rapid spread of household gadgets and directly countered by political opposition to changing woman's primary role of non-wage-earning housewife. When the depression added economic policy to popular moralism, most women with education sufficient to obtain good jobs gave up claims to paid work and accepted housework and voluntary activities as their social role, filling days with a rigorous schedule made possible by the expanded number of servants unable to find other jobs.[3]

World War II freed many working-class women from the necessity of taking domestic work, but it did not liberate middle-class housewives from their primary obligation to care for children, husbands, relatives, and homes—jobs construed as war work such as planning the healthiest use of food, clothing, and morale-raising leisure.[4] When the second great war ended, these middle-class women found their ideal images and their work firmly attached to housewifery, but with decreased servant labor force. The stage was set for them to follow working-class women into the paid labor

force and for increasing tension between full-time housework and more frequent, though often part-time, employment. In the early 1960s, this tension
would burst into a renewed critique of private housework, as well as of
women's status in the paid labor force.

The argument thus far summarized is unorthodox. Some historians of
housework between the wars have found the central theme in technological
innovation and dispersal of goods through commercial advertising and in-
stallment buying; they have shown middle-class women accepting household
confinement in return for an ease supposedly brought about by newly available home appliances, whether or not these actually lightened housework.[5]
For others, the primary theme is male conspiracy, with manufacturers and
physicians, aided by advertisers and abetted by female home economists,
giving women an obsessive concern with their children, their furniture, their
food, and their attractiveness as sexual and social partners.[6] Women felt
"modern," according to this view, if they could buy new, streamlined appliances, even if they were doing more of the daily drudgery of cleaning and
cooking, as well as more child care.[7] The common assumption is that women
generally were unable to hire domestic service, which became a prerogative
of the rich and was, therefore, of only minor interest to women's history—an
evaluation apparently confirmed by the shrinking proportion of women's employment in private household service. Service remained a significant part of
life, this interpretation goes, only in the South, where a labor force was held
captive by racial discrimination and a relatively undeveloped economy, and
only for the black women who predominated in the occupation.

My story, on the other hand, stresses the transitional nature of the interwar years. It seeks to understand better how educated middle-class women
came to accept a career in the home, rather than a paid job outside, as a
sensible use of a college or high school degree and a satisfying adult existence. What happened to the progressive impulses released by higher education and solidified in the suffrage victory? How did an intelligent, well-
trained woman come to believe that developing her sexuality (including its
maternal side) brought greater emancipation than earning an income? These
choices were certainly pushed by many forces, including the cultural power
of Freudian psychology's animosity to lesbianism and praise of heterosexual
intercourse; economic recession that reduced job opportunities; political
hostility to Bolshevism that was presumed to underlie feminist demands;
and feminism's own confusion about what constituted liberation for women,
that precluded escape from, or reevaluation of traditional female roles.[8] One
underestimated factor was the sustained conviction that educated women
might become housewives without devoting most of their energy to housework; they would direct servants.

Appliances lured such housewives to accept traditional housework arrangements, but only the ability to turn over much of the work to other

women—less powerful in age, class, or race and ethnicity—sealed their acceptance. Instead of cooperatives or commercial services, housewives settled for household equipment and the prospect of some domestic service.

Women able to buy some domestic labor retained thoroughly traditional attitudes about servants. Throughout the period labor reformers and home economics experts advocated businesslike treatment of servants through contracts, limited hours, and higher cash wages, but little improvement occurred in these areas. As women of color came to make up even more of the group of potentially employable servants, patterns of racial dominance and deference formed in slavery, agricultural peonage, and reservation policy may even have reinforced notions of the housewife's superior intelligence and culture and the domestic's inferior ability and character. Appliances improved, and relatively scarce workers bargained for shorter working hours and more freedom away from the job. Housework, nevertheless, continued to dominate life for middle-class wives, and they, in turn, sought as much docile service as they could pay for or coerce. Indeed, only the ability to hire some work kept the middle-class woman from looking like a working-class wife whose days were absorbed by housework.

Middle-class matrons not only got work done but also confirmed their self-worth as women through a mistress–servant relationship amplified by class and race distinctions. That such service came from working-class women, the majority of whom were from racially subordinate groups, provided confirmation for the housewife that she was a superior person and would be honored as such so long as she remained a homemaker. Judith Rollins's *Between Women: Domestics and Their Employers* describes how social and cultural patterns of maternalism and deference have characterized domestic work throughout its long history.[9] In the mid-twentieth century, the rewards of the contrast between housewife and servant were as important as the attractions of consumerism to the middle-class woman who decided to spend much of her adult life as a housewife.

The use of a cheap labor source, kept inexpensive by systemic social inequalities, is as important as the spread of electric appliances—perhaps more so as we seek to understand how barriers to interracial and cross-class cooperation were maintained in the past. With middle-class women now in the labor market and facing the need to find caregivers for children and the elderly, the same danger exists in the 1980s—that such women will advance their own economic well-being and social status through the low-paid labor of the low-status, primarily immigrant, older, and dark-skinned females who take these jobs. Documenting the circumstances and means through which middle-class women chose to accept the image of the housewife during the transitional period of the 1920s and 1930s may alert us to contemporary political and cultural dynamics in this era of choice.

A Brief History of American
Mistress–Servant Relationships

Housework is women's work and has been in the United States, as elsewhere, for the past two hundred years. Its antiquity should not lead us, however, to imagine that housework remains essentially unchanged, except for modern innovations of gas and electrical appliances and running water. A domestic revolution accompanied the industrial revolution, and housework changed as much as manufacturing work did. Between 1780 and 1840, much of women's home production was taken over by factories, leaving the wife to oversee purchase and use of factory-made goods and to turn her attention to child nurturance and household morals. By the turn of the eighteenth century, bourgeois women living on the eastern seaboard in burgeoning cities or small towns along commerical routes became responsible for domestic life more than for family economy. (Women on the frontiers of population movement or in rural economic backwaters continued to be active producers. Civilization's westward expansion was measured, throughout the nineteenth century, by how much housewives were freed—or displaced—from home production by access to and the means to buy manufactured products.)

Barbara Welter has described ideals of early nineteenth-century, newly urban housewives, norms purveyed through magazines and novels for all proper women, whether married or only aspiring to marriage, as the "Cult of True Womanhood." Whatever their particular household arrangements or skills, women were uniformly enjoined to be "pious, pure, obedient, and domestic."[10]

By midcentury, growing food, keeping animals, making candles, soap, and cloth—respectable activities for female ancestors—were considered out of place in the urban home. Domesticated women filled their days not with spinning thread but with tending children, shopping for food and furnishings, preparing meals, cleaning up, and supervising the servants who took over as many of these tasks as the housewife felt she could entrust to them.

Directing servants was a new task for many. In the urban environment, as Faye Dudden has shown, a wife's new or newly enlarged obligations appeared dialectically with new conceptions of servant labor. The wife no longer needed an assistant to help produce goods and process food. She needed a servant to take over much of the physical work of the home so that she could concentrate on expanded social and emotional duties: seeing to her husband's comfort,[11] developing the moral and intellectual capacities of her children, and organizing charities to assist the poor, ill, and untutored. The wife also had to learn to evaluate and purchase food, furniture, clothing, and entertainment for family use. Middle-class wives filled their time with tasks of sociability and consumption that required much of the remaining work of the household to be turned over to a servant (or servants) who could perform manually what the housewife willed.[12]

In northern cities by the mid-nineteenth century, the social rank of households could be ascertained by a domestic as well as an occupational scale. At the top of the scale, homes employed several full-time, live-in servants; at the bottom, homes sent out women to service as "dailies." Among the wealthiest, the wife did no physical labor. In the middle ranks, wives expected that some portion of their labor could be turned over to other women, even if only for one day a week or for the years when the house was full of young children. In the artisanal working class, wives could not afford to pass on any of the labor, but they might be prosperous enough not to be obliged to work in someone else's home. Among the poorest, especially newly arrived immigrants and urban Afro-Americans, women were likely to do the work of their own and their employers' houses.

Southern cities before the Civil War imitated the southern countryside, relying on black slave labor for the work of the house as well as field and factory production. Slave labor made possible an aristocratic ideal of personal service, including a wet nurse to spare the new mother disfigurement from months of breastfeeding. Meals were cooked and served, clothes washed and ironed, children tended, errands run—in the hottest summer heat or the deepest winter cold—for no wages and no restraints but the owners' good sense or kindness. Even though plantation mistresses remained responsible for production work, much of which they did themselves, service was a job for slaves.[13] After emancipation the imagery of service remained intact.[14]

White Americans were trained in or learned from the southern model after the Civil War, and northern beliefs in the housewife's duty to supervise labor meshed with southern beliefs in leisured ladyhood. Coincidentally, the rise of corporate wealth created a northern version of the well-staffed household. During the 1890s Mount Holyoke and Wellesley colleges ended a tradition of students' doing their own housework and hired domestics to tend the students' dormitories, recognizing that students' families could afford the extra service and expected their daughters *not* to need training in domestic work.[15] Racist beliefs in black inferiority combined with racial–ethnic hostilities toward new, non–Anglo-Saxon immigrants. By 1900, white women, as soon as they had enough money, turned their housework over to a variety of less powerful women—Afro-American, Mexican-American, Asian-American, Indian, European immigrant, or rural migrant—whom they perceived as inferior. Just as white men derived status from a racial–class hierarchy, so did white women.

Into the early twentieth century, marriage remained a life goal and domesticity a center of women's existence, but ideals focused more on man than God. By then, women were encouraged to be beautiful (and youthful), sexually alive (but not immodest), and intelligently charming (but not overly intellectual).[16] Carroll Smith Rosenberg has concluded that the modern woman organized her life much more around men and heterosexual rela-

tions, whereas her predecessor lived in a female world designed to complement men's. By the 1920s, women's magazines purveyed a picture of sexy,
well-educated partners in companionate marriages.[17]

The deployment of household labor shifted in accord with a number of
economic, social, and demographic changes: substitution of purchased products and services for household-processed goods (e.g., heating canned vegetables instead of cleaning, cutting up, and boiling or steaming fresh ones),
using electrical appliances for tasks such as vacuuming, and a generally
smaller household because of fewer children and smaller dwellings.[18] The
work of housewives became less physically demanding, with or without servants, even though the required time and emotional commitment may have
increased, an ironic outcome that Ruth Schwartz Cowan notes in her study
of household innovations, *More Work for Mother*.

As Cowan indicates, the expectation that mothers would spend more
time with children was linked to the belief that psychological development
depended on mothers' scientifically informed supervision. Marriages based
on the couple's mutual satisfaction required that wives develop themselves
and entertain husbands socially, intellectually, and sexually. In addition to
these tasks, middle-class women had to serve meals, keep house at a high
level of physical and aesthetic comfort, and manage laundry—all at a higher
standard than in preceding decades.

Most housewives sought a subordinate worker to relieve the load, even
if only a part-time "daily" or "hourly." Wives in the 1920s and 1930s still aspired to have domestic help and welcomed having any work removed from
their shoulders. Wives reluctantly acquiesced in the transition from servant to wageworker that accompanied their own transition from mistress to
housewife.

By 1940, the balance was shifting and housewives were doing more
housework, able to hire other women's labor only for day labor. Postwar films
such as *Mr. Blandings Builds His Dream House* (1948) persisted, though, in
depicting typical family life as upper middle class, signaled in this movie by
the family's being served by the live-in, affable black maid Gussie.

A Statistical Profile of Service from 1920 to 1945

"Personal service: Private household" was the category in which the
largest number of women worked until the 1950 U.S. census (when it dropped
to fourth position). Until the 1980 census, when 51.4 percent of women over
age sixteen held paid jobs, the majority of women listed their occupation as
"housewife."[19] The number of domestic servants "increase[d] substantially—
roughly by a third—from 1900 to 1940," with expansion ending during the
1930s. But population expanded even more rapidly so that "the ratio of servants to private families fell 16 percent . . . from 1900 to 1940."[20]

Most historians have calculated the proportion of the population able to hire servants by taking the total of servants reported in the decennial census and dividing by the number of families. This method yielded a ratio of about one in fifteen housewives employing servants (about 7 percent) in 1900. Throughout the 1930s, commentators concluded that 5 percent of homes had servants.[21] By 1950, that possibility had declined to one in forty-two (2.5 percent). All of these figures seem small, and the inference is that most women did most of the work of their households, which certainly explains why power-driven appliances were so eagerly welcomed.

Gross census numbers are deceptive, however, for several reasons. First, all households in the country, including those of domestics, were included in calculating the ratio of servants available, a ludicrous method because it implied that all households, including those of servants, had access to hired domestic labor.[22] Planners throughout the period often spoke, indeed, as if every household—or at least those with young, sick, or elderly members or other special problems—should be able to count on domestic aid.

Second, these ratios assumed that each domestic worked as a full-time servant for one family, which was not accurate by the 1920s. After 1920, housewives hired dailies and part-time workers who came for half a day all week or a full day for part of a week. In fact, many domestics worked for two or more families. Though the full-time, regular-duty, live-in or live-out maid remained the image of the domestic, housewives and advice-givers began to admit that a part-time or day worker earning an hourly rate was equally welcome and perhaps more efficient and practical.

Servants were concentrated among particular groups. If the poorest households are excluded from the statistics, the percentage of homes with service increases dramatically, as indicated by 1930–1931 studies of urban, college-educated homemakers, or middle-class families, from 20 to 25 percent of which had a servant.[23] Studies of members of the American Association of University Women (AAUW) and of self-described career women–homemakers published in the late 1920s concluded that two-thirds of the AAUW working wives and 90 percent of the career women who combined marriage, motherhood, and professions had some domestic help (and half the AAUW set had full-time help[24]). A 1937 survey for *Fortune* magazine reported that "70 percent of the rich, 42 percent of the upper middle class, 14 percent of the lower middle class, and 6 percent of the poor reported hiring some help."[25]

Likewise, a comparison of urban with rural households, which were sharply divided by income during this period, discloses higher concentrations of domestic hiring. Ignoring the 23 percent of farm families in the total population and considering only the 74 percent nonfarm families, that is, people living in small town and urban areas, reveals a distinct urban profile—households with higher incomes and for which servants were the norm. In 1929, 27.8 percent of nonfarm families had yearly incomes of $3,000 and up. Households earning between $2,500 and $3,000 added another 8.9 percent who might compare themselves to families just above them in the income scale and feel that service was something to be bought as soon as added income allowed.[26]

The young economist George J. Stigler, with the clear eye that would later win him a Nobel Prize, reminded readers that domestic service in 1939 had as many employees as "the railroads, coal mines, and automobile industry combined" and deserved study. Though Stigler found great elasticity in demand for servants, with "savings and expenditures on domestic service . . . the most responsive to increases in income," he believed that demand was beginning to fall during the 1930s because families were having fewer children and buying more appliances to ease the hardest labor. By 1940, the percentage of paid servants in households out of the total of women in households had fallen from 8 percent in 1900 to 5.9 percent.[27]

In an effort to reconcile my own impression of continued reliance on domestic servants with the data showing their decreasing availability, I looked for local data and found a source in "Family Disbursements of Wage Earners and Salaried Workers, 1934–1936," a project conducted by the Bureau of Labor Statistics.[28] Drawing a sample consisting of every household in six of the forty two cities surveyed yielded a record of more than sixteen hundred households in six cities from different regions of the country: Portland, Maine; Lansing, Michigan; Jackson, Mississippi; Indianapolis, Indiana; Denver, Colorado; and Los Angeles, California. Three of these, Jackson, Indianapolis, and Los Angeles, had substantial populations of Afro-Americans and Mexican-Americans. The others were racially homogeneous. Interview protocols recorded household composition, employment, earnings, and an exhaustive list of expenditures over a fifty-two-week period.

The sample is especially interesting because it represents the income middle of the population—households with annual incomes between $500 and $3,000, which some commentators considered the minimum needed to hire a servant. In 1929, 22 percent of American households earned more than $3,000 per year and another 19 percent between $2,000 and $3,000.[29] Average education levels of wives in these households ranged between tenth and twelfth grade. A scrutiny of women in this lower-middle-class group indicates the depth of middle-class reliance on domestic service and reveals how central domestic labor was to a household's self-definition as middle class. Moreover, the data point up a truth often hinted at in the 1930s—any woman with enough income would manage to hire some of her work done.

Of these lower-middle-income households, approximately two-thirds in Lansing and Portland could not afford, or did not choose, to hire another woman's labor. Even in Indianapolis, with a substantial black population, just under two-thirds of households did not hire any help with domestic chores. In Denver and Los Angeles, however, almost half of the households paid for some work, with 45 percent and 42 percent of homes, respectively, having laundry done commercially. In the South, where severe racial discrimination limited black women to domestic work, only 19 percent of Jackson's white households did not hire some housework labor. Half hired a domestic and half got their laundry done, either by the domestic or by a laundress.

Such a distribution of paid home services is considerably more extensive than the 5 percent figure usually cited on the basis of decennial census statistics. In addition to revealing the persistence of homemakers' desire for help with their work, it shows the importance of regional economic and racial-ethnic differences in determining how women managed housework.

Many spent regularly for a laundress or commercial laundry service. From a low of 21.8 percent of households in Lansing to a high of 50.7 percent in Jackson's white homes, women with household incomes insufficient to buy appliances sought relief from those chores by sending the laundry out. Lansing's low percentage of commercial laundry use may have been supplemented through its domestic service hiring, 16.5 percent of households and the second highest of the six cities (after Jackson), since laundry remained a regular job for many servants.

How much of the laundry chores were done by hired help also varied regionally. In Jackson, almost half of white families paid to have their clothes washed and ironed. In Denver, and among Los Angeles's Anglo and Mexican families, the most common laundry service purchased was "rough dry," thus leaving the ironing to the housewife. Poorer families could afford only "wet wash," which was the most frequent choice among the 16 percent of Indianapolis's black families buying laundry work and was as common a recourse as rough dry and ironed among the 22 percent of Lansing families sending laundry out.

Even these lower-middle-income families purchased some domestic work. Not surprisingly, 50 percent of Jackson's white households took advantage of the large number of black workers unable to find better jobs to hire some service. Other cities offered considerably less opportunity for housewives to hire help. In Denver, only 6.5 percent of households could afford any domestic help; in Lansing, the percentage reached 16.5, with Portland just over 7 percent, and Indianapolis's white and Los Angeles's Anglo households at about 9.0 percent. These households rarely had full-time help.

What factors made a family decide to hire some domestic or laundry help? The most obvious, and the one found to be most significant in my data analysis, was income. Except for black families in Jackson, total household income was a significant determinant of families' having laundry done; the other significant factor was the number of weeks the homemaker worked at paid employment.

Hiring a domestic servant seems to have been determined by slightly different considerations. Though income remains important, in white and Anglo households the homemaker's level of education was a significant indicator in every city except Lansing. That a better-educated housewife (one with at least a high school diploma, as my data analysis was organized) had better things to do than spend all her time on housework was part of popular ideology of the 1920s and seems to have been acted on by as many housewives as could afford to do so.

The occupations of households that could hire laundry work out or hire some domestic service vary according to the predominant industries in a particular city; in general, white-collar workers and artisans whose work required literacy and writing or computation hired domestic help.[30] In Denver, for instance, most of the husbands able to hire domestic help worked in sales and clerking jobs, including drug clerk, retail clerk, bookkeeper, and credit manager. In Lansing, a more industrial city, husbands supporting households with some paid service worked at clerical jobs but also in skilled artisanal jobs such as machinist, draftsman, toolmaker, crank inspector, and electrician. Portland husbands' occupations were split between clerical and skilled artisan, including a linesman, chef, and monotype operator. In Jackson, with its ampler opportunities to hire black domestics, the presence of a railway center enlarged the class of regularly employed skilled workers. In addition to clerical, sales, and artisanal jobs, households were headed by men with jobs as motorman, railway switchman, railway engineer, railway hostler, and night yard master assistant. Los Angeles, as the largest city and with the most diverse economy in the sample, in addition to the jobs already mentioned, also had carpenter, electrician, and freezer men's families with some service.

Many of these households were also in need of domestic help because the homemaker was employed or because the woman designated as homemaker was supporting the home. Homemakers worked primarily in clerical and sales jobs and a few were skilled artisans. Homemakers hiring domestic help were often clerks, retail clerks, stenographers, and salesladies. Jackson, once again, had a diverse list of genteel female occupations: music instructor, commercial telegrapher, elections clerk, and magazine-subscription seller.

Households that could afford only to hire their laundry done were slightly lower on the economic scale. In Portland, homes hiring laundry were supported by carpenters, truck drivers, policemen, laborers, painters, gas station attendants, and mail clerks. Among black households in Indianapolis, those with wives working as maids and domestics and with husbands as janitors, laborers, and servants could hire laundry work done. People who might be expected to get dirty on the job, or who wore uniforms, seem to have hired laundry work done when they could afford it.

Hiring of domestic servants, however, was limited to households supported by workers who did "clean" jobs: supervisory, clerical, technical, and selling. In such homes, not only did working men and women need to have garments appropriate for their work and their work status, but they also did not expect to perform, or to have their spouses limited to performing, dirty physical tasks. Status divisions in the workplace were replicated in private life.

Women who took housework service jobs were usually the least powerful employees in the labor market. Employment in the category "domestic
and personal service" declined from 52 percent of women workers in 1870 to
28 percent of the female labor force in 1920.[31] Separating private household
work from personal service work in beauty shops, restaurants, and hotels left
an estimated 15.9 percent of women wage earners in service in 1920, 17.8
percent in 1930, and 20.4 percent in 1940. Though exact calculations are
difficult because of changes in the census's instructions to enumerators and
its occupational categories, in general the 1920 figure is probably an undercount; private household work, then, probably continued to employ about
one-fifth of women throughout the interwar years.[32] Its incidence varied
greatly among different groups of women. For the majority of both native-
born and foreign-born white women, 1920 represented the culmination of a
rapid downturn in reliance on domestic and laundry jobs: from 26 percent in
1890 to 8 percent in 1920 for native-born white women and from 52 percent
to 22 percent for foreign-born white women.[33]

By contrast, domestic work was the primary occupation of women of
color—Afro-Americans, American Indians, Mexican-Americans, and Asian-
Americans—who were usually untrained to compete for more attractive jobs
in clerical work or were excluded from such jobs by racial discrimination.
For Afro-American women, the group whose history and geographic concentration were most closely linked with the unremitting servitude of slavery, employment as domestics remained steady from 1890 to 1920, hovering
in the high fortieth percentile, and rose in importance in the next twenty
years, from 46 percent in 1920, to 53 percent in 1930, to 60 percent in 1940.
In the Southwest, Chicanas "worked primarily in domestic service or agriculture until World War II. Forty-five percent of all employed Chicanas
were domestics in 1930."[34] Japanese-American women also were heavily represented: 27 percent in the occupation in 1920, 18 percent in 1930, and 10
percent in 1940, though they were dispersing into agriculture, trade, and
manufacturing.[35] American Indian women, employed as domestics at rates of
11 and 15 percent in 1920 and 1930,[36] were not identified separately in occupational statistics, but the content of training programs in Indian schools
indicates that Indian women expected to find employment in domestic work.

White women, who remained a significant but not dominant segment
of domestic workers, were more likely than before World War I to be native-
rather than foreign-born. Women were often forced to take these less attractive jobs because they needed income; they were widowed, divorced, or
single, with no male income in the household, or married to men whose
earnings were so low that the wife's income was essential.

My 1934 sample included households of Afro-American domestic workers in Jackson and Indianapolis. Comparing these households with those in
which the wife was not employed in domestic work reveals that domestics'
families had lower total income, lower husbands' income, and lower home-

makers' income than other households. Husbands worked fewer weeks during the year, which was probably the reason for their relatively low earnings. Wives were forced to take domestic work because of family need and lack of alternative occupations.

With the Depression exacerbating family need, breaking up households, and diminishing job options, domestic work that had remained steady through the decade of the 1920s increased during the 1930s. War-related employment promised an end to such work because other opportunities increased, and the occupation became much less significant for women workers in general during World War II, dropping, according to one researcher, from 17.7 percent of all women's employment in 1940 to 9.5 percent in 1944.[37] Even for black women, the occupation was less dominant, employing fewer than half the working population by 1944 instead of 60 percent as in 1940. Ironically, however, domestic work became more completely identified with black women, who increased their labor force participation in all arenas, including an increase of fifty thousand women in domestic service; by 1944, black women made up over 60 percent of domestic workers.[38]

The years from 1920 to 1945 may be viewed as a transitional period during which middle-class homes changed from being *directed* by a lady-housewife to being *served* by the wife. The image of the housewife did not change, but work changed in content, and so did the relations between housewives and servants. Both at the beginning and end of the period the housewife's existence was to be devoted to her home and family. By the end of the era, however, she was less able to hire another woman to take over many of the physical tasks such devotion entailed. As a consequence, housewives lost some benefits of the angelic image of the middle-class wife, which not only derived from their attachment to the home but was enhanced by the contrast between the housewife and the domestic servant. With declining access to servants, the housewife not only did more work, she also felt herself to be a drudge. Without a servant to emphasize her superiority, this wife found her role considerably less tolerable.

Theoretical Viewpoint

Throughout the interwar and war years, domestic service remained a constant that defined the elevated status of middle-class women and the degraded status of working-class women of color, especially married women of color, who might be expected to have their own homes to care for. Unmarried white working-class women were most likely to seek domestic work, and often in the 1930s they needed a place to live as well as a wage. Few married white working-class women became servants. Unlike the nineteenth century, service did not represent a stage in a woman's life (doing service as a girl and being a housewife as an adult), but rather sharp divisions in the status of different groups of women. Hiring a maid enabled a middle-class woman to accept confinement to her home and still believe she had escaped traditional domestic servitude. The modern housewife was not so different from the housewife without appliances. Her work status still rested on old patterns of race and class oppression.

This book develops the idea that divisions in status do not represent simply divisions of class or race, systems of domination based on one group's holding superior resources that enable it to turn over unpleasant or unprofitable work to less well-endowed groups. Rather, inherent in the division of housework with its system of tasks, relationships, and the meanings assigned to them were notions of womanhood, of whiteness and nonwhiteness, and of middle-classness as well as working-classness. Through the social assignment of different jobs to different categories of women and through cultural significances attached to particular jobs performed by different groups of women, women learned their appropriate social identities in relation to those other women. They learned to act and to feel white or nonwhite (a category divided by color, class, and ethnic differences); they learned to fill and to embody their class position; and they learned to exhibit the characteristics of heterosexual females in ways appropriate to their race and class.

Though I think that people of color learn their social parts and internalize them in the same way white people do, how black people do this self-consciously and incorporate resistance to degradation is a topic much investigated since the modern civil rights movement challenged stereotypic notions of "innate" or "inherent" black behavior. The new issues opened to question in the last two decades are how white people learn their social parts and internalize feelings of whiteness. Although this book offers some information about social and cultural structuring of the lives of people of color, my analysis focuses on the question that has been less studied and that is more central to my own identity: how do white women learn to embody whiteness? How are they shaped to fulfill a racially-based (and class-based) ideal of female identity that limits their actions and warps their humanity into narrow shapes?

In this book, therefore, I confront one issue now being studied by numerous feminist scholars: the racialization of white womanhood. Whiteness is now considered as much in need of explanation as blackness or Indianness or Latinness. I assume that no one of the traditional racial-ethnic groupings in America is "natural" or preferable or represents a progressive advance over another grouping. The characteristics of any group are neither static nor essential to that group. Rather, behavior we observe in a group is a social (cultural, economic, legal, and psychological) creation and often one formed in relationship to the behavior and ideals of reciprocal groups. Much of this insight has emerged from gender studies, which have illustrated how notions of male and female are formed as dualisms changing across time and space, with what is female being the opposite, the complement, the Other to what is male. These theories built on earlier work in labor history that pointed out whose subordinate position gives them reason to question the "naturalness" of white dominance, just as white women had reason to question the inevitability of male dominance.

The book focuses on the connection in American culture and history between white middle-class women and purity and between working-class, immigrant women or women of color and dirt. These oppositional ideas of womanhood—as angelic or slatternly, frail or strong, virginal or sexual, served or serving—have been connected with images of home and the organization of housework since the mid-nineteenth century. The linked images of good woman and dainty house or bad woman and dinginess show surprising durability and remain vivid even amid the well-furnished consumer paradise of the modern home. The theme of white women's delicacy runs through more modern representations of them as witty, well-educated, and sexually attractive. They need to be cared for. And they get care from men and from other more robust and vulgar women who seem "made" to serve.

Chapter Seven theorizes about the place of housework in maintaining the psychological differentiation between women of color and white women, between working class and middle class, that is fundamental to the self-esteem of middle-class white housewives. The chapter clarifies why, given this relational identity, middle-class housewives did not protest against doing housework but, nevertheless, denigrated its value. I argue that white women should reconsider the ways in which whiteness has been formed and how it is integrally linked to their subordinate relations with white men. It is pleasant to have privileges, but pedestals are confining. White women have not only given up the masculine parts of their humanity to enjoy their privileges but have thereby accepted narrowly defined notions of womanhood. When class, race, and sexual inhibitions are added to those of gender, women's freedom to move through the world is greatly limited. When these identities divide women from each other, they reduce their ability to form coalitions for the improvement of all women's lives.

that "class" was a relational concept and not an absolute existence.[39] Race and sexuality are the final significant categories of our society to undergo this scrutiny.

The shift to not seeing human life as made up of essential biologically based essences of innate race, homosexuality or heterosexuality, native intelligence, or gender is part of the shift in Western thought sometimes described as postmodernist. This book is grounded in ideas developed in feminist theory that are generally grouped with postmodernist thought—that there is no one single truth or point of view through which historical accounts can be told; that history is an account of how people learn to act as if some parts of themselves naturally require such behavior; that categories of humanity such as race, gender, and sexuality are formed as mutually exclusive dualities in relation to each other; and that historians cannot retreat to biological categories or natural law to explain motivation and behavior.[40]

In following these precepts, Chapter Two seeks to understand what messages and images white middle-class women received about who they were. Chapter Three looks at how, within a society in which race and class divide groups into the more and the less powerful, these women constructed their primary work—housework—and their daily existences so as to confirm their beings through and in relation to other women who had to take jobs as domestic servants. Chapter Four reveals servants' views of the work and of the women for whom they worked. Chapters Five and Six turn to the public, institutional context within which housewives and servants negotiated their relationships. Chapter Five examines home economics and domestic service training courses funded and overseen by government agencies that taught women their appropriate duties in relation to housework. Chapter Six recounts battles for reform between domestic servants, who organized like other workers to gain regulation of their work conditions, and middle-class women, who responded ambivalently to the call to aid women workers when reform threatened their domestic service arrangements.

Men are present and set the terms of the racial–class negotiations among women by establishing what household-based work men will not do and will not accept as masculine responsibility, and this study points to moments when men's actions define the limits within which housework can be organized by women. But it focuses on tensions among women and struggles for dominance and equality among women of different race and class groups. In this sense, it examines how white women formed their identities in relation to other women, while leaving their relations with men relatively unexamined. Serving men, however, defines women, and their relationships are built around accomplishing this service. I hope to clarify the postulate tha' gender is never an identity formed in isolation from other identities tha have significance in twentieth-century America, but is an amalgam of rac and class with gender. This idea has long been advanced by women of colo

Two

The Housewife in
a Modern Marriage

What is home?
What does it mean to us?
The woman Within—the man Without—returning at
night to the Home Centre—his day well-spent. . . .
The World Without—the business day—is like the
home World Within.
The Man at work—
Driving the trolley, that others may ride to work.
Guiding a bank, that money may do its most for business.
Managing a store.
   For What?
   For his own home—and for all homes.
That is why business exists.
The woman's work is more than
   Scrubbing potatoes—
   Preparing the meal—
That the family may be fed.
   Washing the floors, the paint—that the home, the Centre
   of Industry, may be clean.
It is comforting the child—
Pouring peace and harmony upon the man—who is disturbed
   by the friction without.

Each tiny task a brick in the structure of
Home—the Centre
For which civilization exists.
—Ida Bailey Allen, "Home!" in *Home Partners,*
   or Seeing the Family Through, 1924

Middle-class housewives (MCHs) had a moral vision of housework at the center of life.[1] MCHs believed they could cherish and impart positive values through homemaking: caring for the young or frail, learning to share responsibilities with a partner, raising aesthetic standards, using physical resources sensibly, and nurturing spirit. Statements and depictions of these aspirations will help us understand what social improvements "good" women thought they could achieve through housewifery. Equally important, domestic success often depended on exploitation of other women, denial of physicality, and limitation of self-development—controlling "bad" impulses.

The dominant vision of twentieth-century domestic life was created during the interwar years. Though the nonworking wife continued to be the norm, the notions of husbands and wives representing complementary but separate natures and existences, which had governed nineteenth-century marriage, ceased to direct married life. "Modern" women and men had to negotiate household arrangements in a more fluid and individualized fashion than had their parents' generation. Couples married, as Elaine Tyler May concludes in *Great Expectations,* seeking happiness, though "caught between traditions of the past and visions of the future. . . . [Men were] attracted to youthful and exciting 'new women,' but they also wanted domestic, frugal, and virtuous wives who would keep house and tend to the children."[2] Women expected their husbands to be financially competent, but they, too, demanded more from marriage than economic support.

The status of housework declined, according to Glenna Matthews, through "commodification of the home" and loss of respect "for housewifery as a skilled craft and for mother as a moral arbiter."[3] Nevertheless, women found meaning in being housewives and did not flee home life. They more frequently held jobs before marriage, and perhaps even until the birth of children, but the trend toward such work outside the home increased gradually. Only when the need for labor in World War II broke through general resistance to wives' employment and postwar economic changes enticed educated women into clerical work (often on a part-time basis in deference to mothers' schedules) did the trend turn sharply upward and MCHs begin to balance wage work and housework.

In the nineteenth century, housewives were, in Barbara Welter's words, "hostages to fortune" upholding traditional values while their husbands created a competitive industrial economy. As the economy shifted from production to consumption as a central element in modernity, cultural norms of housewifery shifted. In the new economy, however, housewives' devotion continued to justify men's economic behavior.[4] The ways women exercised their power as consumers determined the moral future of the country.

During the years 1920 to 1945, when middle-class women married at high rates and accepted the home as the center of existence, how did these relatively well-educated women, who wished to be up-to-date, conceive their role? How did they reconcile personal sophistication with traditional house-wifely jobs? What values took hold in the consumer household of the 1920s to replace those of self-denial and self-sacrifice on which the nineteenth-century business and domestic economies had been built?

Most recent explanations have been guided by a feminist imperative that holds that women were seduced, duped, misled, and gently coerced into buying unnecessary products. They were not free agents in choosing housewifery, which, by its oppressive nature, could not possibly have attracted adherents. Such judgments treat women as victims and belittle their devotion to an ideology that offered positive alternatives or correctives to the male-directed world of commerce and politics.

To recover the ethos of MCHs during the 1920s and 1930s, I have relied on three sources: advice books women bought to learn about homemaking or marriage and family life; novels about courtship, marriage, and family life by popular writers; and movies about husbands and wives. All these sources gave women advice about marriage, as well as elaborate and romantic images of wifedom. The nonfiction writings are a sample taken from the Library of Congress and the Schlesinger Library of Women's History. The novels are by four best-selling women authors who wrote regularly for women's magazines, Fannie Hurst, Dorothy Canfield Fisher, feminist playwright Susan Glaspell, and Kathleen Norris, and by three men, Norris's husband, Charles, a popular writer and younger brother of novelist Frank Norris; Sinclair Lewis, whose *Main Street* debates the virtues of small-town domesticity; and Christopher Morley, whose heroine Kitty Foyle suffers the hardships of the single working white-collar girl (WCG, in Morley's acronym). Except for *Kitty Foyle*, the movie version of which is compared with the novel, the movies examined are about married couples: Marlene Dietrich and Herbert Marshall as Helen and Ned Faraday in *Blonde Venus* (1932); Katharine Hepburn and Cary Grant as Tracy Lord and her divorced husband Dexter Haven in *The Philadelphia Story* (1940); William Powell and Myrna Loy as Nick and Nora Charles in *The Thin Man* (1934, the original) and *Another Thin Man* (1939); Fredric March and Myrna Loy as Al and Millie Stephenson in *The Best Years of Our Lives* (1946); and Cary Grant and Myrna Loy as Jim and Muriel Blandings in *Mr. Blandings Builds His Dream House* (1948).

Scholars continually debate the links between published writings, film images, popular imagination, and people's behavior. Certainly, most Americans did not live like fictional heroes and heroines. Most movies and novels set their characters in well-off households, where disagreements about money rarely interfere with discussions about human toleration, forgiveness, and love, the material of relationships. Heroes and heroines are always beautiful and well dressed.

In *Parallel Lives*, literary critic Phyllis Rose tells how five Victorian couples negotiated their existences through the narratives they created about marriage. Her assumption that all persons "need to decide upon the story of [their] own lives, [which] becomes particularly pressing when we choose a mate, for example, or embark upon a career," seems as true of the twentieth century as of the nineteenth. Rose's observation that marriage is a particularly rich and culturally supported narrative that occupies women's imaginations is true of popular novels and films of the 1920s to the 1940s. I accept Rose's notion that we use imaginative material to "impose some narrative form in our lives," giving them meaning and significance, though not necessarily determining behavior.[5]

By the 1920s, movies shared with novels the task of demonstrating appropriate attitudes. These images constitute billboards on the American mental landscape. Pervasive images offered directions on how women should act in particular situations: smile here, look tenderly now, forgive this indiscretion, and, more important, conceive of your character in this way. These signs are important for their positive vision of the housewife. Instead of the weak and easily manipulated creature we find in histories of advertising, or the educated woman duped out of professional work, or the housewife seeking to defend her service work in an economy with a producer ethic, images from popular culture reveal an American woman who saw herself in the vanguard of female self-development.

By 1920, with women's suffrage passed, completing the domestic promise of U.S. commitment to democratic ideals in World War I, writers outlined home practices appropriate to politically equal adults:

> The family must be democratized in that sense in which each individual within its bond shall be sustained in seeking and in maintaining the conditions of personality. No one human being is to live solely for others' service or to have his or her value estimated in terms of contribution to other lives, but all to seek the utmost perfection of individual life as a contribution to the common life; this is the democratic ideal.[6]

Women and men would not play the same roles in the modern family, but their distinct parts would achieve equal recognition, most notably as partners presumed to contribute equally to family well-being.

The woman of this period, a twentieth-century analogue of the nineteenth-century "American girl," the adventurous, inquiring innocent who represented America's newness and freedom from artifice, illustrated the casual sophistication and informal elegance that resulted from a hybrid of American freedom and European cultivation. She "ha[d] good taste and such special abilities as making good pies, playing sonatas, or earning money. In short, she [came] up to [a man's] idea of a capable, attractive, modern woman."[7] Like the American girl, the New Woman pursued knowledge but voluntarily limited its benefits to her own family. She was plucky, witty, sexy, trustworthy, and domestic; though she might attract men with her vibrance, she would never cheat on "her man," and she would devote herself to his physical as well as emotional comfort.

A woman, more than a man, had to mediate tensions between experimentation and stability—between the old norms based in separate spheres and female self-sacrifice and new norms of comradeship and self-expression. She had to be fun, to have fun, and to keep it clean. She had a responsibility to express her individuality and a duty to align it with her husband's.

Carol Milford Kennicott, heroine of Sinclair Lewis's best-selling 1920 novel *Main Street*, appears at the beginning of the era as a clarion. College-educated and a librarian in St. Paul for a year before she meets Dr. Will Kennicott, Carol is slender, imaginative, and ambitious to acquire culture. Will, by contrast, is phlegmatic, realistic, and able to ride through prairie blizzards to treat trauma cases. He offers Carol the opportunity "not to have to live in Other People's Houses, but to make her own shrine."[8] Carol wants to build a temple to good taste, spontaneity, and authenticity, not only in her house but in Gopher Prairie, too. When the town holds out only mass-produced newness and conventional judgments, Carol flees with her son to Washington to clerk for a government agency during World War I. Will is astute enough to give her time to learn that superior culture in a large, impersonal city is not satisfying. At the end of the novel, Carol returns voluntarily to her marriage and her home in Gopher Prairie, strengthened by a wider vision of the world to uphold truthfulness in herself and in town:

> "I've never excused my failure by sneering at my aspirations, by pretending to have gone beyond them. I do not admit that Main Street is as beautiful as it should be! I do not admit that Gopher Prairie is greater or more generous than Europe! I do not admit that dishwashing is enough to satisfy all women! I may not have fought the good fight, but I have kept the faith."[9]

Carol learns to believe in the worth of her own efforts from a "generalissima of suffrage," who points out that large causes accomplish no more than "'looking at one thing after another in your home and church and bank, and ask[ing] why it is, and who first laid down the law that it had to be that way. . . . Easy, pleasant, lucrative home-work for wives: asking people to define their jobs. That's the most dangerous doctrine I know!'"[10]

The MCH could challenge philistines in her community and home, and she could provide a model for children, friends, and husband. Much of this she managed through intelligent consumption. Despite Lewis's criticisms of mass production, his heroine Carol distinguishes herself through consumption: inventive party favors and food, well-tailored and dainty clothes, and redecorating Will's office to give comfort to his patients.

A housewife's role in consumer culture was not just buying. Rather, her choices and decisions in buying expressed her household's standard of living and defined its social connections, sustained the family's standard of living through intelligent purchases and support of the income earner, justified consumption by transforming goods into use for healthy and moral families, and exemplified the best qualities of American life as a well-informed and articulate person. No longer trapped in the home by a theory of separate spheres, by inferior education, or by political exclusion, women of the 1920s chose dedication to homes, to husbands, to children, and to community. Not self-sacrificial like their mothers and grandmothers, these modern women sought self-fullfillment as partners and companions. Feminist demands for self-fulfillment were appropriated and applied to marriage.[11] In a free union, women could choose the "self-mastery and altruism" of housewifery;[12] their voluntary restraint would ennoble consumption.

Choice was essential, moreover, because the qualities of good home-making were not innate to women; rather, they were skills to be cultivated. Dorothy Canfield's (Fisher) *The Homemaker* (1924), in which the mother earns income and the father "is homemaker in spirit and in fact," was often cited to make the point that, though women were generally the ones "occupied with the details of the work and management of the home," both men and women were makers of homes.[13]

Descriptions of the MCH's role focused on her relationships to society, to husband, to children, and to herself. When specific jobs were mentioned, they were to be done so efficiently and cleverly that the house would seem "to run by itself." Housework had to be done well, but it could be accomplished by anyone—a hired servant, a commercial firm, a machine. Only housewives could make a "home," which required intellect, sensitivity, and diplomacy. Man brought home the raw materials of money, but "woman work[ed] them up into products of material and immaterial value."[14]

Though attitudes do not shift neatly by decades, in general the language of partnership pervaded home and family writings of the 1920s and the language of companionship the manuals of the 1930s. In the 1920s, wives could still increase family income through home-based projects; by the 1930s, the wife's intelligent use of money raised the family's living standard but not its income. Emphasis on marriage organized around conjugal compatibility, including sexual pleasure, characterized the 1920s; by the 1930s, more explicit instructions about beauty, cosmetics, and diet appeared. Being intellectually worthy of a husband was important, but in the 1920s a wife also aspired to action in the community and civic world outside the home; by the 1930s, the wife cultivated her intellect for private pleasures and enjoyment within the home. At the beginning of the era, democratic principles were carried from politics into family life. By the end of this era, "home [had become] a microcosm of sanity in a world that is plainly mad."[15]

Defining a Living Standard

A wife organized social life according to aesthetic criteria that embodied the family's essence. She arranged the household, organized its entertainment, and set its intellectual and spiritual standard. Her decisions directed her children toward a secure future, soothed and refreshed her husband, and enabled her to pursue self-development, preferably in activities outside the home. Home-centeredness was, however, the essence of middle-class life. The home provided a stage for presentation of oneself as a cultivated person, worthy of success and social respect. It was the idealized setting for "those ceremonies and informal hospitalities that are the cherished memories of many men and women—reading at bedtime, picnics, birthday celebrations, Sunday night suppers."[16]

While working-class people began to spend money on commercial entertainment, especially the movies, middle-class families persisted in the tradition of large family suppers and dinners for friends.[17] Middle-class households served three meals a day; cookbooks recommended four courses for each. As the center of social life, these meals were to be surrounded with uplifting ornaments and served with grace.

Cookbooks, etiquette books, and novels gave fashionable advice to the eager novice or the experienced housekeeper seeking innovations. Radio recipe-giver Ida Bailey Allen accompanied instructions about household finances with illustrations showing a centerpiece made of poppies and grasses and place servings for a four-course lunch.[18] Novelist Kathleen Norris's *Barberry Bush* (1927) forecasts Nora Ephron's 1980s *Heartburn* in providing ingenious recipes for difficult occasions and troublesome men. Norris's heroine Barbara Atherton, or "Barberry Bush" as she is nicknamed, marries the moody poet Barry du Spain instead of the richest, and nicest, young man in town, Link Mackenzie. After Barry abandons her, she gets Link. The reader is aware, almost from the beginning of the novel, that Barberry Bush even more than her sister Amy, merits a good man because of her culinary skills:

> Peas, and asparagus salad, and brown muffins, and cherry tart. [Barbara] began to mix her batter easily and comfortably; she had been able to make muffins for Granny before she was twelve. . . . "Amy, if

you mix up what was left of the French dressing with what was left of the Thousand Island, there'll be enough, and it might be kind of nice and light, with asparagus."[19]

When Link visits the du Spains on their run-down ranch, he is impressed by Barbara's "fresh blue linen, with the immaculate white collar," and by her seemingly effortless speed in preparing a lunch of omelette with "*sauce barbare*," which she has invented from abandoned goods—"jars and jars of pickled tomatoes, all coated with mothwing, in the cellar, and bags of onions, and some roots of Chinese ginger, and . . . dry peppers."[20]

Barbara's plucky resourcefulness on these occasions is bound to result in a raised standard of living, which she personally achieves. Though she has borne a daughter, Kate, and will not consider divorce, when Link discovers that the priest who married her to du Spain was a fraud, she happily acquiesces to Link's proposal of marriage and prepares to become mistress of the largest house in town. She tours the drawing room, billiard room, and library and finds

> in the kitchen, Tilly Smith, [who] displayed her wide range, shining black[,] her new white gas stove, her cabinet, sink and storerooms, her ice box—a little room in itself—and the small room where the maids and men had their meals. Tilly's daughter was to be Kate's nurse, an arrangement that made Barbara want to laugh. It seemed ridiculous that her wild gipsy baby should have a maid to herself.[21]

But, of course, this baby will have a maid, and Barbara will teach her daughter the natural dignity with which to adorn her new position.

Barbara, the daughter of an academic, represents the good taste and social grace of a class that values ideals. Wives of professional men such as lawyers, physicians, academics, and accountants saw household space for entertaining as more important than clothing or elaborate food.[22] Businessmen's wives might entertain less at home and more outside it, but they needed to be able to manage some events at home. All could aspire to turn out food as dainty as that of a tearoom and as "piquant" as that of a good restaurant.[23]

An excellent wife could guarantee her family's suitability on the most trying occasions. Myrna Loy as Mrs. Nick Charles provides an unusual example of the wife's good-natured hostessing; in *The Thin Man*, she arranges a formal dinner party, with candelabra, place cards, and full European service, for all the suspects in a murder case. Her husband's revelation of the killer breaks up the party, but not before her proper attitudes about good food and service are noted.

The least effective way for a wife to help improve the family's social standing was through employment. But it was acceptable for her to run a small business out of the home. Possibilities suggested in 1922 were truck gardening, baking for a school snack shop, operating a camp on vacant ground, and speculation in real estate:

> With what she saved by stopping [household leaks] she made a down payment on an inexpensive lot . . . and persuaded her family to camp out on it and wear their old clothes during the summer. Her husband and sons did one thing and another to make the place pleasant . . . and along in August a real-estate agent persuaded her to sell her equity. She made two hundred dollars on the deal, and she had the amount of her original payment back and a good deal besides. . . . Now she owns her own home and spends her spare time in her car looking around for the best investments of this kind that she can pick up.[24]

Social advisers tolerated employment as an outside activity through much of the 1920s, though the working wife risked focusing on her career to the detriment of her husband's and of her own charm. The image of the New Woman imperceptibly modulated from that of educated careerist to that of well-informed partner. A working wife did not shame a middle-class man by showing up his ineffectiveness as a wage earner so much as she cheated the family of social éclat. An up-and-coming young man needed the stimulation and refreshment of a mentally active and sexually attractive young woman. If she did not marry wealth, then her accomplishments signaled her husband's worthiness for higher position. "It may interest young wives to know," said one adviser, "that a large number of corporations have recently begun systematically to investigate the domestic environment of their employees. If it is found that it is not happy, that they do not enjoy a restful and congenial home life, they discharge them."[25] Without the wife's tending, the husband failed. With attentiveness, the wife designed an appropriate "setting for both of you in the eye of the world. It is your background. It represents your taste, your experience, your knowledge of how things are done."[26]

By the early 1930s, the tradition of wives' making money at home had largely passed, but, faced with the Depression, women's use of income became more important. "It is not wealth," admonished one popular text, "that marks the difference" between a noisy, untidy home and a comfortable, orderly one. "The difference in each is determined in part at least by the homemakers upon whose skill and ability the qualities and atmosphere of the home depend."[27]

Housewives kept social order, just like excellent companions, "the kind of person old ladies hire—for a good round sum [who can be] the social secretary of the home, seeing that the children make the right friends, and that father's interests are properly looked after through social contacts."[28]

Servants provided backup, at least for special events, that enabled the wife
to entertain in a calm, gracious fashion. "In the upper middle class in general, a certain amount of domestic service [was] considered essential for a
well-ordered household. The approved standard of living [could] not be
maintained without it."[29]

Christine Frederick, who advised housewives on home efficiency during the 1910s and advertisers on the psychology of the housewife during the
late 1920s, denoted the shift from management as money-saving to morale-
raising in a little book titled *The Ignoramus Book of Housekeeping*. "A standard of living," she said,

> is a set of attitudes toward certain values, toward articles to be bought
> and used, services to be paid for, and conditions under which we pre-
> fer to live. It is almost impossible to draw the line between economic
> or money standards and ethical or more spiritual values, for our spend-
> ing, or wise or foolish purchasing or managing, affects character and
> the lives of each one in the family.[30]

The wife decided whether she spent money on children's music lessons or on
domestic help, on elaborate dishes or on an insurance policy. She determined the standard of living, which was not what a family *could* buy, but
what it *did* buy.

Aspiring to live at the highest social standard one's income could support was considered courageous. Magazine writer Charlotte Adams set a
1940s vignette at a bridge table in a high-income New York suburb, where a
young woman lamented not being able to afford a maid *or* to live in the
neighborhood where

> "all our friends are: . . . Of course most of them have more money than
> we have, and all of them have maids. . . . I'm a good soldier, and if
> Johnny lost his job, I'd be willing to live in a two-room shack some-
> where. But that would be different because we wouldn't be in a nice
> community like this with friends who all have more than we do."

Adams sympathized and said the young wife could choose between "peace of
mind" by giving up the struggle to live well or the unease of pushing to
achieve a high standard of living. Perhaps the wife should encourage moving
to a less wealthy neighborhood. On the other hand, "sometimes keeping up
with the well known Joneses is just the spur that Johnny needs to get to be a
partner of the firm!"[31] Though she must consult with her husband about
what the family could and should do, an astute wife carefully evaluated her
husband's capacities and adjusted their social standard accordingly.

Refining Material Goods

Women and men could purchase a house, furnish it, fill it with appliances and goods, but still not make a home. "A house," as Emily Newall Blair wrote, "may be made into a home, but it may also exist and house a family and not become a home." What makes a home is the care that gives a dwelling "Comfort, Peace, Beauty."[32]

Wealth was inadequate without a talented wife's superintendence. Radical journalist–writer Fannie Hurst depicted a variety of well-to-do households in her 1923 novel *Lummox* in which the title character, the wordlessly sympathetic servant Bertha, expresses values of sexuality, care for parents and children, and artistic responsiveness better than most of her mistresses. As a book uplifting domestic workers and exposing unfair employers, *Lummox* preceded Hurst's organizational support for labor regulations and unions to protect domestic workers. As a gallery of profiles of housewives, however, *Lummox* carried a different message: aesthetic yearnings, sexual honesty, and kindness comport with good housework.[33] Without these qualities, a family fluctuated in social standing and kept only such friends as it could buy.

No matter what income the husband earned, possessions attained their high worth only when infused with the wife's spirit.

> The home without a woman in it . . . is cold, unfeeling. Clocks go unwound. . . . Rugs and draperies have a cold and clammy feeling to their touch. Flowers wither. Books stand primly on their shelves, their characters silent and morose, not garrulous and friendly as are the characters in those books which home women leave about wherever dropped while they run to look at the gingerbread in the oven.[34]

True homemakers created aesthetically pleasing settings, while maintaining intellectual life *and* baking special food.

To manage such a household, women had to control money. Home advisers analyzing Sinclair Lewis's *Main Street* could have predicted trouble in the marriage between the young schoolteacher Carol Milford and the older physician Will Kennicott. Unwilling to accept his wife as a partner in the business of the household, Dr. Kennicott doled out household money in proportion to the charm of his wife's requests; he had a distinctly patriarchal aspect, feeling "generous" and "liberal" when he gave her cash. His wife finally rebelled because she "hate[d] it—this smirking and hoping for money—and then . . . spending it on double-boilers and socks for you."[35] Instead, he and other husbands were told to "place the work of wife and mother on the same financial footing as that of any other labor, and allot so much weekly or monthly on that account."[36]

Wives had to be financially independent for two reasons: to plan family expenditures most effectively and to be self-respecting marital companions. The harshness of modern business required that the husband pay full attention to his career and left his wife responsible for decisions about housing, furnishing, food, and child care. Her management in these areas was as important as her husband's business success in determining the family's social position and considerably more influential in its day-to-day well-being.

Both in her purchases and her use of them, a woman could diminish or increase the household's standards, not through "niggardliness" but by demanding good quality from merchants. In ordering meat, for instance, unwary housewives might telephone the butcher an order and trust him to treat them well. This was a mistake because, in the words of one manual, by their "very indifference, they throw before him temptations such as few men can resist in this money-seeking age." Instead, housewives should cultivate the butcher through visits until he felt more interest and acted like a good friend, "willing to tell you facts about his wares that would be much to your advantage to know."[37]

If the housewife of the early 1920s used her moral sense to keep merchants up to standards, her counterpart of the early 1930s used her aesthetic sense to buy the most "uplifting" goods. Wives were assured that "we are judged no longer by the quantity or value of our possessions, but by what those possessions show us to be. . . . Harmony of colors and simple forms agreeably assembled, even at the minimum of cost, have a far stronger message than a mere show of extravagance."[38]

The items the wife purchased depended on the household's particular character, which she divined and served. She purchased equipment that met her household's needs. For instance, "If a woman bakes a cake about twice a month, she is foolish to invest in an electric beater. But if she serves mashed potatoes frequently, likes finely sieved apple sauce and cranberry jelly, she is foolish to use up her energy in beating, mixing, and mashing. Let the machine do it."[39] Advice books emphasized each family's uniqueness and the housewife's choices; nevertheless, descriptions such as the above established standards for various tasks and not standards for forgoing one item or choosing another. Not to purchase meant to deny a possibility of improvement or development of a particular skill that might please or improve one's husband, children, and friends. Through creative use of money and buying, housewives elevated husbands and children to more creative, playful, self-expressive people; they taught self-development through consumption.

Finally, the housewife studied and nurtured the growth of individuality and self-expression; the home encouraged the growth of unique spirits, as opposed to the uniformity of big business. Social science language described "the general goal of homemaking . . . as *the optimum development of the individual members of the family*."[40] Efficiency expert Lillian Gilbreth may have been using examples from her own family of twelve children when she advised that

> each member of the home must not only be able to express himself, but urged to do so, and given not only the opportunity but the rewards of expression. Home, "a place to rehearse," "a place to show off," "a place to cooperate"—each phrase raises a need and a satisfaction! Mary, who is eating so slowly and daintily that the boys are impatient and laugh at her, is practicing for the dinner party to which she is going Saturday night. Tom, who gave his current event shyly and briefly in school and is dissatisfied with the result, is reciting it at great length and at the top of his lungs to make up for his previous mediocre performance and to revel in the friendly family audience. And Jackie, who is carrying off plates before the family is really finished and rushing for extra spoons which no one needs, is actually only trying to show that he loves every one.[41]

Mothers and fathers had the job of recognizing distinctive characteristics and encouraging them among children and between themselves. Whatever purchases eased or ornamented such labor were justified by love.

These helpful ideas and useful items could be discovered only through constant self-education and study. Some portion of every day's schedule had to be devoted to reading and to assessing new products that might increase the family's share of well-being. "A homemaking woman, no less than any other, has to keep abreast of her profession. You'd hate to trust a doctor, wouldn't you, who never read a medical journal or book?" queried one writer. There are, she continued,

> books and articles in magazines on nutrition which you must read. . . . [and] on the nurture, care and upbringing of children. How to clothe and feed them; how to distinguish their characteristics, tendencies, inclinations, physical defects or perfections. These you can not afford to neglect, for the upbringing of your children is your most sacred responsibility.[42]

Women's magazines were the housewife's source of up-to-date information and hence not frivolous.

Husbands learned more indirectly, and usually from wives, about their part in family life. By the late 1930s, one book warned wives that

> making *each other* happy is *your* business. . . . Your husband, being the right sort, can and should be expected to do his part of the readjusting necessary. Nevertheless, the fact remains that most of the burden

of turning four walls and some furniture into something more than a glorified boardinghouse rests entirely on your shoulders.[43]

Transforming the commercial—the mass-produced for general consumption—into enhancement for individual humans was wives' work.

The housewife's work should also be fun, and she could make it so by dramatizing it, for instance," in planning and serving meals."

> An exotic decorative touch here and there will transfer the most commonplace menu into a festive one, besides giving you the thrill of having expressed your personality. Make an occasion of everyday dinners by using colorful pottery, candlelight, unusual centerpieces (fruit or figurines will be just as effective as flowers), or by decorating your platters of food. We guarantee this a sure cure for any irritation you may have felt in the past about having to cook.[44]

Women's refinement of mundane objects was immeasurably valuable, popular writers intimated. If the emotional and aesthetic qualities of family service could be purchased, they would yield a fortune. In Fannie Hurst's 1933 *Imitation of Life,* widow Bea Pullman earns a living for her infant daughter and paralyzed father by wholesaling maple syrup to Atlantic City hotels, restaurants, and hospitals. Unable to care for her family and to maintain her selling, she luckily finds a widowed black woman, Delilah, who also needs to earn a living and support her tiny daughter. When Bea gets the idea of opening a diner decorated like a Pullman car and serving Delilah's hot waffles and rich coffee, the enterprise booms into a national chain of restaurants, all staffed by middle-aged, heavy black women cooks trained by Delilah, and all offering a homelike atmosphere.

When Pullman plans the first new diner, adding New York to the Atlantic City original, she sees that

> the major need was to succeed in duplicating the genius of the certain quality which had got itself born into the first B. Pullman: Delilah's savory coffee, Delilah's hot waffles, Delilah's Hearts [maple candy], Delilah's smile, Golden Maple Syrup, candlelight at dusk, thin china dishes, odors, the little pampering something that came so readily from Delilah.

Though Bea Pullman's decorating—homelike curtains and her own Delft blue-and-white plates, in the first diner—is mentioned, the spirit is Delilah's. For marketing the concept, however, Pullman garners the credit to herself, as she muses: "Some people have talent for writing poetry or building towers or singing arias. Mine must be to surround people for a few moments out of a tired day, with a little unsubtle but cozy happiness of body and perhaps of mind." Pullman draws inspiration from her housewife's vision, impossible to achieve personally after her husband's death. In the business world, Pullman can be rewarded for her talent, her "ability to provide people with a few moments of creature enjoyment,"[45] though her contribution is planning the atmosphere in which Delilah does the physical and emotional work.

A central characteristic of the wife's refinement was her good-natured self-control; she never nagged or responded crossly. Men might speak unthinkingly and sharply because they were hard-pressed. But husbands did not set the tone of the household; wives did. For the wife, good humor was a job requirement. "No one can afford to let a hasty temper, a sullen mood, and tense feelings ruin the life. The woman who is thus afflicted should not become a wife until she has become master of her disposition, and can speak and act calmly under annoying circumstances."[46]

Myrna Loy embodied Sinclair Lewis's advice for Carol Kennicott—to adopt a stance of "unembittered humor" to meet life's ugliness. In *The Thin Man* (1934) and its sequels and in the Academy Award–winning *The Best Years of Our Lives*, Loy, as Nora Charles and as Millie Stephenson, confronts drunken husbands with aplomb and wit. As Nora Charles, whose inheritance frees her husband from the need to pursue his detective work, Myrna Loy keeps their New York hotel room supplied with Scotch and matches her husband drink for drink. When warned about his former girl friends and faced with his former chums—crooks he has sent up—Nora says with dry aplomb, "I love you because you know such lovely people." In *Another Thin Man*, the former crooks round up babies and bring them in to celebrate Nickie Charles's first birthday; Nora is amused and charming through this chaos. Whenever husband Nick faces danger, however, she stops the repartee, hugs him, and lets tears well up in her eyes; her witty exterior is for his pleasure and not a defense against sentiment.

In *The Best Years of Our Lives*, banker Al Stephenson returns home from World War II and escapes the uncertainties of his first night home by going on a nightclub crawl with his wife Millie, who drinks with him, and his daughter Peggy (Teresa Wright), who stays sober to drive. Both Al and fellow former soldier Fred Derry (Dana Andrews) are carried home drunk, and the wife and daughter get them to bed and tuck them in. As Nora Charles, Myrna Loy also fixes a bed for the hungover William Powell—"Get out and let me straighten that bed; you're worse than an infant"—and in both versions the point is the same: men who are hurt, angry, confused, or celebratory are like children and must be guarded and cared for.

Caring for men and being their clever and entertaining companions occupied so much energy that child rearing became secondary. Historian Nancy Cott has remarked that "the extraordinarily large proportion of women maturing in the 1920s who remained childless, point[s] to the high tension surrounding modern motherhood. . . . People were marrying younger and more uniformly and wives were testifying to more sexual satisfaction, but fewer of them were producing children."[47] Indeed, as one writer warned,

> Too common today are people like Mary and Jim, who, in their eagerness to do all that books and lectures recommend for little Peter, get so involved in his welfare that they lost all their sense of fun. They are today thoroughly dull people, no longer interesting socially. Jim has failed to rise in his business, for he mislaid the spark of enthusiasm which made him an asset to his employer.[48]

A refined household had children but was not child-centered. Wives had to manage resources so that children had caretakers and devote their improving impulses to men.

Indeed, the wife who was so little interested in problems of consumption that she had too many children to sustain the family's living standard was a burden and not a partner. In *Seed: A Novel of the American Family* (1930), Charles G. Norris follows a California family through two generations from 1890 to 1930. Captain Dan Carter, who founds a ranch that prospers in the California agricultural boom, has spread his seed liberally, having nine children with his wife Matty and one with his brother's wife, a treachery that leads his brother to murder him. His youngest son, Bart Carter, an aspiring writer and the novel's protagonist, marries a first cousin, Peggy, and finds that her prodigious fertility, which quickly results in five births, traps him in a dull commercial publishing job. (Children no longer have the value they did when they could work a developing ranch.)

Desperate to free himself for writing, Bart begs his wife to use birth control, but Peggy, a devout Roman Catholic, refuses, and also discourages his novel-writing, which takes time from her and the children and brings in no income. When Bart has an affair with a supportive and successful editor, his wife packs up the children and leaves. For ten years, he enjoys success, with his novels popular and turned into screenplays. At the end, he returns to his family and argues with his dying brother, a priest, about whether Peggy should have agreed to use birth control. Norris evenhandedly presents both sides of the abortion argument. But the novel's shape leads us to think Peggy should have put her husband before her loyalty to the Catholic church; then they could have shared his success instead of enduring a painful and potentially irreversible separation. Bart loves "his Muggins," but her childlike adoration should have focused on him and not on priests. She is too old-fashioned for her husband's good.

Exemplifying Consumption's Benefits

The American woman was the world's wonder: educated, a voting citizen, intelligent and independent, good fun, sexy and attractive, but also domestic, homeloving, and monogamous. Her spirituality was not, as should be clear by now, developed and expressed through religion but through aesthetic ambition, spunk, beauty, and devotion to family. These qualities inspired men like Sinclair Lewis's Dr. Will Kennicott, who tells his wife Carol,

> "One time I said that you were my soul. And that still goes. You're all the things I see in a sunset when I'm driving in from the country, all the things that I like but can't make poetry of. . . . I go around twenty-four hours a day in mud and blizzard, trying my damnedest to heal everybody, rich or poor. . . . And I can stand the cold and the bumpy roads and the lonely rides at night. All I need is to have you here at home to welcome me." [49]

Being a man's "soul" meant not getting bogged down in household chores. Women's devotion to home required the consumption of helpful products, as well as access to servants, and these were the rewards women reaped for choosing to be home partners: the tributes of grateful men.

Household equipment was justified from the beginning by its ability to lighten the housewife's load. To demonstrate its effectiveness, though, wives had to appear fresh, cheerful, and attractive, even in the midst of housework. "Tidiness" and "daintiness" were the watchwords of the early 1920s, qualities with which any wife could transform housework, even scrubbing floors and doing laundry. Doing work in old clothes demoralized the wife and depressed her husband. If she bathed every morning, wore clean, becoming clothes and comfortable shoes, if she was not one of the "kimono-and-ragged-shoes army," and combed her hair simply, her work would appear pleasant. Such a wife and mother was "pretty all the time" because she found "'clean methods of doing dirty work.'" [50]

Housework was no longer drudgery. Machines performed like magical servants to elevate women's status and to give leisure, a social good justified in one book by paraphrasing Plato: "Tell me how the people of a nation organize their leisure time and I will tell you the destiny of that nation." [51] Women had proper tools available, and they needed only to manage them properly to create leisure time for themselves, time for "reading, an afternoon for club or bridge, tennis or embroidery, . . . time each day for study, rest or play." [52]

Toward the end of the 1930s, emphasis on fitness and a slender figure justified the wife's doing more of the physical labor of housework. In a piece titled "The Serious Business of Cleaning," illustrated by a drawing of a stylish young woman in shorts and a bandana wielding a wet mop, the author offers the upbeat advice that housework is "as good and better exercise than golf. It increases the appetite and slims the figure." It was only a matter of attitude. [53]

Self-sacrifice vanished from advice literature, except as a negative attitude inflicted by old-fashioned women who did not understand the need for a cheerful, energetic, playful household. Even efficiency expert Lillian M. Gilbreth instructed wives to plan housework so as to pursue their own interests and to remember that "it is really selfish to be too unselfish in the matter of giving up to others" in the family.[54]

Feminist playwright and novelist Susan Glaspell teaches this distinction with the story of "Blossom" Atwood Holt in *Ambrose Holt and Family* (1931). Poet Lincoln Holt has married Blossom, daughter of the town's wealthy manufacturer, and become manager of his father-in-law's cement business. Blossom manages social life for the gregarious Lincoln and cares for their large house with a maid and a nanny, who supervises their two sons. Blossom establishes her superiority when she welcomes the return of her father-in-law, a charming wanderer and seeker after life who abandoned his wife and young son years earlier. Through her intervention, Ambrose Holt, the father, is returned to his family's bosom in death. After refusing insulin and voluntarily giving up his life to diabetes, he is laid out in the Holt house and his burial service conducted there.

Reconciliation frees the son from anger at his father and fear of the restlessness that led to desertion; through Blossom's action, Lincoln will be able to open himself to life and to become a great, instead of simply gifted, poet. Though their daily routine "would slip back, and often seem a good deal as it had before [Ambrose Holt came], there had been life. . . . There lived in Lincoln something that was Blossom and lived in Blossom something that was Lincoln, because they had known together what neither could have known alone." Blossom concludes:

> She could be more patient now. She understood more so she need ask less. It was all right. One took what was there, and went ahead. It was all a journey, a pretty good journey. "Death is swallowed up in victory," the rector had said. "Make it victory," she said to something in herself. "Make it victory."[55]

From the beginning, the reader knows that Blossom has extraordinary sensitivity that will enable her to achieve a moral triumph. She manages a perfect house, partially because her sympathy is greater than her servants'. Only Millie and Blossom are allowed into Lincoln Holt's hideaway study, Blossom "to make sure Millie, who cleaned it, had not put books where papers should be, or changed ash tray and pens."[56] Blossom also hides in this room, and Millie, who never rings the bell to disturb its inhabitant, tells callers that her mistress is out. Except for cleaning, Millie honors the sanctum.

The governess, Miss Jewett, also lacks the independent empathy necessary to raise two very different boys: a strong, inquiring older son and a sickly, complaining younger one. As she gains maturity, Blossom realizes that "I must be with them more myself" to keep the sickly one from becoming a crybaby and the strong one from being oppressed by self-sacrifice.

Glaspell works variations on the old theme throughout the book. At the conclusion, Blossom gives up her desire to be called by a proper adult name—Harriette—instead of her infant nickname. Her new-found recognition that her wish is relatively unimportant echoes Glaspell's statement at the book's beginning: "Blossom did not like the idea of sacrifice, though she could not have said why, or rather, would not have permitted herself to know why. One should not know that it was sacrifice; one should know only that it was love and natural to do so."[57] Blossom's "sacrifice" is not to daily housework but to organizing her life around her husband and sons, giving them courage to live in a world bent on making money and destroying the natural environment. Her attractive moral character is rewarded with material comfort and servants.

Popular, sophisticated writer Christopher Morley puts a similar sentiment into the mind of his honest, upwardly mobile, working-class Irish heroine in *Kitty Foyle* (1939). Having failed to defeat Philadelphia's Main Line aristocracy for the soul of Wynnewood Strafford, her charming and weak first love, Kitty muses about whether to give up her successful career as assistant to a cosmetics magnate to marry an astute physician, Marcus Eisen. She is reluctant partially because the self-contained Mark seems to need so little help from her. He does not understand that "a woman loves most where she gives most. She loves you for letting her give. A person wants to give everything." The recognition that Mark's Jewishness, his "being so racial," is a hardship that needs pluck to get through life convinces Kitty, finally, that he needs her support and that she can love him.[58]

In no movie is women's loving men with hardships to overcome more lyrically expressed than in *The Best Years of Our Lives*, which won a special Academy Award for Harold Russell, a former serviceman who had lost both forearms in World War II. Returning to his tree-shaded neighborhood and his high school sweetheart Wilma (Cathy O'Donnell), Russell's character Homer Parrish puts her off and pretends not to love her so that she will not marry him out of pity. They are reconciled when he finally tests Wilma by letting her put him to bed, which requires removing his prosthetic arms and hook "hands." As with the other men in this movie, maimed by anger and the nightmares of war, Homer is tucked into bed by the woman who loves him. All three men are saved by a woman's respectful, attentive, loving care. Not self-sacrifice but a self-conscious giving defines womanly goodness.[59]

Women were no longer to act like self-sacrificing mothers, and they were not to look maternal. Despite Depression constraints, manuals of the 1930s urged wives to create enjoyments for themselves and to luxuriate in physical care. Advertisers and domestic manuals advised women that

> the first step in good grooming is cleanliness. The trouble with cleanliness is that most of us associate it with the hard, scrubbed, shiny kind, with hair screwed back into a knot. We have neglected to think of it as a luxuriant cleanliness. Use bath salts or bath liquid that have

glamour and make you forget dishpans, and dust cloths, and diapers. Make yourself feel like a lady of leisure in your bath, and you'll take more of them. . . . [Followed by creams and oils, they will] keep you looking years younger than you really are.[60]

Wives could aspire to the radiance and beauty of movie stars. Makeup used to lift women's morale, and not to entice men, was acceptable.
Cosmetics were no more artificial than clothes.

Long ago we grew into the habit of clothing our hands with gloves, our feet with shoes, our heads with hats; yet we went along for years with unclothed faces. Then some of our more adventurous sisters learned how our feminine ancestors solved the problem of protecting their faces from cold or sun, and gradually make-up edged its way into our habits. Make-up wants its rightful place after years of neglect.[61]

Makeup no longer signaled moral looseness or physical filth. Rouge was applied only over a "scrupulously clean" face, topping a meticulous body. New brides had to learn about deodorants, depilatories, soaps, skin oils, and astringents.

Cosmetics implied physical attraction, which implied sex. By the 1920s, sex was going through a metamorphosis from a dirty unmentionable, an unpleasant necessity, to a physical elixir and the foundation of marriage. For women, sex was often associated with the joys of motherhood, though this was not to be its goal. Intercourse itself should please, regardless of the complicated consequences of pregnancy. "Marriage advice books now made sex the centerpiece of marriage."[62]

In its new status, sex even outside marriage no longer ended in punishments that had been the staple for Victorian popular writing. Bertha, the silent heroine of Fannie Hurst's *Lummox*, is essentially raped by her first employer's son, a foppish aspiring poet named Rollo Farley. But in her arid life, the scene remains vivid. Though she initially protested, when Farley touched her, "She began to cry inwardly. There *was* a little heart in her throat that beat up against her silence. It was terrible to be dumb. She could have shrieked, 'I am all locked! You hear! Prairies are flowing in me and oceans and I am under them. Locked!'"[63] Farley takes her sexual longings and transmutes them into his only successful poem. He also takes Bertha's virginity and costs her the job because Mrs. Farley turns her out when her pregnancy is discovered.

Bertha, however, is betrayed by a man and not by her own sexual desire. Adopted by a wealthy couple, Bertha's son grows to be a handsome and sensitive pianist, endowed with the genius that brought his mother to his conception. At the novel's end, Bertha has become surrogate mother and housekeeper for a widowed, jolly, loving baker.

Kitty Foyle represents a different class of woman and a different di-
lemma. A white-collar girl (WCG), she finds passionate happiness with the
rich, attractive, morally weak Wyn Strafford. After romantic scenes in speak-
easies, a Pocono resort, and a New Jersey beach hotel, Wyn arrives in New
York on Halloween, and Kitty, happy with her first raise and a new room of
her own, forgets to take "precautions." When she discovers she is pregnant
and begins to fantasize about her life with Wyn—who "liked me practically
naked"—she reads the announcement of his engagement to an appropriate
Main Line debutante and decides to abort. Again, Wyn's weakness, his not
being "big enough to have a bastard," and not sexual indulgence, causes
Kitty's abortion. The cleaned-up movie version, in which Wyn's parents an-
nul his secret marriage to Kitty (stunningly played by Ginger Rogers), is
more painful. Kitty bears the baby, legitimate because of a secret and soon-
to-be annulled marriage, and then loses him to an infant illness.

Sex, women heard, was necessary and pleasurable, and its consequences were predictable in an era of birth control. Sexual satisfaction was
premised on the notion of companionate marriage. The idea that sexuality,
even without children, justified marriage, joined men and women in durable
social bonds. For women, this required one more psycho-emotional bal-
ancing act. They had to be sexually reticent before marriage and then be
sexually responsive in marriage. Wives had to keep husbands sexually interested. The stability of the American family rested on their success. Appearance and personality kept husbands attracted and alive. As the academic experts Ernest and Gladys Groves told their readers, "The wife . . . will always
add a bit of illusiveness [sic] to her comradeship with her husband—not
enough to annoy him, just enough to prevent her becoming a dull companion, lest their life together lose its zest when each thinks he knows all there is
to know of the other." [64]

Myrna Loy embodied the stunning and likable woman who attracted
men without making any effort to do so and who would never think of cheat-
ing on her husband. In *Another Thin Man*, she dances with a debonair
Frenchman only because she thinks he has a clue to the murder her husband
is investigating. William Powell, as Nick, watches with the amusement of the
perfectly confident husband and then, when a ruckus puts out the lights,
slugs the Frenchman and takes over as his wife's dance partner to surprise
her when the lights go on. She is grateful, saying, "Why Mr. Charles, I do
believe you care."

In *Mr. Blandings Builds His Dream House* (1948), a hackneyed film
about all the ways a well-to-do city slicker can be cheated when building a
Connecticut commuter house, much of the dramatic tension comes from Jim
Blandings's (Cary Grant) suspicion that Muriel Blandings (Myrna Loy) is
being pursued by his "lawyer and best friend," Bill Cole (Melvyn Douglas).
When Muriel and Bill are snowed in at the newly finished Connecticut
house, with Jim trapped in New York and his daughters marooned at school,

we know the film is heading toward a hysterical confrontation between Grant, Loy, and Douglas. In the end, Mr. Blandings has a dream house and a perfect wife and no reason for suspicion.

Marlene Dietrich's *Blonde Venus* (1932) provides a different version of how to reconcile vamping and virtue. In this film made for the American market, Dietrich plays housewife Helen Faraday. She is a German chorine, who met and married American scientist Ned Faraday while he was studying in Germany. When Faraday discovers that he has contracted radiation poisoning from his experiments, Helen resumes a show business career to earn money for him to return to Germany for treatment. She attracts rich Nick Townsend (Cary Grant) and gives him sexual favors in return for money to save her husband.

When her husband returns to Germany and she moves with their son into Townsend's mansion, Helen remains torn between her fascination with Townsend and her loyalty to Faraday as husband and father of her son. Dietrich has opportunities to perform sexy nightclub routines, singing, for instance, "I'm beginning to feel like an African queen; I want to be bad." But this is a facade. She is doing this work only because she loves her son and has temporarily lost the stability provided by her husband. In the end, Helen, Ned, and Johnny are reunited. In the reconciliation scene, Helen bathes the boy before bed, and then the parents repeat his favorite story about how the young American scientist found the beautiful princess bathing in a country pool and won her hand. Dietrich gives up being a nightclub star in return for being the princess of one home, and her affair is forgiven.

A girl's learning to play the part of a homemaker with a bit of siren in her began during adolescent dating, according to Beth L. Bailey's *From Front Porch to Back Seat*.[65] By the 1920s, youth culture clearly approved of necking and petting as enjoyable and natural activities. In addition, as one boy said, "'When a boy takes a girl out and spends $1.20 on her (like I did the other night) he expects a little petting in return.'"[66] Though sometimes stated so crudely, petting was not exactly a payoff for a boy's dating expenses but rather an expected fillip to the evening, and one increasingly believed to be regulated by the female.

Girls controlled sex on the basis of character. A "lady" knew how to have fun and yet to convey the limits of familiarity. She should never have to say no. "The convention of women's responsibility absorbed this seeming contradiction. If the man took sexual advantage (which, in very early days, might mean only hand-holding but might extend to rape) or even tried to do so, the woman must have not *really* been a lady. She must have, somehow, invited or encouraged him."[67] (When the married man, Dana Andrews, kisses young Peggy Stephenson in *The Best Years of Our Lives*, he immediately recognizes her virtue, saying, "That shouldn't have happened.")

In 1940, in *The Philadelphia Story*, Katharine Hepburn's Tracy Lord illustrates a young woman's difficult search for the mean between the extremes of frigidity and moral looseness. Described by her former husband

Dexter Haven (Cary Grant) as a goddess unable to accept human frailty, Hepburn rails against her father's philandering and her uncle's drinking. She was not touched sexually by her marriage, it is implied, but is one of that widespread "class of married maidens," "perennial spinsters no matter how many [their] marriages," as her father observes.

On the eve of her marriage to ambitious, successful businessman and politician George Kittredge (John Howard), Hepburn is attracted to young Macauley Connor (Jimmy Stewart), a bashful and talented writer covering the society wedding for a gossip magazine. Annoyed at her husband-to-be, Hepburn dances and drinks until dawn on the eve of her wedding. She and the now-smitten Stewart kiss and swim, and then Stewart gallantly deposits his almost unconscious queen in her room, observed by Cary Grant and Lord's younger sister. When Hepburn staggers into the garden on her wedding morning and learns that she was drunk and affectionate, she assumes that she has had sexual intercourse and tells the bridegroom Kittredge that he must not marry a woman of "easy virtue."

Connor, a man of honor, corrects the mistake—he would never take advantage of a drunken "lady"—and Kittredge tries to persuade Lord to marry him, with the warning that he expects her "to behave herself, naturally." Former husband Haven immediately echoes his own desire that she "behave herself naturally." With her future balanced on the meaning of a comma, Lord dismisses Kittredge and, in the rapid turnaround of farce, re-marries Dexter Haven, promising this time to be "yawr," like an "easy to handle" sailboat.

With movie stars providing models, women learned how to be sexy without being "loose." By the time she married, a woman knew that she had to be sexy, for her own satisfaction and her husband's. She was responsible for her husband's fidelity as well as her own. A woman shouldn't think,

> "Now I am safely married, I don't need to fuss so much over my appearance" [and become not] quite so fastidious about her hair in the morning. Or perhaps her negligee or house frock is soiled or mussy looking. *Remember you are still competing with women who are putting lots of time and thought on their looks and clothes,* and men always have a wandering eye for feminine charm. Remember, too, that they are by nature polygamous; they simply can't help it. You have to hold your man against the girls at the office, and the women he meets socially.[68]

Wives had to tend the romance on which marriages were based. "Carry on a love affair with your husband just as you did during your courtship," one adviser wrote. "Forget about the dishes and cleaning up if the moon is high, the air flower-scented, and the night glamorous. Knives and forks can wait, but sentiment is of the moment."[69]

In the ideal world, the wife could leave the knives and forks for the domestic to wash when she came in first thing in the morning. Otherwise, the wife had to give over being a housekeeper to be a lover. She planned her emotional and physical self-presentation to entice and reassure her husband, just as she planned and served balanced meals. Her greatest trick was juggling her own needs and her family's desires to create the exquisite picture of an independent *and* domestic *and* pretty female: the ideal woman of the second quarter of the American century.

Such women—who held together marriages, men's souls, and social standards—deserved all they could be given—and certainly the assistance of less sparkling women. In novels, movies, and advice books, women got images of the MCH as a woman with personal resources but also a woman whose manifold tasks "deserved" help. Carol Kennicott has Scandinavian maids like Bea Sorensen; Kitty Foyle's widowed father hires Myrtle to keep his house and help raise his daughter. Myrtle gives Kitty spontaneous love, since "colored people don't have to stop and think in order to be wise; they just know about things naturally, it oozes out of them."[70] Marlene Dietrich also finds friendly, responsible black women to watch over her son Johnny while she is performing. Black Gussie (Louise Beavers) not only serves the Blandings family but saves its house when an advertising slogan which Mr. Blandings realizes is catchy and can salvage his major ad account, pops out of her mouth.

On the morning he is to lose his job because he has not invented a slogan for a ham substitute called WHAM, Gussie says, as she calls the family to breakfast, "If it ain't WHAM, it ain't ham." Jim Blandings knows it's a great slogan and tells Muriel Blandings to give Gussie a $10 raise. Gussie is then pictured in the ad campaign to represent good cooking, just as Delilah symbolized Bea Pullman's restaurants in *Imitation of Life*. This is the dominant fictional narrative for black women's lives, assistants to white women and caretakers of white family life.

Only the immediate postwar film *The Best Years of Our Lives* pointed to an era without servants. When Al Stephenson's daughter washes dishes on his first night home from military service, he asks: "Is this the maid's night out?" With some amusement, the wife and daughter point out to him that the maid took a "night out" three years ago and has not come back. Life goes on comfortably, however, because daughter Peggy took a course in "domestic science."

For MCHs of the 1920s, 1930s, and 1940s, the ideal vision of wifely womanliness translated into arduous and important tasks that could not be completed without assistance, even by the wife trained in home economics. The complementary story of the enduring and self-effacing loyalty of women of color, spinsters, and working-class women led MCHs to expect to find help from these sources.

Three

The Businessman's Wife at Work

The home is a place for leisure, where the amenities of life are to be fostered, where the spiritual values are to be conserved. . . . The home undoubtedly exists primarily to build the personalities of the next generation, to surround children with that environment which will call out the best that is in them; but to do this adequately, the personalities of both mother and father must also be released, and those of the workers within the home.
—Amey E. Watson, "The Homemaking Industry," 1928

Husbands and children expected to find the home a healthy, sustaining retreat from the outside world, as it had been depicted in popular culture since the mid-nineteenth century. At home, one found appropriately cooked food, charmingly served; clean clothes; clean, orderly, and refreshing spaces for bathing, sleeping, eating, and socializing; and happy, well-mannered children. The time-consuming tasks required to meet this ideal represented a labor of love—of service to the family's members.[1]

Physical labor, hundreds of diligently performed tasks, made possible this pleasant existence. These were not, as we saw in Chapter Two, to require that the wife sacrifice her existence to her family's; rather, she must

41

organize the family resources so that she, too, joined in the home's gracious living. How a wife got the necessary housekeeping done so that she retained time for the demands of homemaking is the subject of this chapter.[2]

First, the MCH reconceived her work as an analogue of her husband's work: management. By the end of the 1910s, middle-class husbands worked as managers and leaders in ever larger and more complex corporate and professional enterprises; these jobs became a middle-class norm.[3] Their wives likewise aspired to transform housework from manual to managerial work. A workingman's wife, caring for a man whose clothes were dirty from a day of physical labor, could easily see the bargain between her husband's work and her own; a bank manager's wife could not.[4] Business-class wives owed it to their husbands' careers and to their own feelings of equality and self-worth to be efficient managers and gracious hostesses, combining professional skills with the social style of the cultivated and wealthy.[5]

"Keeping up with the Joneses" became an American cliché in the 1920s. For middle-class wives, it was an imperative. A workingman's wife might shop for the cheapest or most durable of goods and expected to raise the family's living standard by buying good food and clothing and imaginatively reshaping it for aesthetic benefit. Business-class wives shopped for style as well as durability; their job was to increase the family's comfort and freedom from mundane concerns. Working-class wives learned about politics and took their opinions from their husbands; middle-class wives continued to develop independent thought in book clubs and discussion groups, following practices begun during the 1870s.[6] It was socially acceptable for working-class wives to work to earn needed income; middle-class wives argued for not wasting their intellectual training. Both middle-class and working-class homes catered to husbands and children, even when wives worked, but the middle-class wife was distinguished by her superior organization and consumption.

With service the central concept of home living, wives had few choices: do the work themselves as servers, buy services in products already made, or buy and manage the labor of other women as substitutes for wives. (Well-to-do wives, of the sort who incorporated local societies into the national Junior Leagues in 1921, presumably had a staff of servants so that they could devote their energies to the public good.) Buying home equipment reduced the wife's physical labor; it did not bring the same benefits as turning the work over to a servant so that the housewife could enjoy the benefits that suffused the warm imagery of home. As one writer said,

> There isn't one of us who does her own housework who doesn't also cherish the hope that one day she will have human assistance in the process. Science has been an enormous help in lightening the white woman's burden, but it'll be a long time before we're offered a satisfactory substitute for somebody else to do the housework, light or heavy.[7]

Surely many women succumbed to the desire to be mothered directly and not just through the vicarious pleasure of their own caretaking. A social system with working-class women available to be hired as servants increased the possibility that the wife could also enjoy at least moments of infantile regression.[8]

Husbands, who paid for the privilege, and children expected every sort of home comfort. Wives acted as the agents to buy things the family wanted and to wangle or coerce them out of hired workers. When they failed, the only recourse was for the wife to do the work herself—and to feel herself sunk unfairly into domestic servitude. A wife was torn between her family's demands and those of the servants she wished to placate; though she was often a mediator between the two groups, the wife's material interests remained firmly bound to her male breadwinner.

An exemplary schedule in such a home comes from a fictional account of one household's day published in the late 1930s by *Fortune* magazine to convey information gathered from a poll of readers yielding seventeen thousand responses and a survey of three thousand local women's clubs.[9] In the house of William and Dorothy Smith, successful and jovial Mr. Smith

> wants to get up in the morning in an orderly room; bathe and shave in a bathroom equipped with clean towels and toilet articles that are in their right places; leave the towels, however, in a soggy heap on the bathroom floor; and returning to his room, find clean underwear, socks, shirt, collar, and handkerchief in the proper drawers. He wants to go into a pleasant dining room for breakfast and find no traces of the poker game of the previous evening. He likes his newspaper at his place, his fruit ice cold, his eggs and sausages sizzling from the fire, his toast hot, crisp, and golden, and his coffee just so—boiling, fragrant, and of an exact strength. He wants to find his hat and overcoat without falling over tricycles and ice skates in the hall closet.

Many of the things that have to be done so that Mr. Smith can get ready to go to work in the morning are done, in this fictional household, by Anna Johnson. She has been up since 6:45 and cleared the ashtrays and glasses from last night's poker game; she has cooked and served breakfast, and she will clear and tidy the bathroom during her morning duties.

Dorothy Smith appears in the *Fortune* account after all these chores are completed, for "Mr. Smith likes his wife to kiss him goodby at the door; and as he leaves he may allow that they had better make it early tonight in view of last night's poker game, which lasted very late. He will be home for dinner at six-thirty, and no company. Mrs. Smith says fine," since she has "already told Anna that to make up for the extra work caused by the poker game she can get off early tonight to go to the movies."

Having seen her husband off, Dorothy Smith consults with Anna and plans "a simple evening meal: tomato soup, hamburg steak, baked potatoes, string beans and apple sauce with sponge cake that Anna baked yesterday." This three-course meal can be served and cleaned up by "quarter to eight" so that Anna can make her movie date. Dorothy then makes the beds for herself and her children, who have been sent off to school. She dresses and goes grocery shopping.

In the afternoon, the children arrive from school, and Anna gives them snacks. Dorothy sets the dinner table and is responsible for an evening chat with her husband and children. The *Fortune* account varies the evening story with an episode apparently common in middle-class households—inviting company for dinner.

Forgetting his morning resolution, Bill Smith responds with instant sociability to a visiting friend from out of town and asks him and his wife to dinner. He telephones his wife, who must inform Anna about this change in plans, and together they make the decision that "hamburger is not good enough for guests," so, at 4:00 the menu is changed, with steak and french fries replacing the hamburger and "homely" baked potatoes.

When Bill arrives home with the guests,

> he wants to find Dorothy smiling on the doorstep and the children restfully out of sight for the night. He wants to find some nice little canapes in the living room to eat with the cocktails, but he wants to go to the pantry to make the cocktails himself. He wants to make Bacardis tonight, and in doing so spills sugar on the floor and leaves lime skins and some juice on the drainboard. He wants to sit around over the Bacardis and canapes until everybody is feeling good and then go in to dinner with a definite sense of pride in his house, his wife, his drinks, his food.

These are the just rewards of the successful man, *Fortune* implies; in addition to the promotions his hard work have earned him, Bill feels "he has also earned a pleasant home, a charming wife, children, an automobile, and every minute of the leisure in which he enjoys them."

Sharing her husband's views, Dorothy's main job is to make certain that her husband is unbothered by the work of keeping him comfortable and enabling him spontaneously to invite guests home to a restaurant-quality meal. To be attractively groomed and able to join the social conversation, Mrs. Smith relies on another woman to cook dinner and to keep it palatable until her husband is ready to bring his guests to the dinner table.

The outcomes, of course, are that the food is overcooked from waiting, Anna misses her date and alienates her boyfriend, Dorothy has to cajole Anna not to quit, and Bill Smith has a hangover the next morning. These problems, however, are not Mr. Smith's fault. He is, as the *Fortune* writer's lightly satirical tone implies, messy like most men and not so careful as women are with domestic tasks.

The problem is Dorothy's management and her assumption "that Anna is of a different, and lower, class." Anna is Dorothy's employee and not Bill's, and it is up to Dorothy to figure out how to mediate between her gregarious husband's spontaneous desires and her domestic's justifiable expectation to be treated like workers in other jobs. Bill Smith's expectations are not the problem; Dorothy's management is. *Fortune* assumes that Bill, like other bosses, cannot make such errors about employees because "he knows, and everybody else knows, that he is giving orders to his political and social equals (using society in its broad sense) and not to menials." If Dorothy wants to do her job properly and cannot manage her time and budget to hire the work done, then she must do it herself.

This version of a "day in the life of the Smiths" was fictional, but the same message pervaded home advice and housewives' own accounts. A significant part of the wife's job was to protect a husband's feeling that achievement in the public world entailed effortless comfort in the private world. Successful men, in this scenario, experienced home with a powerful bliss of infancy, when physical wants were served by a congenial mother. (Children in this account were kept out of the father's way so that they did not compete for attention and services.) He could be as messy as he liked, and the products of his waste would disappear with no effort on his part. He could violate the order with which he ran his business and suffer no penalties. He could make a mess and not have to clean it up.[10]

Between 1920 and the end of World War II, American housewives had a three-part job: managing labor (their own or someone else's) to produce cooking, laundry, cleaning, and child care for a middle-class household; displaying graceful aplomb in purveying these service products; and maintaining a social life with their friends and husbands. Manuals, textbooks, popular writings, and women's personal accounts convey the weight of the multiple demands. Yet once the flurry of cooperative experiments during World War I had passed, no one conceived the job as other than the problem of the individual housewife. To achieve the level of service described in the *Fortune* story, wives had to get particular household jobs done and maintain a social existence for themselves.

Women's clubs offered a sociable way of meeting two responsibilities: self-development and gathering information about child rearing and home management techniques. A New England tradition since the 1820s, secular mothers' clubs revived in Cambridge, Massachusetts, in the 1870s and continued for almost a century. Cambridge wives, many married to Harvard University faculty members, formed four generations of mothers' clubs, discussing child rearing and nutrition in the early years of each club's existence and turning, when the children that occasioned the clubs' formation were grown, to travel accounts, literature, and politics. The Cambridge clubs met at 2:30 to have time for presentations and tea before the members returned home to supervise dinner, indicating their reliance on servants to attend to children in the afternoon.[11]

Two Seven Sister colleges set up institutes to aid educated women such as those who met in the Cambridge mothers' clubs: Vassar College's Institute of Euthenics and Smith College's Institute for the Co-Ordination of Women's Interests. Under the direction of Ethel Puffer Howes, the Smith College institute developed a project to locate and place older and younger women as assistants to Smith College alumnae who had "household responsibilities, such that [they are] enabled to continue some measure, at least, of the work for which [they] have been trained," released "from care, or interruption." [12] The Vassar institute responded to "the unrest among women [who] want adequate rest, exercise, recreation, mental stimulation, times for personal upkeep" with a recommendation for better "household organization" through the use of "business methods" and putting "in all the time-saving equipment possible." [13]

As college women met in clubs to discuss means for running their households and to sustain their identities as educated women with interests outside housework, they also imbibed and perpetuated rising standards of service production. During the 1910s, and in greater numbers in the 1920s, many college women enrolled in expanding departments of home economics. Women majored in the field, took courses, or became aware of advanced knowledge from their friends who were in such classes. Having learned theories of food chemistry and experienced standards of laboratory hygiene, as well as learning chemical analysis of textiles and cleaning methods and preparations, middle-class women brought new ideals to running their own homes and to assessing their friends' homes. Standards developed in high school or college courses were reinforced by vast amounts of publicity and public writing on how to design, furnish, and use the home, much of it created by home economists who found jobs with commercial companies and retailers. One listing of "education work in Home Management . . . being done by many manufacturers and wholesalers" found eleven categories in use: "Daily paper advertising; Daily paper reading articles; Magazine advertising and reading articles; pamphlets, samples and circulars; Demonstrations; Lectures with or without demonstration; Motion pictures; Display and Exhibits; Bill Boards; Special reports of Laboratory and Research Work." [14] Some women gained incomes purveying standards that all MCHs were expected to meet in their own homes.

What were these standards, and how did an MCH in possession of a full-time or a daily domestic organize her work? What chores did housewives feel they must do themselves, and what tasks did they think appropriate for turning over to a hired worker? Which tasks did wives feel particularly stigmatizing as signs of an inadequately funded or improperly ordered household? [15]

At the beginning of the period, a popular home economics textbook offered a skeletal schedule for a week: "Monday—1) Put house in order, 2) Cook for Tuesday, 3) Prepare for laundering. Tuesday—Do Washing. Wednesday—Iron and bake; do thick starching. Thursday—Finish ironing.

Friday—Put house in order. Saturday—Bake and plan for Sunday."[16] The
heavy emphasis on laundry left little time for putting the house in order,
though the time was allowed for baking. Such an outline assumed that a few
large tasks defined the week's work and that the housewife did not need instruction about the other tasks that fit in between the big job of laundry.

By 1940, by contrast, a daily schedule for "a full-time housekeeper"
delineated the upkeep that a husband like fictional Bill Smith had come to
expect. Every day the bathroom was cleaned to meet standards of hotel
hygiene; the housekeeper was to "wipe tub, basin and floor. Wash glasses.
Clean toilet. Change or refold towels and washcloths. Check toilet paper,
soap, and mouth wash for replacements." After cooking lunch and dinner,
she was to "brush kitchen floor, wipe working surfaces and stove." The
weekly tasks, still arranged day by day, were as follows:

Monday: Laundry.
Tuesday: Ironing day. Marketing day. Sort and put away laundry.
Wednesday: Day off!
Thursday: Thorough cleaning of bedrooms (including vacuum-cleaning
     rugs, turning mattresses and changing bed linen, wiping finger
     marks from woodwork with damp cloth, dusting moldings, mopping
     closet floors).
Friday: Thorough cleaning of living and dining rooms (including
     vacuum-cleaning rugs and upholstered furniture, vacuum-cleaning
     cloth lampshades and washing others with damp cloth, wiping finger
     marks from woodwork with damp cloth, dusting all moldings). Clean
     icebox. Marketing day.
Saturday: Scrub bathroom floors and walls.

Finally, what were called the "Do-When-You-Can-Duties" could be fitted
into spare time: "polishing silver—when it needs it. Polishing furniture—
when it needs it. Waxing kitchen linoleum. Vacuum-cleaning beds. [And]
washing windows (we hope you can hire someone for this.)"[17] This was a
housewife's schedule, but it could be adapted for hiring a "general houseworker," who would, of course, have Thursdays off instead of Wednesdays
and not enjoy the flexibility of the housewife in taking extra time off or shirk-
ing some tasks.

High-quality housekeeping incorporated equipment advocated from
the beginning of the 1920s by experts such as Christine Frederick. Frederick
thought that housewives who lacked servants could manage most of their
work by purchasing "fireless cookers," which would reduce "ashes, soot or
smoke, to make further cleaning labor for the homemaker," and vacuum
cleaners, washers, and dishwashers, which would "replace a large share of
the work usually done by a permanent servant."[18] Electric irons were so
widely used in the early 1920s that Frederick did not even mention them.[19]

As the above roster of a week's housework showed, such equipment eased the physical burden but did not release the wife from the home. An MCH's actual schedule showed the advantage of servants: no dishwashing, no dinner to cook, and no heavy cleaning or washing. Instead, the wife expected to "assume responsibility for children . . . [do] cooking, baking, planning, marketing, and occasionally help with straightening the house." The schedule for this model household was "very flexible because uppermost in the minds of the parents in this household [were] the three children."

General Daily Schedule
    8:00 A.M. Breakfast prepared and served by maid
    12:00 Luncheon for two youngest children
    6:00 P.M. Dinner (early hour to give maid free evening)
Monday
    Wash day. Extra help for twelve hours. Finishes all washing and ironing including maid's.
    When mistress is out maid puts laundry away (which is seldom)
    Maid washes breakfast dishes
    Makes bed and straightens up house
    Gives children luncheon
    Scrubs bathrooms and kitchen
    Bathes youngest child while mistress prepares dinner
    Maid sets table and serves dinner
    Two older children usually help with dishes, unless they are legitimately engaged elsewhere
Tuesday
    Same as Monday
Wednesday
    Same as Monday. Silver is cleaned this day. Mother and children usually assist
Thursday
    Extra help for ten hours for thorough housecleaning and window washing
    Maid makes beds, washes dishes, straightens up
    1:00 P.M. Free for day
Friday
    Same as Monday. Extra work: cleaning ice box, stove and pantry
Saturday
    Children are at home, consequently things do not get finished promptly as usual
    maid scrubs kitchen and bathrooms, prepares food for Sunday's meal; changes bed linen
Sunday
    straightens house, assists with lunch while mistress goes to church
    Children help with lunch dishes

Maid is off every Sunday right after lunch. The family helps her get away by two o'clock.

2:00 P.M. Free for day[20]

This housewife's high standard of hygiene required daily scrubbing of bathrooms and kitchen, daily straightening of the house and making beds, weekly change of bed linens, and weekly cleaning of windows, silver, and all rooms. She maintained the standard by purchasing the full-time work of one woman and the part-time, one-day-a-week work of two other women.

This housewife also considered herself a full-time worker. Her day presumably began with dressing three children before the 8:00 A.M. breakfast; moved into morning meal planning and marketing apparently accompanied by the preschool-age child; switched after lunch to afternoon child care and dinner preparation; and concluded with evening social time (notably absent from the schedule) with her children and husband.

The essentials of good housekeeping, as revealed in these accounts, were cleaning, laundry, cooking and serving meals, and child care. These tasks had to be accomplished in addition to the wife's managing her own labor or that of servants, marketing, and planning social life, as illustrated in Figure 1.[21]

Cleaning, laundry, cooking, and child care, however, required a workweek longer than that put in by most industrial workers by the 1920s. A more detailed account helps one imagine the demands reluctant housewives felt were placed on them.

Cleaning, that one simple word, covered a series of tasks that any proficient housewife or domestic should have in her head. Tedious though it is to list them, it was probably no less tedious to execute them. Of the usual six rooms in a house (living room, dining room, kitchen, bathroom, two bedrooms), the dining room required the following work once a week:

Assemble cleaning equipment.
Pick up and put away papers, magazines, and linens.
Carry out and clean rugs and scarfs.
Remove from room and dust small pieces.
Dust walls with wall brush, vacuum attachment, or broom.
Dust woodwork, windows, and door casings.
Shake and brush curtains or use vacuum attachment.
Dust pictures.
Clean and polish mirrors, glass doors, china closets, and cabinets.
Dust and polish furniture, taking higher pieces first. Be sure to polish legs and rungs of chairs.
Use vacuum on upholstered chair seats.
Use dust mop on floor.
Clean rug with vacuum.
Replace furniture and small articles and rugs.

Figure 1. Chart Showing Organization Needed for Two Maids

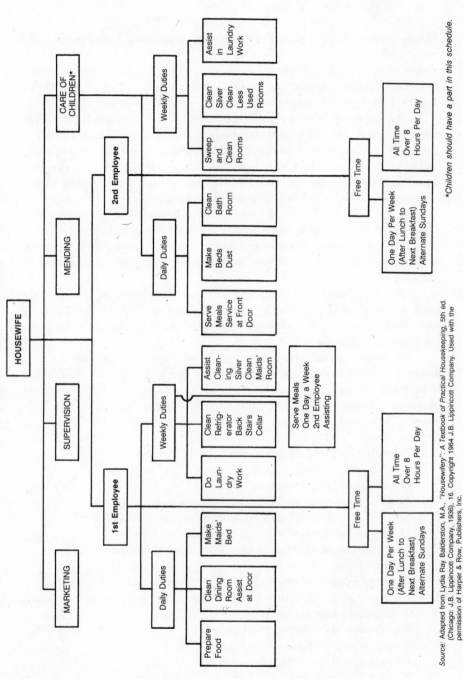

Source: Adapted from Lydia Ray Balderston, M.A., "Housewifery": *A Textbook of Practical Housekeeping*, 5th ed. (Chicago: J.B. Lippincott Company, 1936), 16. Copyright 1964 J.B. Lippincott Company. Used with the permission of Harper & Row, Publishers, Inc.

Straighten shades and pictures.
Check before leaving room to make sure everything is in order.

Each day the housewife checked that the room was "straightened," wilted
flowers were discarded and water changed, pictures were dusted, and crumbs
were swept from table and floor.[22] The other five rooms got the same attention. I have recounted these tasks in detail so that readers may mentally walk
through them; my hope is to convey the laborious attention required to keep
houses in conformity to middle-class standards of hygiene and orderliness.

Such high standards of cleanliness required more than one worker or
long hours of work. A wife could ask her family to make beds on the weekend
but not during the week: for schoolchildren and her husband, "It's just one
thing too heavy in the morning." She could leave straightening and dusting
of the children's rooms for them after school. Older children "should certainly hang up their own clothes. But never be too great an optimist: some
people have spent a life-time being taught and forced and begged to hang
their clothes up, and they never, never learned how."[23]

Instead of relying on her family, an MCH could hire a domestic. One
author gave the model of an ambitious schedule for a "part-time employee,"
who came in six days a week at 1:00 P.M. and left at 8:30 after serving dinner,
which included cleaning the dining room and kitchen before leaving each
day. She thoroughly cleaned the bathroom and kitchen on alternate days,
lightly cleaned the apartment twice a week, and thoroughly cleaned it once a
week. The housewife's cleaning responsibilities were making the beds and
straightening the house each day.[24]

A survey of college-educated housewives in Bethlehem, Pennsylvania,
found that only 45 percent did all the work of straightening up "toys, night-
clothes, and magazines" before a domestic worker arrived. The same group
of women expected their servants "to keep bathroom and kitchen in order at
all times" but were

> evenly divided upon whether or not they expected all pieces of fur-
> niture to be moved on cleaning days. 57 percent preferred having rugs car-
> ried out and shaken to having them merely cleaned by [vacuum]
> cleaner. 65 percent wanted their floors waxed by maid. 82 percent
> wanted their cushions taken out and cleaned. Half wanted floors done
> up on hands and knees and a little less than half expected unseen parts
> of furniture to be cleaned weekly.[25]

Cleaning entailed maintenance of heavy furniture. Varnished furniture
had to be washed and polish reapplied. Old wax had to be removed and new
rubbed into waxed furniture. Upholstery had to be scrubbed with a home-
made soap jel or a commercial cleaner. Bedsprings had to be turned and
dusted, mattresses and pads aired and scrubbed, and pillows washed. Kitchen

stoves had to be taken apart and grease removed; refrigerators had to be defrosted weekly and odors removed with baking soda. Most controversially, windows had to be cleaned—a job that domestics resisted and argued should be hired out to men.[26]

Laundry, like cleaning, became an obsession. In the 1920s, laundry work that had been done outside the household began to return home, with scientific warnings about the danger of infection adding emphasis to manufacturers' claims on behalf of new home washing equipment. Even though home economics expert Benjamin Andrews thought that the economics of laundry production would ultimately take the work out of the home, home laundry was in the early 1920s "the most universal kind of domestic help in America. The advantages of this arrangement are its opportunity to give oversight, to control the processes," which might otherwise risk infections.[27]

Large quantities of clothes and linens had to be laundered because people expected to change clothing frequently. One innovation that increased weekly laundry was the passing of the detached starched collar. For almost one hundred years, from the 1820s to the 1920s, gentlemen wore shirts for many days running, needing only to change the collars and cuffs. Experience in World War I with attached collars on the shirts to military uniforms created a fad, and by the late 1920s the detached collar had passed from the scene. The new fashion, of course, required that the entire shirt be washed and ironed to clean collars and cuffs. With the addition of colored shirts to men's wardrobes in the mid-1920s, men's clothing choices proliferated and so did their wardrobes. By the late 1920s, caring for men's clothes had become a complicated and laborious job.[28]

As home equipment returned the weeks' washing to better-off households, wives found they had a more complex task than sorting clothes for the laundry and checking that all items were returned intact. First, clothes had to be sorted into "slightly soiled pieces" like table linens; "body-soiled pieces" like bedding, underwear, and shirts; and "colored clothes" divided among cottons and linens, lighter and darker. Before actually laundering, pockets had to be checked, stains removed, and clothes soaked for ten to fifteen minutes.

To begin washing, a batch of sorted clothes was dropped into the churning machine, while the launderer prepared rinse tubs, one with hot water and one with cold water, and bluing or bleach for dark or white garments. Clothes were fed by hand from the washer through a wringer directly into the first tub, and a second batch of clothes was put into the washer. While the second batch churned, the launderer wrung "the first batch into the second water, and finally from here into the [carrying] basket. . . . If any article require[d] starching, [she stirred] up a solution in a shallow pan, and dip[ped] it into this before consign[ing] it to the basket." Starch was mixed in heavy, medium, or light concentrations depending on its use for stiff collars and draperies; on "house dresses, slacks, smocks, and children's play clothes"; or on "sheer cottons, lawn, dimity, dotted swiss, and men's soft shirts." Old garments of silks, rayons, and linens might be given light starch "as a restorer."[29]

It is little wonder that one writer warned that though "the swishing, churning suds, the constant vital motion [of a washing machine] seemed to symbolize . . . the very epitome of energy and cleanliness, [which] we know, is next to godliness . . . *after* the suds came the wringing, came the hanging. . . . You [might] love washing machines in the aggregate and shy away from them in the flesh."[30] A woman might well choose the hazards of sending clothes out or, if she possibly could, spend part of her household budget on a laundress to operate laundry equipment in the house.

Ironing completed the laundry task. By 1940, the standard still required ironing bath towels; one writer, however, suggested putting them "through the ringer neatly folded, and lay them with reasonable care in the basket. They will turn out tidy and pressed, ready for the shelf, and much more absorbent than if they had been ironed." A more daring suggestion: "how about simply folding the dish-towels—and the sheets—and the underwear—or are we going too far?"[31] Certainly it was too far for the household that expected "never to hang away any garment . . . without pressing it."[32]

Maintaining high standards of cleaning and laundering enabled the family's appearance to exemplify its inner state of purity and "godliness." These tasks required hard physical labor and time. Even though the carpet might be vacuumed instead of being carried outside for beating, heavy furniture had to be moved so the vacuum could cover every bit of floor. Even though the washing machine worked on electricity, the clean clothes that emerged had to be lifted, starched, hung, and ironed. If a housewife could afford to hire only day work, it was little wonder that she hoped to get laundry and the major week's cleaning out of her purchase.

Cooking was another matter. Though meals were simplified by comparison with the prewar era, the housewife was assaulted with new information about nutrition and diet as keys to good health. Her duty to her family required producing three "protective" meals a day and making meals that could be the centerpiece to social life.[33] Holiday, Sunday, and party meals inspired unusual efforts. Everyday meals defined a day's treadmill: breakfast by 8:00, lunch for children, and dinner at 6:30 or 7:00, followed by dishwashing. One cookbook hinted at this inexorability when it finished instructions for each dinner with a list of "preparations for the future" meals that could be completed while fixing that night's dinner.[34]

Breakfast began the day; usually it was cooked and served to a variety of tastes. Often, breakfast preparation included cleanup from the previous night. In a parody description, one Vassar critic saw a young domestic's morning: "She does not say she minds the stench of the ash-trays and empty glasses from last night's party, nor being up to clear away their traces before she gets the three-minute egg on the table in time for the [husband's] 7:55 train."[35]

Lunches were for children and the housewife, though she might entertain friends on a regular basis. Even if she had no "help" with entertaining,
she could

> cut down her output, not perhaps, on the amount of entertaining but
> on the type? For example, if she [found] she [could] not swing a lun-
> cheon party during a certain week with a menu of chicken in patty
> shells and souffle, suppose she [gave] the party anyway and serve[d]
> frankfurters and potato salad?[36]

Dinner was a central event of the day, the time for husbands and wives
to socialize and to sustain friendship with each other and the time to create a
sense of family unity. One textbook told the cautionary tale of "a social work
student sent to aid a family that was hardly if at all maintaining its unity. . . .
She insisted as the first step that the family meal be regularly prepared and
that they sit down and eat together, and out of this beginning she remade
family life."[37]

Social dinners increased the everyday demands of regular family cooking. One YWCA club member who believed in the 48-hour week for domestics, found that "our Sunday dinners made that impossible. It had been the
tradition of the household that the family should have a gathering of the clan
every Sunday, and I had no desire to give up that tradition when it fell to my
lot to be responsible for carrying it on."[38]

Well-served families expected three meals a day, served formally, with
multiple courses. Such service was not to require the mother to leave the
table because this was disruptive of the gracious manners displayed at meals.
(This is in striking contrast to working-class households in which the housewife often served the meal and did not eat until after the husband and children.) Ever ready to advocate mechanical innovations, Christine Frederick
assured housewives that

> the serving of meals can be accomplished gracefully and with ease,
> even without a servant. Some form of portable wheel tray and either
> warming disks or electric plate warmer or disk stove turned at "low"
> heat, and platters with covers are needed. . . . The reason meals with-
> out a servant are frequently interrupted with rising and confusion is
> not that it must be so, but because there *has not been sufficient
> planning*.[39]

Having a server was preferable, and special entertaining and parties
required extra hands. Etiquette for table-setting and serving regularly appeared in advice books, classroom texts, and even specialized guides. The
family might not enjoy such service every night, but the forms of "English or
family style" serving were clear: food platters were placed by the host, and

the servant brought two hot plates at a time to be filled by the host and then served, from the "left side using the left hand" to each guest beginning with the hostess. Water glasses were filled, dinner plates cleared, and dessert and coffee served without interrupting conversation.[40]

Housewives able to employ a full-time domestic to serve regular or special meals still had to gain nutritional knowledge to plan balanced meals and consumer information to get the best prices and products, "tasks requiring initiative, managerial ability, and a knowledge of scientific principles."[41] Meal planning required the housewife to study nutrition, meal plans, and products available and to plot the use of leftovers. Two innovations especially encouraged this endeavor. The proliferation of refrigerators made it inexcusable to throw away food that could be hygienically stored and reused. "Scraps," a rural term to indicate that food left after the meal went to animals and was not necessarily incorporated into the next day's meal, ceased to be relevant in urban society. Proliferation of commercially canned and frozen foods encouraged greater diversity of menus and enabled attractive presentation of foods. "Eye appeal was regarded as important because so much of the struggle to have people eat what was good for them, rather than what they liked, involved persuading people to eat things such as canned spinach whose taste was not widely appreciated."[42]

A menu that showed the elegant incorporation of leftovers and canned goods started with "cream of corn soup," made from canned corn, had a main course of "vegetable salad with stuffed eggs" accompanied by melba toast, and concluded with a "cottage pudding" covered in "lemon or chocolate sauce." The menu-maker opined, "A vegetable salad is a great convenience every so often to use up those bits of vegetable that we just can't bear to throw away."[43] With a refrigerator, the housewife could serve her family desserts of healthy milk disguised as ice cream, as well as leftover meats and vegetables served up in elegant aspics.[44]

Drama made meals an occasion. Though the housewife might use "cans or frozen foods with a simple sauce; serve cold cuts or chop suey or barbecue brought home from the delicatessen; or use packaged and semi-prepared foods," she should also "feature" favorite foods of her family:

If your husband speaks feelingly of the beauty and aroma of a standing roast, it's up to you to provide one even if it does take time to cook. If your son likes bisquits, why not have them often? . . . Families often get tired of too much semi-prepared food, but if you include one good "home-cooked" dish which will go with packaged or canned foods, you'll acquire the reputation of being a marvelous cook and manager.[45]

Once the meal ended, all dishes used for cooking and eating had to be washed and put away and the kitchen cleaned for breakfast. One of Christine Frederick's time-savers for a "servantless household" was to set the breakfast table with the cleaned dinner dishes so as to save the steps of putting away and getting out of dishes.[46] In typical households, an 8:00 A.M. breakfast required that someone begin work by 7:30, and the day concluded with washing, drying, and putting away dishes after the 6:30 or 7:00 P.M. dinner.

Cooking and meal cleanup occupied the largest segment of time in a housewife's weekly schedule: 14.6 hours in cities of 50,000 to 250,000 and 11.7 hours in cities of 250,000 and more.[47] Even with devices to reduce actual cooking time, many housewives wanted help. In a Chicago study of 1930, 84 percent of employers stated that they needed assistance with cooking, with washing dishes and weekly housekeeping as the second items listed in preference for work to be performed by hired domestics.[48] In Philadelphia, "nearly half of the women (49.2 percent) in the four major occupational groups [care of food, shelter, clothing, and psychological and social needs] were engaged in occupations concerned with the preparation or serving of food."[49]

Of all her tasks, cooking was the one in which commercial products made the greatest inroad on the housewife's domain and work load. As live-in servants declined in numbers, housewives accepted a decline in the quality of food, though they might aspire to service for dinner. "While 'cleaning women' [hired by the day] may have taken over the house cleaning, laundering, and even child care duties of the ex-live-in servants, food preparation was usually a casualty of the new arrangements."[50] Food so processed and removed from its origins as to be "dead" was one price of removing mess from the home and reducing the housewife's contact with the residue of living food. Refrigeration and cans protected the home from food contamination from live animals and from garden dirt; they made the manual work of cooking faster, though they required more cerebral study and planning. And they enabled women to count newly understood calories so as to attain new standards of slim, fit, youthful beauty.[51]

Child care was the ineradicable link with demanding life. Caring for children was a 24-hour-a-day job. Children could not be left alone and, before entering school, were the full-time responsibility of the mother. Middle-class mothers learned the elements of good infant care on their own, in discussions with friends and from reading. They were expected to sort out advertising claims about nutritional baby foods,[52] know the correct temperature for the baby's bath, and balance play and development of the child's imagination with constraint and development of self-discipline.[53] By the mid-1920s, psychology was a popular topic, and one group in Cambridge, Massachusetts, gave its entire 1926–1927 study calendar to "psychiatry and social adjustment."[54] Mothers found the new dangers to children more complicated and worrisome than older ones like "teething, indigestion, mumps or measles, [and even] tonsils and adenoids, [which you could have out], but you can't subtract the unconscious."[55]

Nurseries and schools were obvious social reforms that benefited house-wives unable to afford servants. Smith College's Institute for the Co-Ordination of Women's Interests established a nursery school intended to ease "the life of the average married woman today [and to enable her to pur-sue] professions that may be adaptable to a married woman's time."[56] The schools made it possible for housewives with children over six to take part-time morning and early afternoon work,[57] and groups such as the Bureau of Part Time Work in New York City sought to place educated women in such jobs.

During the day, any wife with small children had her hands full. As one said, "I have small children so that a maid is a necessity rather than a luxury. My maid's work is always the same. Her job is the laundry and cleaning and mine is the care of the children and the cooking" (to Jean Collier Brown, Women's Bureau, August 1938, Garden City, New York). In this household, washing the dinner dishes was included in the cleaning, which the maid finished before getting off at 7:30 or 8:00 P.M., enabling the wife to prepare the evening meal and then change her role to hostess, leaving the scullery work for the maid.

One employer described her own duties in a model schedule:

Get up, help children dress, start breakfast;
Eat breakfast, get children off to school;
Read paper, bathe, dress.
Clean upstairs;
Children's laundry twice a week;
Marketing or gardening, or baking.
Children's lunch if home;
Adult's lunch if husband is home
Free until 4:30 when children come home;
Children's supper. Start dinner

This wife also supervised a full-time, live-in domestic who washed dishes, served meals, and cooked the adults' meals; did the heavy cleaning and all the downstairs (public) spaces; and stayed at home at least four nights a week "on call" for children's emergencies,[58] while the wife gave her attention to her husband in the evenings.

Child care was considered a constant, unmanageable job until children were grown and had left the maternal house. In all discussions of limiting domestic workers' hours, housewives finally retreated to child care as the most worthy and least controllable job that made home scheduling impos-sible: "A code for maids! I hope it fails. . . . I work far harder now than my maid does, and longer hours. Besides, no home that is a home, with children and frequent guests, can run strictly by the clock."[59] Never having a claim for time of her own, the housewife was unfriendly to the idea that the domestic—a social inferior working under the housewife's direction—might make such a demand.

At the same time, the housewife had strong emotional incentives for accepting her own bondage to child care and enforcing the domestic's position as her backup. As one said, the family "was the one place in the world where she *was* indispensable":

> I know that under the [John B.] Watsonian theory almost any trained expert can care for a child more efficiently than his own mother. . . . But what expert, without years of training in my particular family, would know that little trick I use to get the baby to finish his milk? Who else could restore Judy's shaken belief in a just and stable universe when a cold keeps her from going to a long-anticipated Halloween party?[60]

This author, however, talked about a 51-hour workweek for the housewife so it is unclear what portion of the time devoted to baby and Judy she considers work and what simply social time with her children.

Even when mothers described the care of children as one of their major duties in the household regimen, they expected maids to take charge during some parts of the day. Mothers did not take infants on morning marketing trips. Afternoon outings often coincided with rest time for children, who could be watched by the maid during the slower on-call period between lunch cleanup and dinner preparations.[61]

In chronic arguments between housewives and maids about hours worked, child care seems to have produced the most tension. This seems to have been the need that led most housewives to want full-time, live-in domestics. Children made housework a 24-hour-a-day job. They could not be left alone, so whether they needed care or social response, a responsible person must be in their presence. "When one has definite arrangements and cannot leave the house on account of children or other dependents, it is extremely annoying and embarrassing when the maid doesn't come."[62]

The freedom from constant child care was the greatest need regularly expressed by the wife. Indeed, wives assumed that normally five hours per day should be spent with children before doing other tasks.[63] After five hours, a woman wanted relief. In an employee–employer dialogue held in 1942, when war exigencies meant that workers were hoping for better conditions and employers were reconciling themselves to labor shortages, workers offered a number of suggestions about how the workday could be constrained and how people with limited incomes could afford adequate service.

The employee-designed schedules envisioned a working day completed by 8:00 after the evening meal cleanup, and most assumed that a

worker returned to her own home after the day's work. To various suggestions, the housewives replied,

> "What provision is made for care of children?"
> "How about child care? evening care?"
> "No evening problem included. How about child care?"
> "How about evening care of children?"
> "How about evenings off? No mention of aid with children."

Or, as one employer put it in ranking "services needed, in order of their importance and qualifications desired":

1. Children (age 6½ and 3½)
   a. responsibility when I am out
   b. dependability, ability to act in case of emergency
   c. enjoyment of being with children and ability to play with them
   d. preparation of simple meals for them
   e. encouragement to cooperate in household tasks whenever possible

Another employer in a household with two adults and four children listed
"Services: 1) someone living in the house who can take care of children when
employer is out. 2) laundry—large on account of large family. . . . Qualifications: 1) ability and experience with children." A third, in a household with
one child, listed her services desired as "1) laundry; 2) night care of child; 3)
heavy cleaning; 4) cooking."[64]

Some housewives did not think evening hours qualified as regular work
to be paid, even though they wanted someone present in the house. A
Fresno, California, employers' committee drafting comments on a 1938 proposal to legislate a 60-hour workweek for California domestic workers described evening hours in the home as

> free time—time spent entirely as the employee sees fit, not leaving the
> vicinity. An example of this would be at night, after the work is done
> and the children are in bed, if her employer is away from home. She
> would be free to read, sew, entertain her friends, go to bed or anything
> else she wishes, so long as it does not take her away.[65]

A task that might represent free choice for the employer was, in this instance, projected to have the same meaning for the employee, a confusion
that occurred more often around child care than any other job. "When there
are children, there is a 24 hour schedule for the lady of the house, who
doesn't complain about it but who does ask the helper to keep ears open for
the children on occasional evenings when the employers are asked out" (to

Louise Stitt, Women's Bureau, January 1941, Brentwood Park, Los Angeles, California).

The need of housewives to have time off from children was the most persistent argument for having live-in service. If the wife could not hire such service, she turned to part-time workers who performed other household duties—laundry, cleaning, and cooking—as well. Certainly, this most consuming of jobs was felt as a burden, as one story recounted by a YWCA workers' advocate indicates:

> In California some years ago a maid strangled her employer's baby. At the trial it came out she had practically no free time. She worked from early in the morning until late at night. She often wished to attend club meetings or to be out with her friends and there was almost always some reason why it could not be arranged. Her resentment toward her employer grew until she did this terrible thing. I understand that after it happened women's clubs and social workers tried to get better conditions [for domestics]. The girl is now serving a life term.[66]

Whether or not this story was true, the desperation of a woman trapped in a house with a baby was a middle-class theme, and the violent impulse was more acceptably assigned to the domestic than to the housewife–mother, who had more freedom to leave.

Housewives indicated their preference for servants who were more available by paying higher wages for live-in, full-time workers than for live-out workers. In a 1936 Connecticut study, cash wages of full-time resident workers were $8.95 a week in Hartford and $8.42 in Waterbury. The wages for full-time, live-out workers were $6.66 and $6.21 respectively. This report concluded that the anomaly that those receiving room and board also got higher cash wages might be accounted for, in part, by longer hours for resident workers, "who in practice, if not in theory, may be considered as constantly on duty; in part by the greater skill usually required of resident servants, and in part by the many elements of personality and adjustability that enter into the employer-employee relationship."[67]

Though housewives preferred full-time workers, they were often not able to hire them. Day work and part-time work increased substantially during the 1920s. The ideal, however, given the work load, was to get as much work from the servant as one could. Shopping for a houseworker, managing her time, and supervising her behavior were central responsibilities for MCHs, no matter what kind of worker she got.

Purchasing service was a complex negotiation. Like any businessman or clever consumer, housewives wanted to spend as little as possible for the most work possible. Following the model of her husband's business world, the dominant model for well-run organizations, the housewife took seriously her responsibility to manage money wisely. Critical and apocryphal stories abounded during the early years of the Depression of a hostess at a "suburban bridge club" who "triumphantly explained that she had fired her $60-a-month maid and gotten another 'who gave her perfect service for $25 a month.'"[68] In a capitalist economy with business standards of maximizing profits at least partially through minimizing labor costs, the housewife emulated her husband, though her actions were interpreted as "bargain hunting [—] a deeply rooted feminine instinct." In Depression America, it became all too easy for housewives to believe that they could get "a perfect treasure for $5 and a good enough person for $3 [per week]," the relief rate.[69] Women were not supposed to exploit their help was the popular message, but why should a wife pay more for labor than she was forced to?

When the housewife made the hiring bargain, her work had just begun. If she purchased full-time work, or regular part-time, she had to cajole the maid into doing the onerous cleaning work to meet a high standard; she had to persuade her to work the hours around the edge of the day from breakfast through evening baby-sitting; and she had to enforce deferential behavior to maintain the feeling of service in the home. If she hired only day work or special jobs like laundry and spring cleaning, she had to define precise jobs so as to get the most work for her money. The servant had to be taught the particulars and inculcated with the vision of the wife's ideal home—clean, comfortable, well-ordered, and oriented to the development of the family members, including the wife.

One of the wife's jobs was to locate servants who did not object to the sophisticated customs of middle-class entertaining. During the 1920s, smoking and serving alcohol made illegal by Prohibition might risk losing servants or being reported to police.[70] Servants' moral sensibilities were often grounded in religious worship, and their disapproval of morning hangovers was supported by legal standards of Prohibition until 1933.

Paradoxically, housewives felt that as guardians of households in which children were raised and morality taught, they must monitor the physical and moral well-being of a worker brought into the home. The ability to control behavior was added to convenience as a reason for preferring a live-in worker. Employers believed that domestics who lived out, particularly

> negro women, . . . demand to go home at night for one of two reasons.
> Either they do really go to their homes to do the work they must neglect during the day, or particularly the younger ones want to amuse themselves and spend much too large a portion of the nights at dances, or movies or festivals & c. In either case they are trying to burn their candles at both ends and their health suffers, while the employer suffers from a tired servant utterly unequal to the requirements of her day's work.[71]

The housewife expected servants to maintain a high standard of hygiene and to master middle-class manners. They were to look neat and professional but not flashy. Hair must always be neat and covered by a cap or net; makeup used in moderation; perfume and fingernail polish eschewed during work; deodorant used; baths taken once a day "after the heavy work of the day has been completed"; teeth brushed; nails cleaned; shoes worn with low, neat heels; hose inspected for runs; and jewelry not to be worn during work.[72]

Manners when answering the telephone and door were important. The maid had to answer the telephone clearly and without using slang, identify the residence and her own status, and take messages clearly, all in language and manners acceptable to middle-class social life. An employee was to be "responsive and cheerful, and always dependable, reliable, and punctual. Her interest in the jobs [was] shown by the initiative she [took] and the way she cater[ed] to the family's preferences and needs. She must be cooperative and resourceful."[73]

The housewife had to persuade or inspire the domestic to cover over her physicality and manual labor with a veneer of cleanliness and neutralized sexuality. Since the domestic worker had to be fresh and neat looking while doing hard work and receiving low pay, the contradictory job demands intensified the housewife's sense that servants were inferior females; they could not be as clean, as dainty, and as well dressed as their employers, not because of poverty or work demands but because of their "nature." Housewives were graceful and cultivated creatures who needed help, and domestics were inferior females who should provide it as a matter of course.

One employer expected a servant to display "courtesy and spirit of service" by calling the household's two teenage daughters "'Miss Anne' and 'Miss Ruth,'" which two domestics had recently refused to do. She was disturbed, also, that these maids "act[ed], for the most part, as if I were going to 'put something over on them'" (to President Roosevelt, November 1934, Bethesda, Maryland). Other families expected the table service at family meals to be the same as when there were guests; one study showed that 45 percent of employers treated family and company meals the same.[74]

An employer expressed her lack of sympathy with servants because she felt that she "need[ed] help too [and was] ready for a sanitarium due to overwork" (to U.S. Department of Labor, February 1941, from Los Angeles, California). The housewife expected the maid to fill in the gaps between what was expected of the housewife and what she was able to do.

> When I hire a maid I tell her that I should like her to be able to 'pinch hit' once in a while because of some task outside of routine duty which must be performed. . . . When a homemaker buys household service she thinks she wants greater freedom for outside interests. She wants

in her employee the skill and experience she does not have. I am very dependent on the maid's time and skills. . . . The employer always prefers, if she has one maid, that she live in instead of out, because this gives her [the employer] the greater freedom.[75]

When experts advised housewives about how to negotiate, they did not suggest changing the service output of the home. Rather, the housewife was urged to identify more closely with the servant. One author advised employers to "realize that a household employee is a person, a very human person, with the same needs and drives which [you] and [your] families have. . . . She must feel valued, appreciated and respected." The behavior that indicated the "respect for the labor which [was] performed . . . [is] not asking or expecting the household employee to do anything which they themselves are not willing to do—even to washing soiled diapers or cleaning out toilet bowls."[76]

Conscientious "home-makers do not," the YWCA reformers continued, "save for themselves all the most attractive responsibilities, but find out what their employee gets most fun and satisfaction from doing, and try to give her as much choice as possible." The authors hinted at what activities middle-class women found fun, when they offered that the domestic might "make cakes or arrange flowers, for example, . . . even if the cakes aren't so good as baker's cakes, or the flowers so tastefully arranged as [you] or [your] daughters would arrange them."[77] The housewife, the authors implied, need not fear losing her status simply because she shared the work of the home. Her superior taste and delicate execution defied confusion with her lower-class domestic.

Beset with standards for housewifery that emphasized homemaking yet required a considerable amount of housework, MCHs of the era between 1920 and 1945 pushed responsibilities onto other women and took credit for their job performance. The conservatism of the post-World War I, the Depression, and World War II crises that pushed citizens to find reassurance in well-tended homes held MCHs captive and organized most of the service production of caring for people in private households. Some MCHs did their "own" work; others hired houseworkers "in order to achieve some degree of freedom from household cares so that she [might] either work in a gainful occupation outside the home or follow such activities as she prefer[red]. [Others] retained household help to provide personal service and to assure a certain style of living."[78]

Though reformers thought that employers in the first category were less exploitive than those in the second, both groups of women sustained a popular belief in a housewife's solitary responsibility for the human care organized under housework. Middle-class women perpetuated the feeling that home was a place for clean clothes, hot food, responsive care, and gracious space—provision of a "good mother." To carry on this performance, how-ever, they relied on economically less powerful women, whom they saw as their social and moral inferiors.

When the services of these women, who bore a large part of the house-hold burden, were not available after World War II, middle-class women ex-perienced "the problem that has no name" discovered by Betty Friedan among postwar suburban housewives. Wives' new-found need for husbands and children to share housework, euphemistically described as family "to-getherness," may also explain husbands' newly expressed dissatisfactions with traditional marriage, which was supposed to be a catered affair and not self-service. Family members, it seemed, did not like housework any better than domestic workers had.

Four

The Domestic
Does Her Job

Mrs. Roosevelt can [you] help talk or organize something that
will cause these dear housewives whom we work for will realize
we are human even if we are a Black race. . . . We do laundry for
the family whom we work and have to pay to get our laundry
done . . . don't have time to work for ourselves or even to cook a
decent meal of food at home for our husband untill Thursday evening [when] we get what is called one evening out of a week, get
off at 2:30 P.M. stores close at 3:30 P.M., a very short time to shop,
clean our own house, cook that one decent meal at home. . . .
—To Mrs. Franklin D. Roosevelt from
  L.G.H., Fort Worth, Texas, 1937

Dear Madam, . . . I have been in close contact with many of the
Girls and Women who were and still are housemaids, cooks and
other houseworkers and can truthfully state some of the conditions are deplorable. Long hours, poor wages, poor living conditions, a regular Slave's Existence. . . . I would you could or
would write and invite all Housemaids to write to you telling of
the unfair and unjust treatment they undergo, and not publish
their names [so they will not get] into trouble.
—To Mrs. Franklin D. Roosevelt from
  "Just a Maid," Pittsburgh, Pennsylvania, 1937

The domestic's workplace was the housewife's home, and conflicts were inherent in the culture's dichotomous vision of work and home.[1] In the period 1920 to 1945, domestics conceived of housework as a job. Like other workers, they devised schemes to make it easier and more efficient, sought employment at the best wages for the shortest hours obtainable, and sporadically organized to press for inclusion within proliferating laws regulating conditions of labor.

Unlike most other wage laborers, however, domestics were expected to feel the same interest in their jobs as in their own homes and families; indeed, throughout the period, the worker was, whenever possible, required to live at her job. Commentators recognized that many workers did not live in, but living out was a variation on the basic ethos of service and its normative structure: being present in the house and accepting room and meals as part of the salary. Since most domestics were women, this often meant that doing a good job taking care of someone else's home required the worker to sacrifice her hopes for a home of her own or to compromise care for her family and social life with her friends. Coping with the varied demands of the employer's family inevitably required a married domestic to set limits on the demands of her own family, or vice versa. For the unmarried worker, often a young woman, it meant fighting for time to meet friends, enjoy her youth, and perhaps meet a man to marry and set up her own household.

Domestic workers' negative feelings about housework largely revolved around issues created by this tension. Workers complained about the job's long and unregulated hours and about being denied recognition that they were "human," with lives just like their employers'. Positive feelings about using skills to cook, clean, launder, and care for children in someone else's home rarely compensated for long hours, especially in a period when working hours were decreasing in most occupations.

Other changes in the technological and social aspects of housework—notably the introduction of more equipment and the shift in middle-class manners to accept drinking and smoking as elements of entertaining at home—exacerbated the central disagreement. At the beginning of the 1920s, housewives and domestics did heavy physical labor, which electric- and gas-driven appliances gradually eased. During the 1930s, the remaining heavy household jobs shifted from housewife to domestic. Social disdain for manual labor manifest in the job hierarchies of the corporate realm now pervaded the home as well, as the middle-class wife turned over some tasks to machines and others to her servant. Exacting heavy labor from the domestic became essential to protecting the health and refinement of the housewife.

Paradoxically, social notions of glamour and sophistication now encouraged middle-class educated women to take on the typically male behavior of smoking and drinking. Housewives entertained at home and, after the repeal of Prohibition, had no excuse for not serving drinks with the cigarettes. Domestics, usually from rural, peasant, religiously observant cultures, found such employers decadent and immoral, their social life as irreligious and questionable as their child-rearing practices.[2] The domestic's picture of serving a spiritually barren home contradicted the housewife's picture of transmitting superior cultivation to the domestic.

Generally, women who took domestic jobs in this period had no other choices; they were socially peripheral and politically powerless and took housework jobs as a last resort when other employment failed. One author constructed a racial–ethnic map of domestic employment in 1930. The southern housewife had black servants. In Arizona was found "the picturesque Indian maid, or the Mexican senorita with her great black eyes and her buxom figure. The Indians may come from almost any tribe, but Pimas, Papagos, and Hopis predominate." Mexican women were servants in El Paso; American student girls, Scandinavians, and some Orientals in Portland, Oregon; Canadian, Scottish, and English, and blacks when the former were unobtainable in upper-class Detroit homes; Scandinavians in Minneapolis; young German farm women in Nebraska; West Indians in Connecticut; French Canadians in Vermont; Irish and "colored" in Wilmington; Poles, Slavs, Lithuanians, and Hungarians in Pittsburgh; and Irish in New York City, though employers preferred English, French, Swiss, German, Scandinavian, and Scottish.[3] During the 1920s, servants were predominantly migrants from rural areas or immigrants from other countries, sometimes handicapped by lack of English, and often nonwhite. During the 1930s, significant numbers of white women desperate for income and housing took domestic jobs,[4] though nonwhite workers, even more hard hit by unemployment, persisted as more than half the work force. Although domestic work offered some advantages, such as not needing to learn English, women took it when they had no other options.

Despite the diverse groups of women who found employment, during the years after World War I domestic service became more racially defined as an occupation. The proportion of white workers declined as second-generation Euro-American women found other jobs. And Afro-American workers "migrated toward the cities of the North and Middle West, . . . [which] relieve[d] the labor market in rural sections of the South [and] made available great numbers of household workers in northern cities that previously had had an insufficient supply to meet the demand, especially since the curtailment of [European] immigration." By 1930, over 30 percent of female black servants counted in a sample of southern and northern states were working in the North.[5]

Black women discovered that racial discrimination in jobs occurred in the North as well as the South, which added gall to the occupation's other hardships.[6] Unlike second-generation Euro-American immigrants, black rural migrants found no job alternatives. Viewing the era of the great migration from South to North, historian Jacqueline Jones has concluded, "The white mistress-black maid relationship preserved the inequities of the slave

system . . . and thus a unique historical legacy compounded the humilia-
tions inherent in the servant's job. In the end, a black female wage earner
encountered a depth and form of discrimination never experienced by [other
immigrant working women]."[7] Only marriage to a man with a steady income
released black women from reliance on domestic work, and because of discrimination against black male workers, even this respite was erratic.[8]

The increased number of black women engaged as domestic workers
may have spurred the major change of the 1920s—the growing use of day
work in place of full-time, resident employment. Throughout this period,
workers sought to transform domestic service from a norm of full-time, resident service to a job with limited hours and clearly defined tasks, which was
most easily gained through day work. The spectrum of domestic work included full-time living out, part-time, and casual hire. All these forms co-
existed during the twenty-five years from 1920 to 1945. One Philadelphia
study of the late 1930s found that among domestic workers interviewed,
"43.3 percent were full-time workers—approximately one-half resident, the
other non-resident workers—34 percent were day workers; 11.9 percent
worked part-time," and 10.8 percent were employed in other jobs. Since
black workers, at 73 percent, predominated among Philadelphia domestics,
the figures may have slightly overstated nonresident work, though the need
for housing during the Depression had increased living in. This study also
found that, though workers moved among statuses, they generally chose full-
time work or day and part-time work.[9]

Which work form was chosen varied according to the economics of a
region, demographic characteristics of the worker, and alternative occupations available to a woman worker. Nonwhite women generally sought non-
resident work. Mexican-American women, like Asian-Americans and Indians, sought day work to protect themselves from "dangers of working in
strangers' homes" and to ease the barrier of not knowing English.[10] Evelyn
Nakano Glenn concluded in her book about Japanese-American women
seeking day work in the San Francisco Bay area that day work might be a
means to bring in income without first having to learn English or invest in
training or equipment. These women might not know how to do housework
in the American fashion, but they had cared for their own houses and were
eager to learn American patterns. Native-born white women in domestic
work tended to be single and either older or younger than the norm of
twenty five to fourty four years and accepted living in, as did foreign-born
white women. For these groups, live-in, full-time work provided substitute
homes.[11]

Black women, whose work for white families in white neighborhoods
meant isolation in a period of rigid segregation of social activities, pioneered
the trend to day work. Day work allowed them time for social connections
with friends and kin, especially participation in neighborhood churches. A
day worker could behave like a regular worker, with her wages in a bank
account instead of a mutual benefit association.[12]

Housewives and domestics argued chronically about hours, which to workers was the worst aspect of resident domestic service. Even more than live-out work, day work enabled workers to limit the hours they worked. Despite the coexistence of work forms throughout the period, day work became more common during the economic boom of the 1920s. In the Depression 1930s, though hundreds of thousands of workers remained in day work, housewives found it easier to uphold full-time work, living in or out, as the norm.

The 1920s

Day workers controlled their hours better than full-time workers, living in or out. One commentator noted that "the large demand for [day workers during the labor shortage of World War I] gave them the leverage of establishing for themselves an eight hour day and a wage commensurate with that in many lines of industry. Day workers have retained since the World War both the eight hour day and the advanced wages."[13] And outside the South, even black day workers earned more than those working for single families.[14]

Home expert Christine Frederick even advised, by 1920:

If the income provides for outside service, part of it may be spent with the greatest advantage on forms of day cleaning service. A competent cleaning woman in one day of eight solid hours of work, will go thru a seven-room house, thoroly and completely, except the fine dusting or bureau top arranging, which would take the permanent worker most of two days, and then not be done so well.[15]

Day workers mainly cleaned and laundered. White day workers primarily cleaned house. Laundry in such households was sent to steam laundries, which developed class-graded services by 1925, poorer homes buying "wet wash" with no drying and richer homes buying full wash, starch, iron, or fold of linens and clothes. Black day workers more often laundered, in addition to cleaning.[16]

Workers preferred part-time and day work because they could have Sundays off. Elizabeth Ross Haynes reported that older black domestic workers, especially, were "willing to accept a [live-in] place at a much lower wage than another if it gives them their Sundays off so that they may attend their churches."[17] Irish women must also have negotiated work hours, because one commentator reported Irish workers were unpopular because of their attendance at early mass.[18]

Part-time workers could arrange their work schedules around caring for their own homes and children. Christine Frederick cited the case of a

woman who comes to work at 10 A.M. and stays until 3 P.M. In this period she washes the breakfast and lunch dishes, serves lunch, bakes bread or cake, and prepares greatly toward the evening meal. . . . This arrangement has been working most successfully for about four years— the woman who has a family of her own that she sees off to school before she goes to work, and to whom she is back before they are out of school, and for whom she has the whole latter half of the day.[19]

Many workers had family responsibilities. The 1920 census recorded that "29.4 per cent of all the female domestic and personal service workers 15 years of age and over were married, while 70.6 per cent were classed as single, widowed, divorced, and unknown." Many of the widowed or divorced women had dependents, of course, and Elizabeth Ross Haynes reported that a 1923 U.S. Employment Office survey in Washington, D.C., found that almost all such black women had from "1 to 5 dependents."[20] For these women, day work or living out was essential.

Domestic workers preferred the specific tasks usually assigned day workers. In one study workers ranked "preferred jobs," with cooking at the top, followed by serving and daily cleaning. The first two, it could be argued, were relatively skilled and self-directed work, making a complete job of preparing a meal and seeing it eaten. Daily care of the house, which meant light dusting, sweeping, and straightening, also might be seen as bringing order into disorder, having the satisfaction of completed work.

Tasks this group of Chicago workers liked least were the same ones housewives liked least: washing clothes, washing dishes, and staying with children afternoons or evenings. The workers did not necessarily dislike care of children, or even of the employers' children, but rather they disliked having the interstices of a full day's work filled with an additional responsible job. Should the employer's children have an oft-mentioned attitude of superiority and disdain for the domestic, any feelings of being overburdened were intensified by the children's arrogance.

Domestics were more likely to have to do unpleasant jobs if they were regular full-time employees, and especially if living in; they were more likely to be asked

to do [a variety of tasks] they consider[ed] no part of their job[:] Care for furnace and for fuel oil; shovel walks; clean basement; Take down screens; Clean woolen garments in naphtha; Bathe and care for dogs and cats; Carry luggage; Make appointments for employer; Manicure nails and perform other personal services; and Make child eat.[21]

Even in the 1920s, women who wanted to live in were primarily those looking for a home, which usually meant white women whose social life was not so rigidly segregated from employers as were those of black, Mexican, and Indian women. A 1929 YWCA survey found that workers who liked living in did so because of "good food," "training in housekeeping and home-making," and "working in pleasant surroundings, among cultured people, which often meant educational advantages such as books, radio and an excellent opportunity to learn American customs and the English language" (implying that many of the group preferring live-in jobs were recent immigrants). Even for this group, the hazards of living in were lack of definite hours, "which would mean more personal freedom and time for outside interests and activities," and restriction of "social life with its larger circle of friends and more association with people." The general feeling was that "the hours [were] too long and the work too confining and too strenuous as a result."[22]

By the mid-1920s, housewives responded to domestic workers' push for day work, part-time work, and full-time, live-out work by mounting investigations and conducting experiments to recruit workers to become full-time, living in or out. Unwilling to accept the transformation of household service into more regularized, live-out, daily employment with hourly wages and limited hours, housewives' groups turned their efforts to rationalizing a domestic's full-time employment for a single family. When economic depression hit in 1929, and numerous women were forced to accept living-in or full-time work as a condition of employment, the emphasis on reforming standards within full-time housework swept away efforts to organize day and part-time work. Even though thousands of women continued to be employed as day workers, employers could more easily uphold the full-time norm that preoccupied commentators.

The 1930s and Wartime

Beset by lowered wages and higher demands during the 1930s, domestics lost ground in relation to other workers, who were gaining coverage under New Deal initiatives in hours, wages, retirement and unemployment insurance, and protections for trade union organizing. These initiatives convinced domestics that federal agencies might offer them protection against exploitation. Eleanor and Franklin Roosevelt were seen as the presiding geniuses who motivated federal authorities.

From 1933 on, domestic workers wrote to agency heads, especially Secretary of Labor Frances Perkins, and to the Roosevelts from all over the United States. The letters, addressed to "Mr. Roosevelt," "Mrs. Franklin," or "Eleanor Roosevelt," "Mrs. Perkins," and so on represent many statuses and levels of education. Some were typed on organizations' letterhead stationery; others were penciled on blue-lined dime-store notebook paper. Some had excellent spelling and handwriting; others showed hands cramped by age or by the unfamiliar exercise of writing. All had the purpose of telling Washington authorities about what life was like for this group of laborers and asking for information about helpful laws, or reminding officials that these workers had supported Roosevelt's election.

The remainder of this chapter relies heavily on that correspondence to recount feelings about the work content and social arrangements of domestic work. Letters in the National Archives do not represent all experiences of the almost 2 million workers. They include only English-speakers and, usually, full-time workers, but they do come from every region of the country.[23] Did only the most hard-pressed workers, or the most dissatisfied, write to Washington? These questions cannot be answered. But the letters are congruent with reports from YWCA workers' conferences and from social reformers. And the writers' tone is more informational than querulous. Writers constructed their pleas within a familiar, societywide vision of domestic work, trusting to familiarity for impact.

Day workers and casual hires did not send letters. One possible explanation is that day workers had gained greater control of their work so that government hours and wages legislation was not so important to them. Women who took casual jobs may also have been acting entrepreneurially or have been too oppressed to write. The notorious Bronx "slave market," where housewives drove up to hire a day laborer, contained both groups. Some of the West Indian and southern black women evaluated prospective employers, demanded reasonable pay, and used the market to tide them over between regular work. Others, however, were the least competent and most vulnerable, often southern women lured north by dishonest employment agents who took the women's money and found them no jobs.[24]

Domestic workers from all sections of the United States depicted a demanding and responsible job, usually poorly paid and nonnegotiable in content. Housewives expected infinite work performed to the direction of the wife–expert; the worker was employed, not for her skill but to execute the housewife's desire and demand. Little or no recognition was given to the employee's knowledge, even that presumably gained from many years on the job. Domestics sometimes echoed employers' ideas that better training would help them and raise the respect of the job.[25] But mostly they attributed poor treatment to poor organization of the job, and especially to its exclusion from wages and hour laws that regulated other occupations; housework was not treated like industrial employment.

> They advertise for a housekeeper. They ought to word the ad "Wanted a slave who will give every second, minute, and hour of her life for 1.00, 1.25, 1.50 a week." (Atlanta, Georgia, 1933)

> It has reached the point where [domestic service] employment is nothing less than slavery and is bondage for those engaged in it—for the hours are from 6 A.M. till 9, 10 and later into the night. (To Mrs. Franklin Roosevelt, August 1933, from Los Angeles, California)

> We are honest to goodness white slaves. It was our believed [sic] that slavery had been abolished, but we are very much in doubt of it. The girls here are made to work for room and board, from 6:30 to no set hour at nite. (To Mrs. F. Perkins, January 1934, from Ironwood, Michigan)

Housewives hired domestics on terms unregulated by any public authority,[26] and peer-group pressure tended to encourage sharp dealing, or at least paying the lowest wages possible for the maximum labor. The housewife had ready cash to pay wages or a home to offer workers who had no savings and no ability to hold out for a better-paying job. Also, as domestics overheard, the local market of employers, the housewives, talked about wages and standards during their social engagements and essentially set a going market rate that they all honored.

As with slavery, the issue was not having a good or bad master but the system itself. As one woman asking for inclusion in maximum hours laws wrote, "I work for the best people in my town, but even this is not enough. If I complain, just think of those who don't have employers as nice as mine" (to Mr. Roosevelt, August 1938, Newport, New Hampshire). "There may be some [housewives] who are kind, but the average demands too much" (To Miss Perkins, December 1938, Seattle, Washington). "We have read in history books and other books about slavery of long ago, but the way the housemaids must work now from morning till night is too much for any human being. I think we girls should get some consideration as every other labor class has, even though it is housework" ("Fifteen weary housemaids" to Mrs. Roosevelt, February 1938, no place indicated).

Slavery remained part of the nation's consciousness in the 1930s, bolstered by films like *Gone With the Wind*, which premiered in 1939. Slavery was the primary story about black people that was known and shared by white Americans. European immigrants with memories of quasi-feudal relations in Russia, Italy, and the Balkans may have used the term with slightly different connotations. Workers constantly used the word, and it contained racial and power meanings.

Three factors metaphorically and structurally linked housework and slavery: not treating domestics as people independent of their employers, designing housework to give domestics the physically hardest tasks, and demanding almost unlimited working hours. In addition, during the Depression, many employers offered room and board and no wages in return for work.[27] Employers accepted and often stressed these inherent elements in the job's construction; to domestics, such acceptance represented willful ignorance and exploitation.

Housewives had many reasons for ignoring the independent existence of their servants, including their own desires to be ideal wives and mothers and yet to be partially freed from the pressures of family service. Unwilling to challenge the dominant belief in housewifery as women's most laudable existence, middle-class women upheld the virtue of homemaking and demeaned the worker who freed their time and energies. To reconcile the search for time and development separate from housework, the wife had to turn over labor to a servant and to see herself, simultaneously, as the home's caretaker. She wanted to get some of the work done by another woman and take credit for it herself. The less said about her servant's competence or importance the better.

Turning over the work of cleaning up intimate areas of life violated strong feelings of family privacy. Servants might gossip about family oddities in their clubs or church groups or make judgments about family behavior. Criticisms of their employers' morality appear in many of the letters to Washington. Hiring someone of no significance, rendered as invisible as possible, mitigated employers' fears of intrusion and revelation.[28]

Housewives may have sought "alienage" between themselves and the domestic, whether of race, class, national group, or age, for two additional reasons. Hiring a servant of a lower economic class, foreign origin, or stigmatized racial status increased the housewife's power in setting the conditions of work; it also protected her sense of distance from the worker. A housewife could more easily feel herself "subject," able to believe that her experiences constituted reality, and to deny similar capacity to her servant, the "other."[29] Organizing the work so the domestic did the heaviest jobs helped the employer to see herself as the "mind" of the job and distinct from the employee, who represented the "body."

Domestics repeatedly complained about not being seen as human, and of housewives' failing to recognize any commonality of capacities and needs. Assertion of need might arouse hostility. One black woman wrote, "I ask the lady whom I work for to grant me a few hours to care for some real business and bills that had to be seen after and I was sorry I spoke about it. I was answered with such grievous [sic] words" (to Mrs. Franklin D. Roosevelt, January 1937, from Fort Worth, Texas).

Hours of work were the major contention through the 1930s and the war years. Housewives expected servants to help them meet the demands of the 24-hour-a-day schedule, and public discussions that accepted full-time service as the norm for the job implicitly encouraged such an aspiration. Domestics argued that they were hired for specific tasks or hours like other workers; anything they could not do in that time was the housewife's responsibility.

> I am working at the rate of 13 hours per day with no days off. (Alexandria, Virginia, 1933)
>
> I leave home quarter of 7 every morning. I finish 9:30 P.M. When I get home it is 10 o'clock. . . . The people treat me as one of their family and I suppose I should not kick. But—I certainly would like to know more about Domestic rules and laws if there be any. (To NAACP, April 25, 1931, from New York City)[30]
>
> Mrs. Franklin Roosevelt
> Dear madam
> I have heard of your great work among the poor and decided to write you asking isn't there any thing to be done about private family work

where girls and women do the work of 4 people and earn half the pay of one. For instance I work for some people they pay $5 a week. I do all of the cooking, laundry, cleaning and stay with the child some night work every day from 8:30 untill 7 oclock except Thursday and Sunday. On those days work from 8:30 untill 1:30 or 2 oclock. Isn't there some kind of a law that could help this dire situation among the working girl.

A Working Girl
Indianapolis, Ind
Nov. 7, 1938

Letters like the above form a litany in the correspondence files of the Women's Bureau, various New Deal agencies, and organizations representing workers such as the NAACP and the YWCA. The complaints are ordinary and repetitious, like housework itself. They gain power from repetition and piquancy from slight variations.

To enable domestics to speak more fully, I will quote from a number of letters and intersperse workers' comments with some daily and weekly work schedules. The following was presented at a 1942 meeting of women workers:

Schedule of a Week's Work

7:00–8:30—Straighten living room and front rooms
8:30–9:15—Breakfast—the family eats in installments. During this time, plan the meals for the day and order from the market.
9:15–9:30—Breakfast dishes
9:30–10:15—Upstairs—beds, bathrooms
10:15–11:30—Monday: washing
Tuesday–Thursday: cleaning thoroughly one room, or scrubbing various places
Friday: thorough cleaning of house
11:30–12:30—Dessert for evening and prepare lunch
12:30–1:00—Lunch
1:00–1:30—Dishes
1:30–2:00—Odd jobs
2:00–4:30—Rest—on call
4:30–8:00—Prepare and serve dinner; dinner dishes
Time off: Thursday after 1:30; Sunday after 2:00
Household: 2 adults, 2 children; 11 rooms, $3\frac{1}{2}$ baths.
Other help, none.[31]

This schedule adds up to a 79-hour workweek, well within the range found in a northern Illinois YWCA survey of 1938, in which the average reported by 263 workers was "84 hours per week with a minimum of 75 hours and a maximum of 92."[32] Servants put in much longer hours than housewives doing their own work typically reported. A 1929 survey conducted by Hilde-

garde Kneeland for the Bureau of Home Economics of the Department of Agriculture concluded that "housekeeping seems to be housekeeping whether
it's north, south, east or west." Typical times worked by the housewives
ranged only between the shortest work week of 47½ hours and the longest of
53½ hours, with "food taking the largest toll of hours." Average time allotted
to jobs was similar in rural and urban households, with minor differences, as
follows:

> cleaning—7½ hours per week
> laundry—5½ hours per week
> mending—1½ hours per week
> sewing—4½ hours per week
> Preparing meals (rural, 15½ hours per week
>   city, 10¼ hours per week)
> Dishwashing, clearing up (rural, 7 hours, 40 mins/wk
>   city, 5 hours, 11 mins/wk)
> Care of family and
> management   (rural, 4½ hours & 1¾ hours
>   city, 6¾ hours and 4½ hours)[33]

This minimalist account of tasks contrasts with the schedule of daily hours:
no serving, less cleaning, and no accounting for being available during afternoon times.

How were days organized to stretch out so much longer for the domestic? How did her day differ from the housewife's in time spent and in jobs
done? One woman reporting to the Women's Bureau described a full week's
work. On Saturday, as an example, she

> got up 5:15 fixed furnace, got breakfast, made beds, polished nickle in
> bathroom and kitchen, polished tub and other fixtures; took floor brush,
> scrubbed and polished tile floor in bath room, scrubbed and polished
> floor in kitchen, washed windows, wiped woodwork, scrubbed and pol-
> ished steps to basement and washed banisters. swept all walks and
> front porch, washed silk stockings, went to grocery, helped make pea-
> nut bread; trimmed dried beef, washed vegetables, put things away,
> scrubbed eggs, cut up vegetables to put in soup, fixed supper, made
> salad and desert. Washed dishes, fixed breakfast, will now fix furnace.
> Was naged all the time I got supper; said I had no pep was too slo.

Unusual elements in this account are the outdoor work, windows, and furnace, generally considered men's work. In addition, husband and wife both
worked outside the home so she could count on no help from the housewife.
In this instance, the domestic had replaced the housewife and did not show
the pep the housewife considered appropriate.[34]

Although many domestics worked in households where the wife was not employed, hiring a full-time domestic to substitute for an employed wife was common in some cities, especially in homes with young children. In a 1935 St. Louis study, 70 percent of households hiring domestic workers had children. In nearly one-third of these households "the employers were engaged in full time gainful occupations with an additional 5 per cent in part-time employments. This places full responsibility for decisions upon the employee—at the same time allowing the worker to work without immediate supervision."[35]

Domestics worked around the perimeters of the family's beginning and ending its work- and school day, so domestic workers' hours began earlier and ended later than for most occupations. Whether the domestic lived in or commuted to work, her days began early and ended late.

> My hours are 7:30 A.M. to 6 P.M. and they want me to look after the [three-year-old] boy two or three evenings while they go out. (To Frances Perkins, August 1933, from Plattsburg, New York)

> The work consists of . . . from 7 A.M. until 8 P.M. everyday but Sunday and Thursday and of course, on those two days I arise at 5:30 A.M. in order to get through with my work by 1 o'clock in order to have the afternoon and evening off. (To Mrs. Franklin Roosevelt, July 1933, from Dayton, Ohio)

Work started between 5:15 and 8:00 depending on whether domestics were on the premises to begin the day as soon as they arose or traveled to work from their own homes. Most seem to have been at work by breakfast time. Departure time for those living out was after preparing the evening dinner or after serving and cleaning up the meal. If living in, their evening hours might be spent "on call" watching children while the parents were out. If living out, servants might still be expected to child-sit two or three evenings a week: "I don't stay where I work and have to pay for my room. If they want me to stay at nights I'm obliged to, and that makes me have to stay there almost every other night."[36]

Days off were socially recognized as half a day Thursday (or Wednesday) and Sunday (a convention that protected the housewife's Sunday lunch but denied church attendance to the domestic). Pressures for full-time service even threatened to erode these free times.

> Even on your supposed to be days off have to do a days work before you leave. Gee! Whizz! you so darn tired you feel like staying there and going to bed to rest up for the next days' 13 hour grind from 7:30 to 8:30. (To Mary Anderson, Women's Bureau, November 1933, from Dayton, Ohio)

> I put in from 72 to 76 hours a week. The only time I have off is Thursday evening and afternoon. Sunday afternoon with every other Sunday

evening off. When I leave in the afternoon every thing has to be done."
(To Miss Perkins, 1933, Racine, Wisconsin)

Dishes [might] be left on the day off . . . for the worker to wash when
she returns.[37]

My day off. I get off after lunch at 12:30 when served. I get off at 1:30 or
2 P.M. I am told by this lady to be back at 8 P.M. to turn on a flood light
in yard. (To Mrs. Franklin D. Roosevelt, January 1941, Los Angeles,
California)

A servant who read about the California Day of Rest Law, which required employers to allow employees one 24-hour period a week off from
work, in her YWCA Employees' Club bulletin and asked for a full day off
reported her employers' response: "She wanted luncheon served and
wouldn't hire a girl who wasn't willing to stay in until 1:30 P.M. on her day off.
What do we do about it?"[38]

Another variation of the argument over hours between housewives and
domestics was the question of time "on call." Most employers did not assign
specific work during the afternoon between cleaning up lunch dishes and
starting dinner. But domestics were not allowed to leave the work premises
and were usually expected to answer telephones and doorbells and perhaps
to mind a napping child. Whether or not this time constituted work, and how
much work, was debated throughout the 1930s. In legislative or voluntary
limitation of hours, how was this time to be counted?

One version would count the following schedule, for instance, as a 60-
hour week:

7:00 Rise, get breakfast and eat
7:45 Sweep 2 piazzas, clean 2 bathrooms
8:30 Dishes
9:00 Make dessert
10:00 General cleaning
11:30 Start dinner
12:15 Dinner at noon
1:00 Dishes
2:00 Rest period, answer telephone and door
5:30 Feed animals
6:15 Supper and dishes
7:30 Free for evening
Time off: Thursday afternoon from 2:00
Sunday afternoon from 3:00 (frequently all day Sunday, especially in
    summer)
Holidays—half day; all day Christmas
Household: 2 adults, one school-age child; dog and cat.[39]

To count this as a 60-hour week, the daily 2 to 5:30 "rest period" was not considered work. Most housewives' groups argued, in discussing hourly wages, that every two hours on call should be counted as one hour of work because no physical labor was required. Most domestics argued that two hours spent at a place the employer required and often serving as the employer's message taker and doorkeeper was two hours of work. So long as the occupation remained unregulated, the vision that prevailed was the employers'.

Hours were significant because housework was physically demanding and solitary. Having to spend hours without pay further deprived the worker of a life of her own. Even when wartime competition for labor forced employers to raise wages, they did not reduce hours. As one group of domestics said during the war, "Time-off is important not only to health but also to morale. The worker . . . needs time so that she may do her share in national defense as an individual in her own right," instead of enabling only housewives to participate.[40]

In general, cleaning and cooking were set tasks, and an array of other jobs might be assigned. Expectations varied by region and by the racial and ethnic background of employers, as well as by the composition of the employing household and its idiosyncratic habits. Little specialization characterized the occupation. The titles of "maid," "general houseworker," "cook," and even "laundress" were used for workers who did approximately the same range of tasks. Although the laundress was more likely to be part-time and to have fewer expected tasks, all of these workers might be asked to range through "cooking, keeping house and nursing all in one job" (to Mr. President, January 1937, La Grange, Louisiana) as well as washing clothes.[41] Particular tasks were not separate and unrelated jobs, but rather the cumulative work performed by a domestic during a normal workday.

Work usually began in preparation for breakfast. Baking for all meals, including breakfast, was not extraordinary. As Ellen Woodward noted in a letter about regional autonomy in Works Progress Administration (WPA) women's training programs, cooks trained for southern households needed to know how to roll good biscuits—not a usual requirement in the North and West. Baking, of course, required a hot oven, and burns and heat were hazards. A Wichita correspondent reported, "It is nothing unusual for a girl to lose 15–20 pounds in a very short time in many of places. In summer they are shut up in hot kitchens, the oven often at 500° F. or not much better, to keep the [rest of the] house cool. The girls' bodies are covered with the prickly heat" (to Miss Perkins, July 1934, Wichita, Kansas).

On Mondays, laundry work traditionally occupied the remainder of the morning. Even with washing machines, the work was heavy:

> My sister works for five dollars a week . . . for a family of five. . . . She must wash clothes twice a week and each time washes enough to clothe a family of ten and not five. You can say the washing machine will do

the washing but it is my sister who must put up, take down, and iron
these clothes. (To Mrs. Perkins, July 1935, no place indicated)

Other mornings, cleaning occupied the time between breakfast and
lunch. Part of the time was spent dusting, vacuuming, and clearing clutter
and debris (such as ashtrays) out of the public dining and living rooms: taking
"care of the general appearance of the home." Bathrooms were scrubbed and
towels cleared away. One room might be given a thorough cleaning, which
could entail moving all the furniture to vacuum more thoroughly and to
clean walls and even, perhaps, lifting rugs and carrying them outside to beat
by hand.[42]

The employer often did the day's shopping during the morning cleaning period. When she returned, there might be packages to carry in. One
letter described the drudgery of working for a particularly thrifty housewife:

Often [she] buys her groceries on week-ends at bargains. She comes
home with those huge paper sacks, a foot in diameter at the base and
three feet high, filled with canned goods, flour and other heavy articles. These, the girl must lift out of the car and carry into the house.
A protest is just ignored. Also 5 gallon water bottles must be lifted out
of the car. These are only examples. (To Miss Frances Perkins, July
1934, Wichita, Kansas)

Then the domestic prepared lunch. The elaborateness of catering varied by household, but it was taken for granted that meals should be prepared, served, and cleaned up at noon and in the evening.

Afternoons had more variety than mornings. They embraced ironing,
mending, child watching, silver polishing, perhaps yard work or cleaning the
auto, "special" jobs added onto basic housecleaning, cooking, and laundry
work. Some time was usually on call, responsible for telephone answering,
message taking, and turning away salespeople from the door.

By 5:00 P.M. at the latest, dinner preparation began. The domestic-
cum-cook seems to have been expected to adapt to the housewife's wishes on
all occasions. As one cynical correspondent described a possible day:

The lady goes out and returns with four extra for dinner after ordering
dinner for only two—dinner ready on time—and Mrs. takes 3 or 4 cans
of beer from the refrigerator out to the front porch where the six relax
and drink their beer—until the dinner is ruined. And the Mrs. says
Julia these potatoes are stiff, and this ice tea is as warm as if it had been
on the stove. Julia dare not say who was to blame, but goes back to the
kitchen and waits again for another hour—and finally finishes her evening work around nine o-clock, tired and weary from such draging along
all day from 7 A.M. (To Miss Anderson, April 1942, Springfield, Ohio)

The convention of dinner service was that the family left the table before it was cleared for washing the dishes. As the same writer put it, "[they] sit at the table and smoke for half hour or so—all which held the maid at least until 8 o-clock."

Domestics could not plan a regular end to the day because of the sociable nature of meals. Promptness at meals was not fashionable, and domestics found their workday lengthened by the family's and guests' lateness in coming to the dinner table. Dinner was served between 7:00 and 7:30 so that the conclusion of the meal and cleanup kept workers until at least 8:00 and perhaps as late as 9:30 or 10:00. Even though the domestic might not have worked constantly from the morning through the evening meal, she was held at the place of work for twelve or fourteen hours.

Cooks regularly complained about the presence of guests at dinner. Either they were given too short notice or too little food, or simply more work cooking for extra mouths, "with no extra money" (to Mrs. Perkins, August 1933, Raleigh, North Carolina, from "an interested colored friend").

After cleaning up from dinner, the domestic might have to turn down beds for the household, "the last straw at the end of a 12 hour day."[43] Or she might have to mind the children. Rarely were domestic workers hired for full-time child care. Generally, domestics "looked out" for children during the day's work. And the domestic worker was considered regularly available for baby-sitting when the housewife and her husband were out during evenings. If she lived in, "after working from 6:30 or quarter of seven in the morning till 8:30 P.M. or quarter of nine (with no rest period), [she] has to stay in 'with the children'—sometimes actually out of bed until one or two. All this though her job be not with the children" (to Franklin D. Roosevelt, August 1937, Ilion, New York).

The question of discipline raised immense tensions. Children took the cue from their parents that the domestic was not someone of consequence. "A great many places the children will strike a person and the women will only say 'don't pay attention to children'" (to Women's Bureau, November 1933, Chicago, Illinois). This domestic "person" described well the employing women's attitude that what happened between children and the domestic was not important, except, of course, that the children were not reprimanded for treating domestics as inferiors.

You can't scold them because they will fire you. (To Mrs. Roosevelt, November 1933, New Britain, Connecticut)

The children treated me as dirt beneath their feet, simply because I was "nobody but the maid." To a girl of my age, such treatment, by such little children, only caused me to dislike them, and I do not want to bear malice in my heart towards anyone. (To Dear Gentlemen, NAACP, June 1934, New York)[44]

Hard physical labor spread over a long day with few social pleasures
led to complaints of ill health that were strikingly at odds with the usual de-
piction of housework as healthy for the housewife because it gave her light
activity. Some problems, such as being confined indoors, were unique to the
domestic. One advocate of shorter hours for domestics pointed out the limitations of indoor work:

> with only a few hours off once a week in the afternoon and evening. . . .
> The cooks and maids are thus deprived of sunshine and fresh air for a
> whole week although some of them are permitted to go out in the eve-
> ning at times. But they are deprived of the health-giving rays of the
> sun. (To Mr. F. D. Roosevelt, April 1938, Chicago, Illinois)

Other problems would seem to be endemic to the work of the house
itself and were avoided by any woman who could hire someone else to suffer
them. Foot pains, for instance, were constant. Though home economists advised that many household tasks could be done sitting down, domestic workers often found household equipment the wrong height and position. Instead,
servants spent hours on their feet, standing to clean, to cook, and to iron.

Lifting was another hazard. Model codes suggested by domestic workers advocated that

> no woman engaged in this work shall do any outside work such as wash-
> ing the automobile, cleaning the garage, sweeping the walks or yard or
> any such work. . . . No woman shall do heavy work such as waxing
> floors, or polishing them, washing windows, or woodwork within the
> house. Nor any other heavy work apt to be a physical strain to a
> woman.[45]

The normal hardships of housework became more acute for women
who did the work full time and every day. One correspondent reported,
"One maid I know was discharged when her hands became sore, and consequently infected from the action of strong cleaning agents which she was
compelled to use" (to Franklin D. Roosevelt, August 1937, Ilion, New York).
By the late 1930s, such agents as lye for dissolving grease, oxalic acid for
bleaching, gasoline and benzine for cleaning, kerosene, and turpentine were
in common use.[46]

Both work hazards and exploitation were felt to fall more heavily on
very young, very old, and nonwhite workers: the less powerful the worker,
the more abused she was in hours demanded and rest denied.

> They are harder on the colored woman. They seem to think that a col-
> ored woman have no feeling tiredness. They put 16 and 18 hour work
> on them and they have to work every inch of their life to get it done

and that is all day and best of the night. (To Mr. President Roosevelt, July 1933, Baltimore, Maryland)

A woman from Washington, probably black, reported the backbreaking load that seems often to have been placed on black domestics: "I cook, wash for two Rooming houses on hand. She doesn't have a washing machine. Scrub on my hand and knees and iron, clean, wash windows, scrub wall[s]" (to Mrs. Roosevelt, January 1942, Washington, D.C.).

When researchers from the New York State Department of Labor interviewed domestic workers in 1948,

> There were [still] many complaints about window cleaning and polishing floors with paste wax. . . . There were also innumerable complaints about having to scrub floors on one's knees[:] "Washing windows hurts my arms and makes my sides sore. They want five or six floors washed on your knees, but when they [employers] do it, they use a mop." "Windows and this knee crawling! Sometimes I come home with my knees swollen."[47]

Hard work and long hours did not pay off in good wages. Throughout the period, wages seem to have had more relation to the worker's power relative to the employer than to available supply or local living costs. In an occupation with almost completely elastic demand, wages depended upon what the housewife could pay and how many women were desperate enough to take the job at that price. Throughout the 1930s stories appeared of women taking jobs for room and board only.

Food was a source of grievance. Most workers, even if only dailies, expected at least one meal a day. Often, they claimed, so little food was provided that they ended the day hungry. Others said they were given "their old food they wouldn't eat their-selves" (to Miss Perkins, April 1933, Chicago, Illinois). Meals were "hastily eaten, causing stomach agonies,—or in between acts, thus usually arriving at the 'cold' stage,—and the night meal . . . eaten at such a late hour, making the fast between the two meals of too long duration for comfort" (to President Roosevelt, March 1937, Los Angeles, California).

Room was often no better than board. One YWCA survey reported from California "examples of what has been asked of girls we have sent out on low-priced jobs in homes":

1. Sleep on davenport in room through which family passes to go to bathroom.
2. Sleep on cot which is put in living-room at night.
3. Sleep on back porch where the wash tubs and garbage cans are kept.
4. In a room over the garage. Numerous cases of this.

5. In room with children.
6. In same bed with a child.
7. In same bed with the grandmother.
8. Maid often refused use of bathtub where there is only one bathroom in the house.[48]

The unregulated nature of the employment, coupled with no reasonable assessment of the value of room and board, meant that housewives could demand full-time work in return for housing. This practice was easier to justify if some tutorial purpose might be implied, and housewives talked of themselves as transmitting standards to the young, the immigrant, and the educationally deficient black and Mexican.

In general, housewives took advantage of many women's need for housing, food, and income and the lack of alternative available jobs to pay as little as possible. Even patriotism did not diminish the search for bargain labor. As one woman reported:

There seems to be much discussion among the officers' wives employing domestic help as to how much should be paid for twelve and fourteen hours' work including room and board on the fort. Some of the wives have taken advantage of the fact that the poor little "private's" wife is so anxious to remain close by her husband on the fort that she will slave all day long in a home for her room and board without pay. This has tended to reduce the morale of the little wife as she has no spending money and no free time to call her own. Officers' wives, above all, should know better. (To Committee of Fair Employment, May 1942, from Fort Lewis, Washington)[49]

Low wages exacerbated health problems:

How can we poor tired of life girls make ends meet, with having teeth looked after eyes and glasses to be cared for and life insurance to pay, with this sinful wages. No wonder they girls help themselves to things when not noticed. I am over 50 and much worried about my future therefor myself as well as other girls doing housework. (To Dear Kind Father President Roosevelt, August 1933, Detroit, Michigan)

Employers paid attention to possible infections transmitted by workers but not to work hazards. By the early 1930s, the Community Employment Service, a black-sponsored and directed training program in Atlanta, sent prospective employers a health history for workers, which gave physicians' reports on "ears, tonsils, teeth, nails, pulse, heart, lungs, urinalysis, and blood test."[50] WPA household employment programs paid for workers to get Wassermann tests for syphilis. And by the early 1940s, twenty-three com-

mercial placement agencies in New York City were cooperating with the city
health department and the child welfare committee of the county medical
society to require tuberculosis testing.[51]

Inadequate clothing also affected health. As a woman wrote from Gal-
veston, Texas:

> Me myself when i go to work in the morning i hadter leave my house at
> Six thurty to get to my work for seven o'clock . . . and what so hard on
> we poor colored women [is] we dont make enought to ride the Bus.
> i walk a mile every morning to get to my work. . . . And you know
> we cant buy a coat to keep us warm going to work. (To Mr. President
> Roosevelt, December 1938)

Mistresses took the responsibility of providing uniforms, but few day
workers wore them; some took pride in carrying work clothes. Workers did
not have to pay for uniforms, a bonus, but they tried to avoid these marks of
service.

Day and Night

I'm a cheerful little earful of "Yes,
ma'am's" through the day;
I'm a merry (oh, yes, very!) maid at
work along the way;
. . . .
Oh, I'm prim and very trim in my uniform
at night;
Dinner ended, house amended, then I'm
out of sight.
Off to dance—there's a chance
of acquiring a beau
Who will change me to a lady with
an M.R.S., you know.[52]

Throughout the 1930s and the war years, domestic workers were generally depicted as young women who took housework jobs in the interlude
before marriage. Images of youth sustained the notion of the houseworker as
helper to and pupil of the housewife. Seeing housework as a life stage instead
of lifetime employment mitigated concern about lack of regulation in the job.
Young people did not have family responsibilities or need adult wages or
time to spend caring for their own households. Images, however, only partially coincided with reality.

Many young women did get wages, room, and board for housework,
especially to support attending school. Most houseworkers, even when described as girls, were adult women and often had families. For them full-time

work generally meant living out and commuting to and from the job. Cash
wages were essential because they purchased food, housing, and transportation and provided for dependents. Wages for living out were typically lower
than wages for living in (adding a moderate value for room and board) and
probably contributed to making the job harder for women of color relative to
white women. As one woman, almost certainly white, said:

> Sleep-in, you do not have to travel back and forth in cold weather.
> Hours are longer, but not as hard, because work is planned for a whole
> week. You get more pay on a sleep-in job. You save on room rent and
> food. It's much easier than day work, which works you too hard.[53]

A major tension for domestics was the pull between an employer's desire for full attention to her home and the worker's need to care for her own
home and family. Depression and wartime economies that deprived households of male income may even have increased the proportion of domestic
workers responsible for supporting families.

During the Depression 1930s, housework was the most accessible job
for adult women. "A special analysis of 1930 census data on gainfully employed
homemakers [found that] 16 percent of 'servants, waitresses, etc.' were the
sole wage earner in their family—a larger proportion than for any other occupational group." Over a third of women homemakers working as domestics
were heads of households. Families with a woman head and without regular
access to male income were the most needy, but even in multi-earner families, many had substantial reliance on domestic workers' incomes.[54]

Studies conducted in Baltimore and Philadelphia during the late 1930s
to collect evidence in favor of domestic workers' inclusion in Social Security
retirement provide selective data that accord with anecdotal information
from other parts of the country. One finding from the all-black Baltimore
study and the heavily black Philadelphia study was that "the large proportion
of nonresident full-time workers, in contrast to the small group of resident
full-time workers, and the relatively large proportion of regular day workers,
are typical of Negro household workers in general. A study of white domestic
workers would probably have shown considerably more resident and fewer
day workers." The studies also found that, among black women in the prime
employment years of twenty-five to fifty-four, most worked in domestic service. And, as accorded with their adult status, the majority of workers were
married, widowed, divorced, or separated. More than half had dependents
to support; 37 percent of the single women in Baltimore reported "other persons dependent on their earnings."[55]

For these women, the return of the norm of day work in the labor
shortage of the immediate postwar period represented recognition of their
family and work responsibilities. By the late 1940s, however, the "job de-

scription—day worker—household" required a hard day's work. Tasks required included

> 1. Cleaning—May clean entire house, including washing and waxing floors and woodwork, dusting and polishing furniture, making beds and changing linen, cleaning blinds, refrigerators and stoves, vacuuming rugs, bed, furniture, and drapes. 2. Laundry—Washing and ironing, white and colored cottons, linens, silks, rayons, children's clothes.[56]

Women taking these jobs could do the work in their own homes only as a second shift of hard physical labor.

For the domestic worker, the halo around the words *home* and *domestic* seemed ironic. She gained virtue by tending another woman's home and earning money for her own. By doing "woman's work," she slighted her woman's duty to care for her own family. With only solitary wives responsible for a home's care, the domestic's home inevitably suffered when the bulk of her labor went into other women's homes.

Dominant cultural images depicted servants as women without independent lives and interests. Domestics were envisioned as single women, young or old, cut off from any attachments except those to the employer's family. Domestic workers' families were not assumed to need care or to engage in the same relationships as their employers. When the domestic worker sought to defend her time and energies for her own home life, ironically she appealed to an image that justified her labor in another's home but not her protection as a worker.

Five

Education for the Vocation of Housework

Home economics training serves a double function,—it prepares for an income-earning occupation and also for a woman's own life needs. . . . The returned [World War I] soldier will demand that many occupations, now taken over by women, be given back to him, but at no time can he replace the woman who is well trained in home economics.
—Henrietta W. Calvin, *Home Economics Courses for Girls and Young Women,* 1918

The U.S. federal government and local state and municipal governments did not coerce girls to choose domestic work as a vocation. There was no need. Young women were surrounded by familial and cultural pressures to become housewives and household workers; they were effectively closed out of other professional and technical fields. In these circumstances, little coercion was needed to strengthen their choice.

Government programs did, however, spread information and ideas about what housework was and how it should be done. Accepting the social limitations placed on women, government agents, educators, and family experts used public schools and federal funds to teach young women and girls what their jobs were.

Often the experts who designed and purveyed these messages were women. Unlike those feminists who fought women's assignment to particular work and segregation from the world of men, seeking the improvement and advancement of women, they accepted segregation and sought advancement through accomplishment within a "woman's field." This chapter does not consider how well the strategy helped women to gain social equality with men[1] but how it led privileged groups of women to design programs and courses that sustained a vision of women as domestic workers and maintained a division of household labor between middle-class housewives and working-class, often nonwhite, domestic workers: a power relationship that persuaded middle-class women to accept their exclusion from centers of male power.[2]

I distinguish here between the educational, school-based programs that predominated during the 1920s and the work relief and training projects that emerged as part of the New Deal response to the employment emergency of the 1930s. First I focus on the vocational education classes funded by the federal government under the Smith-Hughes Act (1917) and guidance given these courses by the Office of Education. I then turn to work relief and related projects run first by the Federal Emergency Relief Administration (FERA) and then the WPA.

Developing a Woman's Profession

The most regular source of employment in the United States, paid or unpaid, for all adult women was housework, whether done in their own homes or in those of employers. Many women did both during their lifetimes, either simultaneously or sequentially: working for wages as an adult outside their own households, or working in domestic service until marriage shifted the work to the couple's household. Domestic work might also be sought at the end of the work life, as the single job available to older women forced into the labor force because of widowhood, divorce, or desertion or the husband's unemployment. Whatever the cause of women's economic need, domestic service was an all-purpose solution.

By about 1900, home economics as an educational discipline to train women for this occupation was taking on all the aspects of a certified profession with collegiate-level degree programs, a national association (the American Home Economics Association [AHEA] founded in 1908), journals reporting research, and curriculum developments. Home economics lacked, however, one essential professional criterion: exclusivity.[3] Every woman in the society was expected to be able to do some elements of household work, and this universal female expectation excluded men from some claim to work in the field. (Men could, of course, qualify through research and writing, and some did.)

To complete the professionalization of home economics as a female-led scientific field, the leadership had to develop subcategories to create ladders of authority and competence that distinguished women along lines of ability, social position, and respect within the professional associations. Not surprisingly, as in other academic fields, university-based scientists working in laboratories ranked over high school teachers in applied home economics, although the latter were more expert than housewives simply practicing home economics. In contrast to chemistry, biology, physics, and other increasingly arcane sciences of the end of the nineteenth century, however, which separated male scientists' knowledge from that of ordinary men, all women were expected to know something about the "science" of the home. Home economics had a different task from that of the male-dominated sciences; it had to rank the "amateurs," as well as establish the professional–amateur distinction. Housewife–employer had to be differentiated from domestic–employee; within the working class, women who performed housework for wages had to be distinguished from housewives who labored for love of home and family. The unassisted housewife was still to reign as the queen of American domestic life,[4] even though the image of maternal and wifely service disguised how different this work was for a wife with servants, a wife with no help, and a wife having to do her own as well as another woman's housework.

Unlike feminists such as Charlotte Perkins Gilman, who advocated taking specialized tasks such as cooking out of the home and making the home a center for emotional and sexual life, leaders of home economics such as Ellen Swallow Richards (Massachusetts Institute of Technology), Martha van Rensselaer (Cornell University), Mary Schenck Woolman (Teachers College, Columbia University, and Simmons College) and Marion Talbot (Wellesley College and University of Chicago) chose to emphasize the home's economic importance in consumption and human development, reaffirming the need for full-time female labor in the household. Many of these college-educated women were not, however, willing to do housework or to have women like themselves do it. Home economists and women's club leaders set out to save the home as a center of female professional competence, and in doing so, they emphasized the image of the solitary housewife. Simultaneously, however, they sought to justify middle-class women's pursuing interests other than housework and to train a class of women to take over the essential manual labor of the home.

Distinctions between housework as wage work, as unwaged work, and as a profession were debated and codified during the 1910s through political debate. Vocational education and teachers' groups lobbied Congress for federal legislation to provide support for vocational training of American youth.

A number of progressive groups, led by the National Society for the Promotion of Industrial Education (NSPIE, later the National Society for Vocational Education, NSVE), sought congressional funding for state education programs to prepare youth for the complicated skills needed in an industrial society. During the years immediately before and after congressional passage of the Smith-Hughes Act, the meaning of vocational home economics, as well as its content and student population, was heatedly debated.

In general, the American Home Economics Association, composed of collegiate experts in fields such as nutrition, sanitation, textiles, and design, and of middle-class clubwomen and housewives, initially favored not including home economics in a vocational training bill, while the NSPIE, composed of industrial educators, labor economists, and youth workers, did want it included. Labor reformers such as Henrietta Roelofs of the YWCA Committee on Household Employment and home economists in favor of education for wage earning also backed the NSPIE position. These women believed that "*non-wage earning occupations* in the household, such as are practiced by the wife and mother, should be considered under the subject of *vocational homemaking education, and wage-earning occupations* in the household . . . should be considered under the subject of *vocational industrial education.*" Clarifying differences between housewives and servants was "an act of historic importance in the solution of the domestic service problem," said Roelofs, "for it signified a recognition of domestic service on an industrial basis with all that this involves in standardization of hours, division of labor, etc."[5]

Throughout the early 1910s the NSPIE tried to persuade the AHEA to join in congressional lobbying and to assuage the AHEA's objections. These came from the "academic Home Economics people who felt it was too trade like"; from the "group who believe[d] that the vocational element will ruin 'the beauties of home life'"; and from those who believed that NSPIE did "not really want to advance Home Economics but to use it as a stepping stone" for industrial education.[6]

David Snedden, a leader of the NSPIE, may have been willing to give up the exclusive use of funds for training domestic servants because he believed housewives were workers. He boasted at one point that he had been trying for years to get the U.S. Census Bureau to include under "gainfully employed" "the approximately 20 million women who are employed in homes but not for wages, or for direct monetary return."[7] The NSPIE may also have believed that protecting funds for vocational training of working-class girls was less essential than for working-class boys because the girls would be employed only before marriage and did not need as much training as their prospective husbands, who would be employed throughout their adult lives.

Some tentative mutual understanding enabled the NSPIE, AHEA, and other women's groups to lobby successfully for congressional passage of the Smith-Hughes Act for Vocational Education in 1917. Building on the Smith-Lever Act of 1914 for federal subsidy of rural extension programs in agriculture and home economics, Smith-Hughes provided for funds to be granted to state education authorities to pay one-half the costs for instruction in three vocational fields: agriculture, arts and industries, and home economics, designated simply as "vocational home economics." Theoretical arguments became practical ones about whether the U.S. Office of Education would authorize expenditures for non–wage-earning homemaking courses, for wage-earning industrial courses, or for both. If money were to be given for homemaking courses, what standards would define "vocational" training as opposed to "household arts" appreciation?

The divisions within and between groups were rarely clarified. Indeed, the Smith-Hughes Act provisions for supporting the training of teachers for vocational home economics gave everyone a reason for being a vocationalist. The act's effect was to provide federal support for about one-third of public school home economics training, with the remaining two-thirds coming from state and local funds without the requirement that it be for "vocational" training. The act also paid land-grant colleges for training teachers of home economics, a significant incentive for the development of collegiate programs, the primary purpose of which was to train women for teaching.[8] These women could have premarriage careers, earn respectable wages, and then be able to care for their own homes at marriage—an ideal mix for middle-class women's education.[9] Despite the rhetoric of the movement, the collegiate programs did train women for work in commercial and mercantile food, decorating, and furniture businesses; by 1928, the Home Economics in Business section of the American Home Economics Association had three hundred members.[10]

Increased professional opportunities for middle-class women were an immediate consequence of the Smith-Hughes Act, and the division between the American Home Economics Association and the National Society for Vocational Education vanished. By 1920, the two groups and organizations in the women's lobbying federation, the Joint Congressional Committee, joined forces to seek more funds for home economics, which was allotted only 20 percent of the funds for trade and industrial education in the 1917 legislation. During the 1920 legislative session, they pushed for the Fess Home Economics Amendment to Smith-Hughes, which explicitly recognized homemaking education as vocational under the act's terms and guaranteed one-third of the allotted funds to home economics work.[11]

The Fess Amendment failed, and no new funds were authorized by Congress until the passage of the George-Reed Act in 1929, which authorized additional funding through 1934 for Smith-Hughes Act classes and equalized expenditures between vocational education in agriculture and in home economics. The George-Ellzey Act of 1934 raised the funding level and gave equal sums to vocational training in agriculture, trades, and industries and to home economics and was perpetuated by the George-Deen Act in 1937.

Collegiate training in home economics could serve the same functions for black as for white middle-class women, except that for black women, with higher rates of sustained paid employment, normal college support from federal funds and possible professional employment in nutrition, textiles, and dietetics could be guaranteed. The career of Flemmie Kittrell, a 1924 Hampton Institute graduate in home economics with a 1935 Cornell University doctorate in home economics, is one such professional success story. As dean of home economics at Howard University, she developed a field in international nutrition education and became a leader in exporting the knowledge of U.S. schools of home economics to Africa during the establishment of independent African nations.[12]

Training of teachers followed racial lines, however. Most black women were trained in the southern black colleges, which had developed during Reconstruction to provide basic literacy and job skills for freed slaves. From the time Samuel Chapman Armstrong founded Hampton Institute in 1868 to the death of his intellectual heir Booker T. Washington, the president of Tuskegee Institute, in 1915, "Negro industrial training" was the preferred beneficiary of northern businessmen–philanthropists and southern white school reformers. Hampton, Tuskegee, Fort Valley (Georgia), and Utica (Mississippi) were teacher training colleges (or normal schools, supported by congressional appropriations for Negro land-grant colleges from 1890 on), founded to train industrial teachers who could transmit the work ethic to the Afro-American working class, which was seen as shiftless and unable to take advantage of its labor market "as unskilled domestics and agricultural laborers."[13]

The pattern developed at Hampton was for four years of high school training. The first two years consisted of 10-hour workdays, followed by 2 hours of night classes; the second two years consisted of classes 4 days and work 2 days a week. The work that financially enabled students to pursue collegiate certification as teachers was chiefly in farm labor, domestic service, and unskilled factory production; the student teachers, who would become the "agricultural and mechanical teachers for the South's black public school system," "were taught 'proper' work attitudes by having to do unskilled work so that they would have no problems in teaching 'the dignity of labor' either to children of farm laborers and servants."[14] Manual labor was a norm for the collegiate peers of the black home economics trainee in the south, and the women's course differed little from the men's.

The southern home economics curriculum for white women assumed that black servants performed manual labor. It was nonmanual and in "such 'white women's specialties' as teacher training and scientific instruction, i.e. chemistry in nutrition or the application of chemistry and physics to cooking rather than applied studies. . . . If an applied course was given it was a special class in fancy cooking, . . . which could not be trusted to the Negro servant."[15] When Texas Technological University sought certification for teacher training in home economics in 1928, it listed at length its equipment for home training, which included one dozen finger bowls and a full set of two dozen soup, dinner, luncheon, salad, and bread and butter plates, cereal bowls, and bouillon cups and saucers. Middle-class girls needed to learn how to use elaborate tableware.[16]

In the Northeast and Midwest, schools of home economics stressed the development of professional skills comparable to those in male-dominated disciplines; home economics departments taught young women scientific standards and their application to individual households. Unlike the South, however, these institutions also nurtured research aspirations such as those Flemmie Kittrell acquired at Cornell. Northern institutions were more likely to provide a research base for, and to teach, new standards for sanitation, child welfare, and nutrition. Middle-class women were being trained for productive adult life: "If [the student] marries, she knows how to run a home. If she doesn't marry, she may have a vocation along homemaking lines such as cafeteria manager, trained dietitian, designer of clothes, according to her talents."[17]

The patterns established in normal schools and colleges were replicated by teachers in the public school programs funded by Smith-Hughes and succeeding legislation: day classes taught during regular sessions, trade extension and preparatory classes taught in the evenings for students already holding jobs, and evening home economics classes for women and wives who had other duties at home or work during the day. Day classes for regular students during the first two years of high school were intended, one advocate said, to prepare the "26,000,000 women [who] are housekeepers," who need "specialized training in such subjects as child care, home nursing, cooking, meal-planning, garment-making, household management, and buying [since] 90 percent of money wage-earners bring home is spent by women."[18]

During the course of the 1920s, an emphasis on education for the vocation of homemaking gradually took over in courses offered during the regular day curriculum. Contrary to Henrietta Roelofs's hope that vocational education would clarify the industrial status and improve the labor standing of domestic workers, in much of the country vocational home economics became equated with preparation for a woman's keeping her own house. By 1931, California's annual report to the U.S. Office of Education listed expenditures under "vocational homemaking education." The director of the Home Economics Education Service of the Office of Education, Adelaide Baylor, admitted to the Texas state supervisor,

> Personally, I prefer the word homemaking in our literature that we send out to the States and through the states, and recommend that while we leave the term "home economics" in the State Plan [for voca-

tional education], you use the term "homemaking" wherever it is possible in your materials. . . . [As to the] "useful employment" [requirement for funds], since that is also the reading of the law[,] it would be well, I think, to leave it as it is without change. A woman is usefully employed in her own home when she is a homemaker.[19]

As was the case with teacher training, particular skills for homemaking varied in different regions of the country and in different school districts, and they changed during the two decades between 1920 and 1940, moving from concentration on generic cooking and sewing to more elaborate specialties in clothes making, meal planning, child study, and home decoration by the end of the period. Within this general scheme, middle-class schools offered more specialized studies in home improvements, while working-class schools stuck to basics. In the mid-1920s, Dallas, Texas, public schools offered evening classes in white schools in interior decorating, millinery, clothing, and foods; by 1927, classes were added in home planning and furniture, color harmony, nutrition and dietetics, period furnishing, and tailoring. Evening home economics classes in Mexican schools in other Texas cities, by contrast, covered subjects like sanitation, personal hygiene and clothing, personal hygiene and cookery, and "how to dress becomingly." In high schools designated "Colored," clothing and cookery predominated, with some work in child care.[20]

California gave no evening classes in home economics during the 1920s, only regular day courses in public schools. By the early 1930s, part-time home economics classes were available in home sewing and millinery, child development, home nursing, and foods, basic courses of particular use to housewives needing to make their own clothes and hats, to conserve food budgets, and to understand their children's emotional progress. Regular school courses approved for federal funds included applied work in "home food preparation, preservation, and service; home sewing, including construction and repair of clothing, linens, and other; millinery for women and children; home laundering; home gardening; home nursing; home invalid cooking; and housekeeping." Supplemental work, eligible for funds when offered by local schools, included house planning, interior and furniture design, interior decoration and furnishing, hygiene and sanitation, household science, dietetics, and home reading, courses that varied depending on the school's interests. California education officials assumed, however, that most training would "emphasize the needs and practices of the home with a small income where the housekeeper must act as cook, maid, butler, hostess, and mother."[21]

Illinois schools, like those in Texas and California, intended to raise the aesthetic standards of students' homes. Required to plan home projects in conjunction with classroom work, students were set exercises:

Obtain a certain sum of money from your parents. Take that sum to buy
kitchen equipment that will increase the kitchen's efficiency and
convenience;

Introduce a "Better Music Month" in your home. Be responsible for
the music bought during that time seeing that it is really good popular or classical music;

Collect and arrange in booklet form twenty-five gift suggestions for
Christmas, giving cost of each and materials which may be used in
making them.[22]

Ohio schools taught meal planning, garment making, and house planning
and furnishing in the first year; clothing budgets, construction of garments,
costume design, house management, child development and family relationships, and food and nutrition in the second year. A suggested home project
in Ohio held out as a "minimum accomplishment" that "each girl should
understand the principles involved in the preparations of candies and simple
Christmas sweets [and] be able to pack an attractive Christmas box of
sweets."[23]

In segregated southern "Colored" schools funded under the Smith-
Hughes, and later George-Deen and George-Ellzey acts, girls took courses
in domestic service, in home nursing and child care, and in laundry, which
included, in one instance, "8 lessons each in bleaching, removing stains,
washing linen, cotton and woolen goods."[24] In El Paso, Texas, the school
board created a segregated school system "which established a home economics curriculum for Mexican girls to enable them to acquire the skills
needed to work as domestics," on the grounds that this training would "best
assist the students to find jobs." In Los Angeles, Mexican schools that taught
students English "were praised for moving Chicanas from the cotton fields to
domestic service," which would speed their Americanization.[25]

In all states, much of the training for domestic service was not taught
under the category of home economics but was funded as "trade extension
and preparatory" classes. In Texas, black and Mexican girls followed part-
time courses in cooking and household service; female students of all races
got training in nursing and dressmaking.[26] Indian women working as "cooks,
laundresses, bakers, and seamstresses were to improve their skills by study
in commercial centers."[27] In California, by comparison, "trade and industrial" courses were available for girls in cosmetology, power laundry work,
cake decorating, and costume design.[28] Illinois devoted most of its industrial
funds to men and gave courses for girls only in nursing and dietetics.[29]

In Virginia, illustrating the maintenance of racial distinctions among
working-class women, three evening trade and industrial classes for white
women were funded in 1935: in Lynchburg one in dietetics for nurses; one in
textile math for textile workers; and one in home economics for homemak-

ing, which was organized for "unemployed, underprivileged women" who needed some "bucking up." Classes organized in 1935 for "Colored" schools, by contrast, were in domestic service, practical nursing, and "Trade Preparation for Housemaids in Coordinating, Children's nursing, laundry, table service, cleaning, [and] general housework."[30]

Black educators supported home economics training for girls, including training for domestic service. Economic hardships and poverty required black women to earn wages in domestic service and to produce food, clothing, and decent housing for their own families on low wages; teaching homemaking to twelve-, thirteen- and fourteen-year-old girls implied not only wage earning but also recognition that black families had needs like white families. "If," as Carrie Lyford, a Hampton Institute home economist, wrote, "better home conditions are to be secured [among blacks], it is necessary that girls be trained when they are young to assume home responsibilities."[31] Black colleges such as Prairie View A&M in Texas and Tuskegee in Alabama received Smith-Hughes teacher training funds (though at a much lower rate than white teacher training programs). Nannie Helen Burroughs's National Training School for Women and Girls, founded in Washington, D.C., in 1909 with Baptist church support, sought students wanting education for "improved home life" and as "every-day workers." All these institutions joined domestic uplift to cultural uplift with the addition of black history to the requirements of the major.[32]

Burroughs also undertook training of adult domestic workers through organization in the mid-1920s of a National Association of Wage-Earners. Intended, like Booker T. Washington's earlier work at Tuskegee, to raise Afro-Americans' pride in the limited jobs left them by discrimination and their skill in doing these jobs, the association's practice house offered women the same educational format as practice houses for college majors in home economics and promised to work with employers to train "green country girls" to acceptable city standards. Students were given tests

> in the actual preparation and serving of food, cleaning of rooms and making beds. . . . Housemaids and office attendants [were] taught how to answer the door bell and telephone. . . . Day workers [were] taught the fundamental things which most employers expect them to know or to do. All applicants [were] instructed in the principles of good conduct, manners and dress.

The association hoped to function as an employment service to guarantee good employers and good workers. For Burroughs, the enterprise's objectives were creation of "working women of whom a community will be proud" and, through the competence and self-assurance of workers, reduction of the occupation's stigma so that the domestic worker could be "just as proud as the nurse is of her uniform." Though economic hardship kept the practice house from succeeding, Burroughs's ideas were close to those purveyed through the 1930s by the YWCA and by WPA projects.[33]

While Burroughs's students learned laundering, plain cooking, and waiting at table to be useful to their employers and their own families, middle-class students learned to purchase such services. Homemaking for the middle class was management; for the working class, it was labor. In married life, the middle-class girl might need technical skills; in practice,

> [she] knows that skill in domestic pursuits is absolutely no asset in securing the masculine attention which she craves. As proof of this lack of interest on the part of the average man it may be stated that it is difficult to find any number of husbands who made a definite inquiry as to their fiancee's ability to cook or who even suggested that marriage be postponed while their prospective housekeepers secure some training for their job. . . . While a man who is not trained to support his household is looked at askance, the girl hopes to "hire someone to do her work."[34]

The Depression necessitated increased emphasis on frugal use of resources and maintenance of family morale. Home economics associations sought government aid to support courses in family life and homemaking to assist housewives in maintaining the family's standard of living. Homemaking as a vocation predominated in public schools that received federal funds and in evening classes that hired unemployed home economists to teach a variety of skills for homemakers. By the mid-1930s, courses to prepare girls for their major role as homemakers and, in some schools, boys for their role as fathers were being authorized for federal reimbursement. To be acceptable, the courses were supposed to include such "social studies" issues as

1. Provision of food for the family.
2. Selection, care, and construction of clothing.
3. Care and guidance of children.
4. Selection, furnishing, and care of the house.
5. Selection and use of home equipment.
6. Maintenance of health.
7. Home care of the sick.
8. Consumer buying.
9. Management of all material and human resources available to home.
10. Maintenance of satisfactory relationships.
11. Application of the arts and sciences.[35]

These broad standards were interpreted with "little unanimity" by home economics experts, but a national survey indicated that "homemaking instruction tend[ed] to be pointed toward intellectual understanding more than toward manipulative skill, and that this tendency is believed to be a desirable one. It also appear[ed] that the need for studying problems of personal living rather than future homemaking responsibilities [was] being stressed, and this tendency [was also considered] desirable." Increased funding so that more courses could be offered in regular day schools was recommended, even though such domestic emphasis might accelerate "a trend already apparent, . . . namely a decrease in the percentage of students taking subjects such as foreign languages and mathematics."[36] Evening home economics classes for adult women, by contrast, enrolled large numbers for sewing and remodeling clothing, as housewives sought to maintain clothing standards by doing the sewing themselves.

Instruction in family relations might keep middle-class and working-class white girls from practicing the skills of cooking, sewing, and laundering, but at least they promised a respected social role. Many black schools were denied any home economics training either for domestic service or for home management. By the mid-1930s, the discriminatory distribution of federal vocational funds was a topic for research by the NAACP, which protested discrimination against black pupils in all three categories of agriculture, home economics, and trade and industries programs. Indeed, as the Depression hit state budgets everywhere, federal grants became prizes that were given to the most favored pupils and schools. Funds that might have trained black girls for domestic service in the 1920s were shifted to training white girls for family living during the 1930s. For black girls, the major hope for some attention and money became the youth relief and work relief projects, which also inculcated traditional women's work positions and skills.

Work Relief and Vocational Training

Principles and practices developed in state vocational education programs during the 1920s carried into the New Deal work relief and education programs of the 1930s. The massive national effort to provide families with income—and youths with hope for the future—expanded the government's role in sustaining and inculcating class- and race-appropriate "women's work" and social roles. During the New Deal, agencies trained girls and women, depending on the assessment for their best hope of income and support, to see housework in one of three ways: as a housewife–manager directing an employee, as a solitary housewife doing the work of her own family, and as a domestic working in others' homes.

New Deal projects had one additional consideration: to avoid aggravating the trauma of job competition during a decade of high unemployment. The protests against allowing married women to benefit from scarce jobs or relief funds have been discussed by many historians. Less often mentioned are the protests against forms of education or work relief that might enable women to compete with men for jobs or black men and women to compete with white men and women.

Racial and gender conservatism underlay the moderate reforms of the New Deal. Girls and women were taught that their work was "service" and that their truest and best work was caring for homes and children, in ways that varied, of course, by class and race. Black men were excluded from skilled work relief jobs and given relief wages lower than those paid to white men; black boys in vocational programs were taught only unskilled hand work or use of outdated equipment; black girls in resident centers were disproportionately pushed into nursery and cooking and cleaning programs. The message in crisis was that no one's position would be changed; beset by falling incomes and threats of joblessness, white men would not be exposed to job competition from women or men of color.

Keeping women attached to the home was an essential element in New Deal relief programs. Stressing women's connection with housekeeping kept women firmly on the periphery of the job market and out of competition for jobs traditionally thought of as men's. Strengthening the image of women as caretakers of home life reassured citizens about the conserving principles of the New Deal. In the midst of the Depression, programs that taught women how to make homes healthier and more cheerful were justified on the grounds that better-skilled housewives would presumably have higher job morale and improved ability to care for families harmed by business failures and unserved by an overstretched government. Preserving dominant ideas of woman's primary social and economic role as wife and mother was so useful to so many groups that it is not surprising the New Deal programs readily incorporated the image into their design.

During the first two years of the Roosevelt administration, women received attention and relief through the medium of FERA-funded, state-directed projects such as camps and work relief projects. Relatively small numbers of women were served, and more radical approaches were taken to women's education and employment in these years than would be after 1935, when stable and large federal commitments were made under the WPA and the Social Security Act. Although housekeeping was a substantial part of opportunities offered to women between spring 1933 and spring 1935, the projects did not put women's homemaker role at the center of project design. Comparison between the earlier and later projects underlines the conservatism of post-1935 projects for women.

There were two major FERA projects for girls and women: camps operated under the worker education philosophy of project director Hilda Worthington Smith and work relief projects. Both projects purveyed domestic ideology. In camps for young women, the residents were required to perform the basic housekeeping duties of cleaning and cooking, which were often described as giving young women practical training to manage homes better: either the parental home to which they returned or their own marital home. The conservative imagery, however, existed amid classes in history, economics, and workers' rights—a context of preparation for industrial income earning and union membership as well as homemaking.

Women's Division director Ellen S. Woodward also concentrated the first FERA work relief projects in production that used women's typical household skills. Women gardened, cooked, and canned food for relief distribution. They sewed and finished garments and mattresses for welfare distribution. They worked as domestics for women heads of household so that those women were able to take relief jobs outside their homes. And unemployed teachers and housewives taught home economics and household skills. Housekeeping aide projects appeared to keep women in traditional roles, paying them relief wages to care for homes of families in which the mother was unable to provide full services of cleaning, cooking, and laundry. In many instances, however, the relief worker was taking over household work so that another relief-eligible woman could get a job. Both were paid relief wages that often exceeded market wages for the lowest-paid female jobs. As Martha Swain and Susan Wladaver-Morgan have pointed out, the effect of this project was to gain relief wages for two women instead of one and to uphold a notion of government responsibility for providing income through work for women as well as men. [37]

Within these women's jobs, class and race distinctions were maintained by the division between manual and nonmanual projects. Relief funds were paid to "non-manual visiting housekeeper[s], preferably a woman with some home economics training [who] visits the homes of families on relief and by means of discussion and demonstrations helps the homemaker make better use of her limited resources," and to housekeeping aides, who were "domestic workers." [38]

By spring of 1935, as FERA funds and programs were redirected toward WPA and straight work relief, programs took on a more conservative cast. The reason, one historian speculates, was a desire to protect the WPA from the charge of employing too many women. One way to respond was to keep women's relief jobs connected to homes. [39]

WPA continued the housekeeping aides project, perhaps because of the large numbers of black women certified for jobs as heads of household and also classified as unskilled workers. For these women, the aide job became a major source of federal employment and one, of course, acceptable within dominant racial conventions. "By 1938, black women comprised 93 percent of the workers in the WPA housekeeping aides program, [and] all supervisory and white collar personnel in this program were also black." [40]

The job changed its character from that of the FERA program, however, so that aides were assigned only to households certified by local relief authorities or designated charities. The work provided was intended to sustain the traditional family when mothers were chronically or temporarily ill, particularly in the periods around childbirth, and in families with aged, blind, or handicapped members. Many black groups welcomed the relief jobs, not only because they offered a reasonable wage at a time of high unemployment, but also because they implied federal recognition for traditionally black and despised work. A magazine story titled "The WPA's 'Good Neighbors'" reported that "humanitarian service is the watchword of the [14,400] colored women who are employed as housekeeping aides by the Works Progress Administration" in thirty-nine states. One could take special pride in working to improve life for families even poorer and more needy than one's own.[41]

The housekeeping aide projects were easy to publicize. Paying government-funded wages to relief-certified women with "no skills or profession through which to earn a living" provided jobs for "trained home economists" to direct the mundane duties of "practical homemakers" of working-class and primarily black families. For their pay, the aides performed a range of "duties under the headings of cleaning the home, preparation of meals, laundering, making and remodeling garments and household articles, caring for children, simple home care of the sick and advice on marketing, budgeting, nutrition and home management." They were domestic workers, but with limited hours and federally set wages. Even though the project offered workers an alternative to domestic service, WPA officials reported that the home economics lessons and supervised housework experience ultimately would enable aides to find employment in private homes.[42]

As was true of private domestic employment, government employment created tensions between the domestic's work life outside and inside her own home. Reports idealized housekeeping aides as mother-housekeepers able to replace the essential work lost when a mother was ill or absent (sometimes the program was labeled "help-a-Papa").[43] Though an aide had to be the head of her own household to be certified as a relief recipient, she supposedly adopted each assignment as "her family." One worker, caring for a family of seven children whose mother was hospitalized for a broken leg and father was "working steadily but at small pay" stayed late each night to bake and cooked Sunday dinner "regardless of her quota of hours."[44] Housekeeping aides were trained to make nourishing and appetizing meals from relief commodities so that they could teach poor housewives to use these items effectively. Courses to prepare the aides also taught them to use "graham flour instead of white flour in baking cakes, and making a meal for four serve eight persons with the aid of stretchers and fillers." The aides learned to make furnishings such as drapes and table linen from flour bags and "a china buffet out of a piano box."[45] In Kansas, housekeeping aides trained in "the safest and most modern methods for canning fruits and garden produce . . . taught hundreds of women how to can these things for use in their own home."[46] Beneath the official mandate to provide care for families authorized by local charity or public health agencies was the mission to teach home economics techniques and attentive mothering.

Housekeeping aide projects were organized in all parts of the country but were essential in the South with its large black population and the highest rates of "female heads eligible for works program employment." The heaviest percentages of female heads of household were in the former Confederate states, excluding Louisiana and Arkansas. From Texas to Virginia, the lowest percentage was 20.1 in Tennessee, rising to 37.4 in Mississippi. Washington, D.C., where 23.9 percent of households among relief-certified families were female-headed, reflected its position as a southern outpost.[47] Planners desperate to assist women accepted surrogate homemaking as a reasonable job for unskilled black women workers.

The housekeeping aide project required constant vigilance by federal officials to keep it from becoming a domestic servant project. The project was intended to have women serve families at roughly a peer level, with race and religion usually matched, but in the South state officials "thought of [it] as a 'servant's project' employing 100 percent Negro women." In Mississippi and Louisiana, where few white women worked in domestic service, no whites were assigned to housekeeping aide projects, and workers sent out on the project were referred to as "maids."[48] As late as October 1940, a New Orleans newspaper reported approvingly that, as part of their training, housekeeping aides were washing and ironing laundry for poor families that did not need service in the home but were "unable to care for their laundry."[49]

In spring 1935, just before the FERA was superseded by the WPA, Ellen Woodward announced a federal allocation of $500,000 to train 7,600 domestics. Woodward may have had a variety of motives. One was the desire to improve standards for workers so that housewives would be discouraged from reducing wages and raising hours. Another was the political need to do something for hard-hit black Americans without offending white New Deal supporters and critics. A third was pressure from her peers to create work relief for unemployed professional women. Whatever the project's origins, news reports indicated the popularity of education in traditional roles. Newspapers seemed relieved that the New Deal might turn back the deterioration of household standards caused by commercial innovations in housework, "fulfill[ing] the needs of a generation that has discovered it is not necessary, it is not profitable and it is not good for the human body to live out of a can."[50]

In the FERA project, Woodward began to develop the pattern that she worked out fully in the WPA after its creation in May 1935. The primary goal was to get women jobs. All advisers and advocates for women assumed this was possible only if women were trained and paid for work already generally accepted as women's work. Woodward was convinced, moreover, that household work as an occupation providing jobs would cease to exist without the "elevation of this occupation to the level of a modern industry."[51]

Additionally, Woodward was beset by political critics of the New Deal, especially by members of the comfortable middle class, who charged that "women's projects" paying security wages, such as sewing rooms, removed needy women from the employment service rolls and from the domestic service supply. Many sewing projects gave one hour at the end of the day for domestic training with the implicit promise that these women were available for hire when the local market demanded additional servants.[52] Woodward could save domestic work as a large-scale job for women, rebut criticisms of New Deal social leveling, and get women off relief rolls through a properly conceived domestic work training program. Her approach was evident from the earliest authorized projects in spring 1935.

Woodward set procedures to design projects for local housework customs; for each city or state, directors of women's work were required to call meetings of "representatives from non-fee-charging bureaus, such as the Big Sisters, YWCA, Council of Jewish Women, Catholic Women's Organizations" to educate them about proper standards in "wages, hours, living conditions, and contracts."[53] The advisory committee was to set the particular content of the local training course within the general categories of cooking, cleaning, laundry, child care, and personal hygiene. Letting housewives determine work content while the government encouraged hour and wage standards and the use of a regular contract was the implicit bargain Ellen Woodward maintained throughout the New Deal.

Training household workers, carried into the WPA in 1936, compensated relief-certified teachers to teach high-school-age girls (though women aged eighteen to thirty-five were accepted) skills that would enable them to enter the labor market and find jobs. The trainees did not have to be certified as relief-eligible (though local relief offices referred girls from families collecting public assistance) and were paid only with "lunches, uniforms, and a dollar a week for carfare to and from the training centers."[54] Teachers got relief funds; young women got skills that would presumably keep or help them off relief rolls; and the public got better-trained household workers. Training programs for household workers were "inaugurated in February 1936 in 17 states, New York City, and the District of Columbia." The program registered 9,272 young women and trained and placed 5,685 in just over a year.

The project was designed to train full-time live-in or live-out workers, who would work for a single employer. Indeed, so set was the notion that a domestic was a live-in worker that the WPA would not refer women heads of families for housework training unless their home responsibilities permitted their accepting live-in jobs.[55] (The housekeeping aide projects, with limited daily and weekly hours, were for these older women.) Government programs also inculcated public health standards into home-based work. Health examinations of trainees became popular, and workers were issued health certificates after passing standardized tests for venereal diseases and tuberculosis.[56]

As Woodward faced increasingly desperate need without increased job options for women, she resourcefully reorganized household training in late

1937 into the Home Demonstration Service.[57] As a widow making her own way, Woodward, supported by her ally Eleanor Roosevelt, had consistently fought for a portion of relief funds for women. Her Mississippi background as a white "lady" also echoed Roosevelt's instinct to base appeals on the image, if not the reality, of women's traditional roles. Training one set of women to be better housekeepers so that they could pass these skills on to other house-wives was a relief form that appealed to public desires for continuity and per-sonal security.

Home demonstration centers for household skills gave relief recipients a respectable location from which they either found jobs or remained in the centers to teach their newly acquired skills to local classes of homemakers and domestic workers. A WPA-certified job, work as a home demonstration expert paid a "security wage," which was a significant incentive for women to accept training. By late 1937, the project had been established in twenty-three states and enrolled almost six thousand women.[58] As late as June 1940, a domestic training program was operating in twenty states and the District of Columbia. There were sixty-five centers, "15 of which [were] for white trainees only; 20 for colored; and 30 for both white and colored," as one ob-server reported.[59] Very few Southern states had such programs, perhaps be-cause lack of alternative jobs for southern black women meant that there was no shortage of servants; additionally, southerners may not have liked the no-tion of federal interference in regulating household labor conditions.

Woodward enlarged the projects' ability to pay stipends, and she sharp-ened the agency's stance on working standards. In most areas, and especially in southern states, the relief wage was higher than the going rate for domes-tics and worked to push up the local standard. When housewives complained that they could not find domestic servants because they were "on relief," it usually meant that the women had WPA jobs and were unwilling to leave them for the "fire-sale" wages of the Depression. In states like New York and Pennsylvania, WPA wages for homemaking aides were about $60 per month for 128 hours of work. "Good" housework wages in the private market were $8 to $10 per week with room and board and more than 60 hours per week; $5 per week was a popular norm. One author noted the tension between government pay and private pay: "Girls can't be expected to work hard around the house all day for $5 a week, but on the other hand the average man in Pittsburgh can't compete with relief salaries. Let's strike a sensible compromise and get some of these people back to work."[60]

The standard accepted by WPA headquarters and local advisory com-mittees from 1936 to 1938 was less stringent than the 48-hour week for-mulated by the voluntary watchdog group, the National Committee on Household Employment, and the YWCA during the 1928 pre-Depression prosperity. All these groups had come round to a harsher standard: 60 work-ing hours a week, with 1 hour of work being calculated for each 2 hours of afternoon and evening "on call" time; "two half days off a week, beginning not later than 2 P.M. on the week day and 3 P.M. on Sunday"; overtime compensated by time off or extra money and not to exceed 12 hours in any one week; and a one-week paid vacation after the first year's service.[61]

WPA-funded training schools worked with local offices of the United States Employment Service (USES) or National Reemployment Service (NRS) to persuade prospective employers that students with certificates deserved regulated jobs. After the passage of the Fair Labor Standards Act (FLSA) in 1938, some training programs used the act's provisions to inform employers about minimum acceptable wages. Hours were not dropped to the FLSA 40-hour maximum, but its existence was used to advocate placement at 48 hours per week for live-out workers and 54 hours per week for live-ins.[62]

Wage standards varied more according to locality than did hours. It was presumed that cash wages were subsidized by uncounted presents of goods in addition to meals and rooms. Consequently, the standards for wages were less exact: advisory committees called for a minimum to cover "cost of living of independent women at a health and efficiency level," minus the cost of room and board for a worker living in. For workers living out, carfare was to be paid, with nothing said about their room costs. The inherent competition of the local rate for relief jobs provided a federal baseline for pay, one always higher than the local domestic rate, according to state news reports collected at WPA headquarters. In some localities, authorities closed down the competing WPA projects to force women to accept domestic work jobs that remained unfilled at the local state employment office.[63]

In return for meeting wage and hour standards, housewives could expect to hire workers trained to meet local norms of service. Workers were instructed in personal hygiene and social etiquette (including judicious "use of lipstick, rouge and powder") at the same time they learned to use cleaning materials, recipes, and child care techniques that met middle-class women's expectations.[64] It was assumed that "girls come from underprivileged homes and need to build up new standards not found in their own homes. . . . They need to be taught new attitudes, poise, etc. Cooperation with employer is set up as a necessary end."[65] In general, girls were to be trained in houses much larger than their own (one in Florida had five bedrooms, three baths, a kitchen, living room, sun parlor, and porches), to learn "how to answer a telephone properly, how to use electrical appliances, how to prepare and serve a smart luncheon or formal dinner, and the care of linens and silverware."[66] They were taught pronunciation; "old methods of accenting words on the wrong syllables until you can hardly recognise the words they mean" were corrected in southern projects.[67]

Whereas in the South girls were taught humility, in the North they had to conform to behavior that was "neither abject servility nor 'irritating displays of independence.' Rather . . . an attitude of dignified service and, as an employer put it in a letter of appreciation, 'that grand willingness to do just a little bit more than is actually specified.'"[68] Northern projects stressed responsibility and cooperation more than southern ones did.

Training to care for children in the middle-class fashion was important in all projects. In a Mississippi project, the objections of employers "to negro nurses, that of frightening the child with 'bugger' stories and superstitions, is done away with for the girls are taught that it is harmful and must not be done."[69]

Table service and cooking varied regionally. In the South, as Ellen Woodward noted in a memorandum to women's project administrators, making good biscuits was more important for a domestic's success than learning to make many dishes in an overall mediocre meal.[70] In Baltimore, "hot rolls . . . light, delicate, crisp," was the specialty.[71] In Connecticut, one was expected to be able to bake a good apple pie.[72] In New York City, the rules for formal family table service were to "carry a napkin, never touch the tableware with a bare hand, serve from the left, don't lean on the diners' shoulders, don't whisper down their necks."[73]

Since women certified as heads of household were not eligible for domestic jobs that required them to live in, much of the domestic training work was carried on in the youth division of the WPA, the National Youth Administration (NYA). Like its parent, the NYA resolutely held to existing race and gender divisions in organizing its projects. Even in the most liberal agency in the New Deal, the Division of Negro Affairs headed by veteran educator Mary McLeod Bethune, the NYA sought to exploit adherence to traditional work divisions rather than to challenge them.

When Bethune was appointed by President Roosevelt to head the division of Negro Affairs of the NYA, she found that racial discrimination did not take the form of offering different projects for black and white youths. Rather, black teenagers were not certified as eligible for projects in proportion to their economic need, and resident work projects were not set up in communities where needy youths lived. Bethune protested actions of southern relief officials to certify white families for relief funds more often than they certified black ones.

Neither Bethune nor other NYA and WPA officials fought the other major limitation, however—the requirement that work projects be jointly funded by the federal government and by sponsoring groups in local areas. White groups rarely underwrote integrated projects, and black communities were hard-pressed to accumulate equipment and materials for projects on which the federal grants would pay wages and staff expenses. Martha Swain points out a similar diminution of opportunities for women in 1938, when the WPA increased local contribution scales to a level higher than women's groups, who had sponsored women's projects, were able to raise.[74]

With such constraints on providing assistance, Bethune's acquiescence in gender- and race-segregated projects is not surprising. State reports provide abundant evidence that the NYA trained women not just for work in the home but also for their appropriate place within the home. In the South black female youth were conditioned primarily for employment as domestic workers, while white female youth were trained for employment as house-wives—to be more proficient in running their own homes. The 1937 report for Mississippi recorded that the state "had enrolled 450 NYA youth in home-making classes and 800 in domestic service classes." The report did not com-ment on the racial content of these categories, but it is likely that the white girls were in homemaking and the black ones in domestic service.

Kentucky state pamphlets issued for use in NYA courses indicated job assignments and work relationships. In four pamphlets for homemaking classes on spring cleaning titled "Look Up for Spring—Dress Up; Fix Up; Spruce Up; Clean Up," the drawing on the covers of the first three showed a young white woman sewing, hanging curtains, and a full clothesline. The drawing on the cover of the "Clean Up" brochure showed a black woman in a bandana bending over a washtub. As we saw when examining surveys of con-sumer expenditures, even the seasonal nature of this relationship was ac-curate. A white housewife without a washing machine could generally plan to do her own housework except for hiring a part-time worker for the heav-iest chores of the year, which included laundry work during the annual spring cleaning.[75]

Other Kentucky reports in the Technical and Training Series illustrate the decorative aspects of middle-class housewifery. Titles in this series in-clude "Hand Questions," "Personal Cleanliness," "Christmas Cookies," and "The Kitchen strikes for Cheer in Color." The only non-household-work pamphlet illustrated with a white woman is "The Waitress." A Louisiana class taught "the arrangement of furniture in the various rooms, for properly fitting out a home. Landscaping was then discussed, with a special demon-stration of the manner in which evergreens could be grown from cuttings."[76]

Hospital work, a major category of personal service performed in a nonhome setting, also sustained racial divisions between women. Texas state reports on hospital training programs record black girls being assigned to kitchens, cafeterias, supply rooms, and laundries. Latin-American girls had similar assignments.[77] White girls were trained on the wards as nurses' aides and in hospital offices as clericals. One reason Texas and other southern states may have rationalized this division was the segregation of nursing schools and the lack of nursing education facilities for black girls in those states. Faced with students desiring to pursue nursing education, the Texas NYA asked the Division of Negro Affairs to prepare a list of hospitals that would accept black girls.[78]

By the end of the 1930s, most young women in the domestic projects were black and Hispanic. Only with the new influx of refugees from Europe would the programs again be racially diluted. Once again, domestic pro-grams were used to acculturate newcomers to the society. As one report said, "German hausfrauen are being given an opportunity to learn the culinary ways of their adopted land," as well as "table service the American way." After training, the penniless refugees, mainly Jewish, could find employment as domestic servants.[79]

The refugees were harbingers of the international crisis that ended domestic training and took women workers, black and Hispanic as well as white, out of kitchens and into factories. The training programs ended when the New Deal officially closed down relief programs in 1942. They had aided numerous women and their households by providing wages and working conditions that may have been ameliorated somewhat by the social pressure of local women's clubs monitoring WPA projects. The New Deal had not, however, challenged gender beliefs that women's greatest contribution to social well-being came through sacrificial care of children and homes, or racial beliefs that the position of women of color was to serve white women in this responsibility, or class beliefs that domestic work was a good education for a young woman whose career would be marriage and housekeeping.

After the war, many middle-class housewives wanted to go back to where they had been before the war eroded the domestic labor supply.[80] A proliferation of alternative jobs for women provided white working-class women an out, however. The escape of women of color waited until 1950s civil rights victories broke down job discrimination by race.

Women fled housework because it never gained the protections and benefits typical of many jobs during the 1930s. Just as vocational home economics became identified with homemaking and ignored paid work in homes, labor reformers and domestic servants failed to persuade employers and legislators that the same problems existed in domestic work as in any modern employment—a need to regulate hours, provisions for unemployment, and security in retirement.

Six

Negotiating the Law of Service

Household Employees Song,
sung to tune of "Tramp, Tramp, Tramp"

1. No more mistress, no more maid,
   No more work that's underpaid,
   Hours that take all your leisure time away.
   We love beauty, art and song.
   We must live, ere life is gone.
   Unity is what we want to pave the way.

Chorus:
   Social Security we need
   Social Security indeed!
   March we forth 2 million strong,
   Workers all, but stand alone
   While all legislative measures pass us by.

2. These are things we must demand
   If high standards we command
   Then a Household Worker we'll be proud to be.
   Hours shorter, wages right,
   Our security in sight—
   Better understanding in the home we'll see.

Chorus:
—YWCA Song, Composed at Tower Hill, Michigan,
Industrial Conference, 1938

————————

In the mid-1930s, household workers sang this song at YWCA summer camps, wrote letters to members of Congress and the president, and collected data to bolster demands for inclusion of domestic workers in labor protections sponsored by the New Deal. Domestics, sometimes organized in clubs and union chapters, found allies among such women's reform groups as the YWCA, the National Women's Trade Union League (NWTUL), and the National Consumers' League (NCL), in civil rights organizations such as the NAACP and the National Urban League, and among union affiliates of the American Federation of Labor (AFL) and the Congress of Industrial Organizations (CIO). Nevertheless, the panoply of labor protections passed during the 1930s explicitly excluded domestic service from coverage, continuing the pattern of earlier state-level labor laws.

During the years between 1920 and 1945, a revolutionary era in American labor relations, little changed in the legal status of domestic work. Domestic workers failed to win inclusion in state and national laws designed to regulate workplaces and to protect workers, did not sustain a labor union, and were unable to gain widespread middle-class adoption of voluntary contracts. Steps were taken to transform a somewhat feudal image of domestic service into an industrial notion of household employment, but these strategies—government regulation, union organization, and voluntary labor contracts—failed. The key actors in the story were women—reformers, housewives, and domestic workers. They voiced their appeal to the men who ran institutions that might help them—unions, civil rights groups, legislatures, and courts.

World War I and After

Women reformers in the Young Women's Christian Association, the National Consumers' League, and the Women's Trade Union League used the labor needs of World War I to push for better conditions for women workers and federal oversight through establishment of a Women's Bureau in the Department of Labor. By the late 1910s, their interests included domestic workers, a group that had declined in numbers as women found alternative war-related jobs.

Although united in the demand for regulating industrial work, reformers had divided interests on the issue of domestic labor. They recognized the needs of domestic servants as workers who deserved the same protections as

other women workers. But as middle-class women, they felt union with
other women of their class who desired to have enough household help so
that they could participate in public life. Instead of advocates, reformers became mediators on the issue of domestic work. They designed reforms to
educate housewives about management and fairness, and they accepted the
housewives' demand that workers be trained to merit better wages and
hours. Reformers balanced the housewives' arguments that service was a
personal relationship best governed by goodwill and voluntary contracts
with domestics' demands that service be treated like a job and covered by
the same laws as other jobs.

The YWCA was the women's organization that was most persistently
concerned with the problems of domestic service. Its first Commission
on Household Employment, formed in 1915, assumed leadership because
"the Young Women's Christian Association exists for the benefit of all women,
and numbers in its membership both employers and employees."[1] From
the YWCA's perspective, reforms should both improve work conditions for
working-class girls and improve home conditions for middle-class sponsors.
Though concerned to raise labor standards to help housewives attract more
servants, the committee followed Roelofs and chair Elizabeth Dodge in
seeking fairer conditions for workers.

In the context of World War I and the suffrage battle for citizenship,
YWCA matrons urged their friends to treat their employees according to
standards "developing in the best industries, where paternal bestowal of
privilege is giving way to comprehension of the rights of all workers as citizens in a democratic community."[2] War shortages encouraged housewives'
clubs to adopt new terminology and work conditions and to organize placement bureaus for "household assistants[,] with standardized pay and hours
and . . . addressed as Mrs. or Miss."[3]

During the war, the YWCA committee sought to persuade employers
to expect to hire limited-hours, live-out household assistants rather than full-
time, live-in servants. An article praising this new system reassured housewives that

> all of this talk of standardizing housework and of making it a profession
> sounds very much more intricate than it really is. When put into prac-
> tice it works somewhat like this: [The home assistant] works eight
> hours a day and works every minute of those eight hours, just as she
> would . . . in a factory. Her working week is the standard 44-hour
> week so arranged as to permit one full day of rest. . . . She comes to
> her employer's home at the hour agreed upon and returns to her home
> at the end of the work period, [perhaps] 7 to 11 A.M. and 12 to 4 cover-
> ing breakfast, luncheon, and four or five hours of general household
> work [or luncheon and dinner and four hours of housework].[4]

Full-time household aid was maintained but full time was reduced to the workweek advocated for industrial workers.

The National Women's Trade Union League, another mixed-class group, promised in addition, as a 1919 resolution "Standardization of Domestic Service" put it, to "do all in its power to promote the organization of domestic workers throughout the country [and] go on record as favoring exactly the same standards of hours, wages and working conditions . . . as for workers in any other occupation." The NWTUL accepted another resolution called "Women's Domestic Service in Their Home," which committed the league to support "every movement or device designed to lighten the labor of the woman in the home, particularly the mothers, and that by the same methods the League do all in its power to secure . . . recognition of the social and economic value of the work of women in the home and appreciation of the fact that the millions of women so occupied are a very important part of the labor world." Amy Walker Field, the resolution's sponsor, argued for its adoption because "the work of families is going on whether there is paid domestic service or not, for the world must be fed and clothed and kept clean, however it is done."[5]

Winning suffrage in 1920 affirmed women's citizenship and their entitlement to larger roles outside the home. Middle-class women aspired to paid employment and to responsible voluntary activities, but not at the expense of failing to meet their standards for family and home service. Faced by the mid-1920s with a reduction of domestic labor that threatened either their mobility or their standards, housewives responded by looking for labor reforms to make the occupation more attractive relative to competing ones—to meet workers' demands "for the democratization of the kitchen and the abolishing of the more or less feudal relations of domestic service."[6]

Embarrassment seconded self-interest. Newly enfranchised housewives were chagrined to discover that the least popular women's occupation was domestic service. How could women claim their public rights if they were incompetent to direct their private realm, the home? For both reasons, after a brief postwar hiatus, clubwomen took up the issue of household employment.

Housewives' organizations had to propagandize for better conditions to attract women to domestic service, because by 1920 state governments were increasingly protecting women workers through hours and wages laws. The Supreme Court decision in *Muller* v. *Oregon* (1908) confirmed the right of state legislatures to establish maximum hours of labor (even if this infringed on the individual's presumed absolute right to contract) to protect workers unable to bargain as full adults—women in the *Muller* case but also adolescent boys and girls. Between 1876 and 1908, twenty-one states passed maximum hour laws. Between 1912 and 1914, twelve states adopted minimum wage laws. Other state regulations about age, night work, and hazardous employment were enacted during the Progressive era.[7] Though by 1920 the impulse for new legislation was dead—the California state assembly, for instance, voted down a bill "providing for a 10-hour day for domestic workers"[8]—new norms had been established. Even the Supreme Court's holding in *Adkins* v. *Children's Hospital* (1923) that the District of Columbia's minimum wage law for women was unconstitutional did not set back some wage gains for women.

Groups like the Cambridge Home Information Center, formed during World War I to plan food conservation, turned into centers for teaching housewives better organization, including better treatment of servants. Other cities had Bureaus of Household Occupations that provided information and also acted as employment bureaus for servants. Model projects like Smith College's Home Assistants pointed the way for scheduling part-time, live-out work. The Philadelphia Council of Household Occupations, formed by socially minded Quakers, began to investigate employment in the city in 1926 and, aided by President Marion Edwards Park of Bryn Mawr College, conducted a self-study that became a Women's Bureau survey, following an earlier Women's Bureau study of a housewives' Domestic Efficiency Association in Baltimore.[9]

Women's groups emphasized education of members, publicity for local standards of wages and hours, and voluntary compliance. They were not successful in stemming the movement toward part-time, live-out, and day work, nor did they raise wages and reduce hours. Most significant, housewives believed that study and experimentation were required to "determine whether long overall hours can be cut down without loss to the employer of adequate service."[10] One YWCA employer, who had heard about labor standards and a 54-hour week from other Y friends, unabashedly confessed:

> After more than three years of experience with having a maid in the house I still do not quite see how it would be possible to keep the true spirit of the home and still have perfectly standardized working hours for the maid. The members of the household who are working on schedule surely need the relaxation that comes from lack of schedule pressure when they get home. And so I have never reached the place where I have said to the maid: your hours are from seven in the morning until one, and from five o'clock in the evening until seven-thirty, and it is your privilege to stop at one and at seven-thirty whether the work is finished or not.[11]

Domestic workers continued to work regular workweeks of 72 or even 84 hours, in contrast to a decline in manufacturing workers' hours from 59 per week at the beginning of the century to 50.3 per week in 1925.[12] In seeking self-regulation, housewives seemed unable to agree on how to change the design of housework.

By the late 1920s, led once more by the YWCA, housewives' groups and reformers began to take coordinated action. In 1928, Lucy Carner, executive director of the YWCA's Industrial Division and a former teacher at the Bryn Mawr Summer School for women workers, contacted appropriate Washington offices with a proposal to hold a conference on household work. She succeeded in gaining support and in September sent out a call for a national meeting on employer–employee relationships in the home. Mary Anderson, director of the Women's Bureau and an advocate for ill-paid women workers, signed the call. Housewives' interests were represented by Louise Stanley, chief of the Bureau of Home Economics in the Department of Agriculture, and Benjamin Andrews, professor of home economics at Teachers College, Columbia University, a founding member of the American Home Economics Association and author of a leading collegiate home economics textbook. Housewives' organizations predominated at the meeting, but Carner insisted on inviting at least one worker representative from the YWCA. Josephine Holmes of the 125th Street YWCA in New York City, at the initial conference, and Nannie Helen Burroughs, head of the National Training School, who joined the committee early in 1929, represented Afro-American interests.[13]

Meeting in October 1928 in Washington, D.C., the conferees constituted themselves a national committee to function as a clearinghouse for information about promising experiments in home relationships and as a research organization. Amey E. Watson was chosen executive director of the National Committee on Employer-Employee Relationships in the Home (hereafter NCHE, though not renamed National Committee on Household Employment until 1933), which existed from 1928 until 1945. Independently, the YWCA National Board created a Household Employment Subcommittee of the National Industrial Committee that lasted from 1929 to 1940.[14]

The initial conference emphasized the usefulness of efforts to "further the organization of voluntary groups and mutual discussions on standards" in dialogues between housewives and servants, leading to "the formulation of working contracts by groups of employers and employees which shall specify minimum standards." It did not, as Carner wrote the AFL, consider such conversations "a substitute for definite trade union organization" and recorded its conviction "of the necessity for organization in this field."[15] Nevertheless, the conference's recommendations envisioned harmony, not confrontation, between housewife and servant. Educating employers about management responsibilities would balance training programs for workers and make the home a model workplace.

Local organization of groups of well-informed employers and employees could together negotiate minimum wages in line with local rates, establish maximum hours and overtime and vacation provisions, and determine value of noncash payments in room, board, and uniforms. Though wages varied regionally, hours could be standardized nationally, and the conference recommended 48 hours per week as a goal. Recognizing that the "work of the home can not be concentrated into a consecutive eight-hour day and a five-and-a-half-day week," the committee recommended "experimenting with work plans and schedules in actual homes . . . to determine what adjustments will be practicable in different types of home situations."[16]

The Chicago YWCA, with Annetta Dieckman as industrial secretary, joined forces with Hazel Kyrk of the University of Chicago's Home Economics Department to survey local wages in various women's jobs and to analyze schedules of housework. Even this modest effort disconcerted some YWCA employers, who felt that the NCHE "should appreciate the personal elements in these relationships and not be too scientific and impersonal."[17]

Housewives' responses to demands for improved work conditions emphasized the personal element. Stressing each home's uniqueness and the need to accommodate idiosyncratic personalities, employers indicated their good intentions along with their unwillingness to regiment home life. Reformers believed that employers could learn to organize their homes and their work better and that only voluntary actions could bring the home within the standards established for other occupations through law. The Depression, however, cost women industrial jobs and made them eager for domestic work. When housewives no longer had to compete with industry for workers and the Presidential Committee on Emergency Employment recommended domestic work as an alternative for lost industrial jobs, hopes for voluntary improvement of standards faded at the same time demands for government regulation rose.

Workers' groups in the YWCA persisted in gathering information to bolster their demands for reasonable working conditions despite the economic downturn. In summer 1930, YWCA groups met at summer industrial conferences and debated the content of a Code of Ethics drawn up by the Twin Cities Club of Household Employees and presented at the May national convention. One New York group criticized use of the term *servant* and concluded that "progress in adjustments could not be made until employers as well as employees are interested in developing a Code of Ethics."[18] The Subcommittee on Household Employment ratified the association's commitment to develop clubs of household employees as well as to encourage employers to study their own practices.

Depression gave a crisis air to household employment. Mary Anderson reported to Lucy Carner that

> Dr. [Louise] Stanley again suggested diverting factory workers to work in the home to relieve the unemployment situation and asked if I wouldn't "agree to let down the bars," and have factory women take jobs in the home to relieve unemployment. Of course we have no bars up . . . and as I understand it there are many houseworkers looking for jobs, at least in some localities, and that there is plenty of unemployment among them. I should be very distressed if our slant would be

that employment in the home would afford substantial relief in this unemployment situation.[19]

The NCHE called a second conference in April 1931 and devoted a
session to "a discussion of the problems brought about by the present unemployment situation." Reports from T. Arnold Hill of the National Urban
League, Edith Dudley of the New York City Employment Service, Dorothy
Wells of the YWCA, and others "presented evidence of a widespread reduction in the wages of household employees . . . and of increases in the number of hours of work required." There were many reports of "increased number of so-called opportunity homes, in which the employee works for room
and board, with possibly a small wage in addition."[20] To counter the deterio-
ration in standards, the conference adopted a model contract to be publicized. The conferees voted to uphold as a standard a 48-hour week for live-
out workers and a 54-hour week for live-in workers, on the assumption that
the live-in worker saved 6 hours a week by not having to commute to her
job. When the worker was on call she was "not free to leave the house but
may follow her own pursuits. . . . Two hours on call should be considered
equivalent to one hour of working time." Wages were to be set according to
local rates, and "a minimum wage for the full-time worker, whether skilled
or unskilled, should be established at a rate that meets the cost of living of
independent women at a tolerable level."[21]
        Although the conference proclaimed its continued desire to facilitate
discussions between employees and employers, the latter apparently opposed such high standards because they were feeling the financial strains of
the Depression. One prominent New York YWCA member reported to Lucy
Carner after the 1931 meeting that "the Y.W.C.A. has been greatly criticized
for the biased attitude taken" and had created antagonisms "among the
people [employers] you have to interest."[22]
        Traditional notions that household workers were well off relative to
other workers, which were given social scientific certification in Lucy May-
nard Salmon's *Domestic Service* (1897), still held even in the Depression cli-
mate. Evidence had to be collected to counter popular impressions that the
occupation was a good one and that workers were irrational to avoid it. The
1932 summer national YWCA convention empowered association employment offices to collect data about placements managed through YWCA offices (in 1931, these offices placed fifty-four thousand women in housework
jobs); in addition, some of the twelve thousand YWCA members who worked
as domestics were canvassed to gather information about their wages and
work conditions.

The New Deal

The election to the presidency of Franklin Delano Roosevelt and the
announcement of federal economic intervention spurred more aggressive la-

bor action, even among domestic workers. By summer 1933, passage of the National Industrial Recovery Act (NIRA) stimulated hope that domestic workers might gain a household workers code enforceable by the National Recovery Administration (NRA).

Business accepted the NRA because it allowed committees to set industrywide wages and hours, which could mitigate competition and produce a manageable wage total. Reformers saw the codes as a means to issue nationwide, federally supported maximum hours and minimum wage rules in response to the *Adkins* rebuff to state minimum wage laws and the fact that "at the peak of the [state-level] protective labor legislation movement in 1930, only one-third of the eight and one-half million women working were covered by regulation of their working hours."[23] The NRA promised to revolutionize working conditions. Even though the Supreme Court ruled it unconstitutional within two years, "the 40-hour week became the norm, [and] arithmetic dictated that the 40- and 48-hour week would bring with them the 8-hour day. . . . A large minority of the codes prescribed a premium rate for overtime hours, more frequently time and a third but often time and a half."[24]

It quickly became clear that these benefits would not extend to the majority of the female and black labor force. For many workers, exclusion from NRA confirmed their secondary status. When groups such as the National Association for the Advancement of Colored People (NAACP) and the National Consumers League protested racial discrimination, NRA headquarters ignored the actual racial and gender distributions in job assignments and responded that the codes did not specify differentials by race and were not, therefore, discriminatory to blacks. As one canny correspondent wrote to General Hugh Johnson, the director of NRA,

> Thanks for your reply of the 3rd instant, in which you refer me to the "cotton textile code" as an evidence of the lack of racial prejudice. I am not fully conversant with this code, but I am informed that it does not cover cleaners nor outside workers, most of whom are colored.[25]

Labor historian Irving Bernstein estimates that 70 percent of black workers were not in covered jobs.[26] In 1934, the Women's Bureau found that 10 to 15 percent of black women were "eligible for participation in code benefits as compared with more than half of all white women workers."[27] White women were better treated than black, though about a quarter of the codes allowed differential wages (lower) for women compared to men.[28]

Advocates for the interests of white women workers and of black men and women soon realized that the NRA was limited by unwillingness to formulate codes for major occupations, especially in agriculture and domestic service, in which black men and women were concentrated, with the latter occupation also of substantial significance to white working-class women. A few weeks after passage of NIRA, the young black government economist Robert Weaver wrote a program, "Domestics and the NRA,"[29] which was quickly endorsed by a black coalition, the Joint Committee on National Recovery, and by the YWCA.

Spurred by Women's Bureau director Mary Anderson, the YWCA raised the issue of code coverage at the 1933 annual two-week summer regional camps held for industrial workers.[30] These workers were accustomed to gathering data about wages and hours and quickly compiled complaints to justify asking the NRA to set a code. Over the signature of Pearl Bobbitt, a domestic from Kansas City who had been elected chair of a national household employment committee, the YWCA workers wrote to Hugh Johnson advocating a household employment code. They reminded him that "there are about 2,469,000 domestic workers in the United States, and more than 1,000,000 of these are Negroes. In all YWCA organizations the Negroes are included."[31]

In addition to YWCA-organized workers, other black domestics formed associations to respond to the opportunity offered by NRA. Neva Ryan, a domestic, called a meeting with the Chicago Urban League to discuss codes. When only blacks attended, Ryan set out to attract white workers and in 1934 began working out of the YWCA offices on behalf of the Domestic Workers' Association.[32] The Domestic Workers of America, U.S.A. wrote from Philadelphia asking for laws to "guarantee the domestic worker . . . a living wage, shorter and more standard working hours," and unemployment and workmen's compensation insurance.[33] The National Association for Domestic Workers, headquartered in Jackson, Mississippi, with officers listed in Jackson, St. Louis, Knoxville, and Baltimore, presented a fully drawn code with a 48-hour week and overtime paid at the minimum hourly wage up to 56 hours per week. Employers could not hire workers under the age of sixteen, and "employees [should] have the right to organize and bargain collectively through representatives of their own choosing . . . free from the interference, restraint, or coercion of employers or their agents."[34]

Workers, civil rights groups, and reformers in the NCHE spawned an effective letter-writing campaign, but no regulation ensued. As Hugh Johnson's secretary, A. R. Forbush, wrote to most correspondents,

> Every since the establishment of this [NRA] administration, we have received numerous communications concerning the status of household help. While we are in full sympathy, there is no possible way we can take direct action in their behalf. The homes of individual citizens cannot be made the subject of regulations or restrictions and even if this were feasible, the question of enforcement would be virtually impossible.[35]

Mary Anderson, answering similar inquiries from the Women's Bureau, advised that "the National Industrial Recovery Act in its present form does not apply to household employees." She encouraged instead working with the NCHE to get "cooperation from employers in the voluntary adoption of [a code]."[36] A drive for a voluntary code seemed essential if a mandatory one could not be adopted, and publicity was easier to get in an environment of code-setting. That was the approach being followed by the fall of 1934.[37]

Though many reformers persisted in a drive to pass constitutionally acceptable national legislation, which culminated in Roosevelt's signing the Fair Labor Standards Act (FLSA) in June 1938, the NRA experience showed that domestic work had no chance of federal regulation. When Congress passed the FLSA, it claimed authority for national regulation of hours, wages, and child labor under the commerce clause of the Constitution, which limited its purview to activities of an interstate character (narrowly defined in the 1930s). If one worked in a covered industry, the act was, as United Mine Workers president John L. Lewis said, "a bill of rights for labor."[38] The implication was that a worker not covered by the act was not a full citizen.

Domestic workers seemed the quintessential case of intrastate employment, though the definition would expand considerably over the decades to enable their inclusion under the 1974 FLSA amendments. Numerous other categories of predominantly female and nonwhite workers suffered implicit or explicit exclusion, however, and many of them shared characteristics of domestic work. Hotel workers such as waitresses and chambermaids; retail clerks performing customer service; workers in charitable or nonprofit hospitals, often cleaners and nurses ministering to patients; and agricultural workers, seen as transient and irregular, or as members of the household like domestics—none of these achieved FLSA coverage, whether because of the interstate commerce provision or, for agricultural workers, because of written exemptions.[39]

White male workers benefited disproportionately from the act, making up, Ronnie Steinberg argues, for women's differential access to coverage under pre-1938 state minimum wage and maximum hour laws. The 1938 act gave minimum wage protection to 39 percent of male adult workers and to only 14 percent of female adult workers. Less striking, the federal overtime hours provisions covered 31 percent of men workers and 23 percent of women.[40]

Requirements that employers pay overtime wages especially aided men. Women's hour protections under state laws took the form of setting an absolute limit on the hours per week a woman could work for one employer. Men's protections under the federal law set no limit on hours worked but simply required an employer to pay a premium wage (usually one and one-half times the regular wage) for keeping a worker longer than maximum hours (in *Bunting* v. *Oregon* the Supreme Court had upheld overtime provisions for men but not for women in the Oregon hours statute).[41] State laws prohibiting any work over the prescribed maximum number of hours restricted incomes as well as hours; a woman had to moonlight at a second job at regular pay to raise her income instead of getting enhanced pay for long hours at one job. The message to employers of women, including house-wives, was that women could work long hours in uncovered jobs and not choose a more flexible trade-off between pay and hours.[42]

Domestic workers were not overlooked because of lack of organization and consciousness. Many wrote to the Women's Bureau and to the White House asking for information to confront their employers' demands that they put in long hours for low wages. Southern black workers, especially, asked for help. After the defeat of the effort for an NRA code, however, the YWCA's at-tempts and local organizing activity were generally rechanneled into efforts to win voluntary agreements or to pass state-level hour and wage laws.

The NRA code activity crystallized the idea of setting national stan-dards for hours, wages, and job descriptions, just as the interstate limitation promoted voluntary rather than compulsory regulation. After the flurry of activity in 1933 to obtain a code, organizations concerned about racial jus-tice, the well-being of women workers, and the condition of homes joined together to urge members to design and adopt a voluntary agreement. Some even hoped to develop an emblem for employers similar to the Blue Eagle "consumers' emblem and agreement."[43]

By 1934, with the appearance of FERA, soon to be succeeded by WPA, YWCA women's groups took on a quasi-official character as local advisory groups to WPA household-training projects. With govenment support for housework training, coupled, at the insistence of Ellen Woodward, with publicity for labor standards, the YWCA intensified its efforts to get local employer advisory groups to set wages and hours appropriate to the area.

For the remainder of the decade the YWCA and other national wom-en's organizations worked primarily to persuade leaders of local clubs and as-sociations to be "progressive" forces leading the employers of their commu-nities to adopt better standards. Though such women occasionally supported state legislation on hours and wages, federal coverage under Social Security, and union organization, women's clubs focused most of their energies on public education. The drive to reform their neighbors and clubmates repre-sented an organizational and strategic alternative to legislative battles. It en-couraged the notion that housework was something for personal negotiation between domestic servants and housewives and not for legislative regulation that the New Deal reforms spread to most occupations. Even this "private" approach did not assuage some members' opposition to considering the issue at all.[44]

As the best-known housewife in the country, Eleanor Roosevelt repre-sented the ideal employer to emulate. Having donated money and time to the NCHE since 1930, Mrs. Roosevelt in 1934 became honorary chairman, with her name heading the organization's letters and bulletins (next to chair-men Benjamin Andrews of Teachers College, Columbia, and later Dorothy Wells, YWCA secretary of the Industrial Division). Mrs. Roosevelt wrote and spoke about good housewifery and put out press releases about such innovations as the redecoration of the White House servant quarters. She said,

> Since the last alterations were made in 1901, we have progressed in our ideas of how people should be treated. I have always felt that public residences, such as the home of a governor, and certainly the White House, should set an example of the right conditions under which people should work, and to the extent that it is reasonably possible, establish standards of decent living for those who have to work in the homes of others.[45]

Eleanor Roosevelt's discussion of her own housekeeping set the pace for numerous surveys conducted by the YWCA and local women's clubs, including the League of Women Voters, the Council of Jewish Women, and women's city clubs, during the mid-1930s. Billed as research projects, the tabulated surveys informed housewives as to where their own practices fell in relation to those of their friends and peers. During the mid-1930s, local YWCA clubs conducted sixty-four studies, often with separate questionnaires for employers and employees, to make certain that each side presented its version.[46]

The YWCA's requests for information in 1933 went to white and "colored" workers. Emily Warrick, a black worker elected to the National YWCA Industrial Council in 1933, polled associations in the fall of 1933 to find data, since

> we [have] very little information on household employees from the Negro branches in the south. . . . As we have the additional job [compared to government code-setting] of getting public opinion behind us, we need the point of view of southern Negro groups on provision[s] which should be included in a voluntary agreement. . . . We cannot let others be more interested in us than we are in ourselves.[47]

The YWCA encouraged interracial cooperation in collecting data with projects in Louisville, Kentucky, and Lynchburg, Virginia, though black workers did not attend the southern summer industrial conference camp until 1938, and then only two at each conference.

Even white southern clubwomen, viewed with suspicion by the national offices of the WTUL and the YWCA,[48] organized discussions under the impetus of mid-1930s legislation and organizing. The Texas Commission on Interracial Cooperation at its 1933 meeting "pledge[d] to secure satisfactory wage and work conditions for all domestic workers, both men and women, of every race."[49] Jessie Daniel Ames, founder of the Association of Southern Women for the Prevention of Lynching, reminded Mary Anderson that "there should be a certain number of state women invited [to any national meeting about servants] for the very simple reason that 55% of all women in domestic service in 1930 were in thirteen Southern States." Ames prepared a booklet on domestic service and used her position as director of women's work in the Atlanta-based Commission on Interracial Cooperation to encourage Southern Methodist, Southern Baptist, and Southern Presbyterian women to emphasize members' responsibilities to domestic servants.[50]

The focus on voluntary efforts led the NCHE to seek "an employer for chairman of the Standards Committee" in late 1934 and to match organizing employees with raising employers' consciousness. Mrs. Kendall Emerson, chair of the YWCA Public Affairs Committee, solicited local association presidents for names of interested employers, because "we feel strongly that whatever is done must be on a cooperative basis and that therefore we must have the thinking of groups of organized employers within our own membership."[51]

Despite its numerous research projects and employer study committees (242, in a 1937 account),[52] almost no YWCA group succeeded in adopting a code. The Chicago YWCA under the leadership of Industrial Secretary Annetta Dieckman and with the aid of University of Chicago home economist Hazel Kyrk, produced a model for a voluntary contract in 1929, which was adopted by the NCHE conference in 1931.[53] This model contract set the terms for discussion and was passed on to numerous U.S. Employment Service offices when they began to accept employers' orders for domestic service in 1935.[54]

In contrast to the pre-Depression model contract, the 1931 version envisioned 60 "actual working hours . . . during which the worker is not free to follow her own pursuits." Two hours of "time on call," when the worker was not free to leave the house but could "follow her own pursuits," counted as one hour of working time. Overtime could be required and compensated by "extra time off" or hourly payments. The worker got pay for four of the eight national holidays, and "some adjustment [should be] made for church attendance." Nevertheless, the two half-days off per week could begin as late as 2 P.M. "and immediately after the mid-day meal on Sundays." Minimum wages would be paid only to unskilled workers and the wage scale increased for more skilled workers, whose wages were to be comparable to those in "local industries." Finally, live-in situations should provide the worker "adequate food . . . access to bath, adequate heat and light, [and] a place to entertain friends."[55]

Though the proposed contract was hardly revolutionary, difficulties in gaining agreement to it reinforced YWCA findings that most domestics worked longer than 60 hours per week, for less than an industrial minimum wage, and with constant demands for uncompensated overtime. A 1936 Connecticut study conducted jointly by the YWCA and the state Department of Labor found the largest number of workers in the range of 60 to 70 hours per week, with an average workday of between 11.4 and 12.5 hours. "The 7-day week was general, but the majority of women covered in the report did not

work full time on all 7 days." (The maximum hours allowed for regulated occupations in Connecticut was 52 per week.)[56]

Housewives showed great distress at the idea of signing a contract.
One Midwest YWCA industrial secretary reported that when she called a
meeting of household employers to publicize a model contract, "Women all
over the city [said] that the YWCA shouldn't meddle in this matter and that if
anything is done it will work to the detriment of the employee."[57] Those
groups that did manage to approve a voluntary code were hardly generous.
One recommended by Buffalo employers in 1932 accepted an actual workweek of 63 hours, with daily overall hours not to exceed 12½. A Tucson, Arizona, agreement between employers, employees, and agencies in 1936 put
weekly hours at 60 with overtime limited to 12 hours per week and set the
time for beginning Sunday's half-day off at 3 P.M. Both of the committees
suggested that employers require certified health exams for employment.[58]

Employers refused to countenance the idea that households could be
regulated by contract like businesses. Amey Watson's analysis in the late
1920s that housewives and domestics needed a good personal "relationship"
to create a pleasant home environment was echoed throughout the era and
across the nation. Even socially conscious housewives expressed sentiments
like those of British scholar Violet M. Firth, whose *Psychology of the Servant Problem* (1934) promised that "no addition to wages or subtraction
from hours will bring peace until the men and women concerned [as ser-
vants] receive their due as human beings."[59] As workers represented their
wage and hour demands more firmly and pursued legislation at the state
level, women's clubs persisted in their ambivalence toward legally defined
relationships.

Nevertheless, all major women's groups, the American Association of
University Women, League of Women Voters, General Federation of
Women's Clubs, National Association of Colored Women's Clubs, and wom-
en's groups in the affiliated denominations of the Federal Council of Churches
sponsored some public relation efforts during the 1930s. Even the Junior
League joined in by the end of the decade. Writing in the association's magazine in 1934, Lucy Randolph Mason, executive secretary of the National
Consumers' League and a member of the Junior League, encouraged members not to take advantage of Depression unemployment to pay low wages
but "to plan one's household in such a way as to combine family comfort with
consideration of the domestic staff, whether it consists of one or a half dozen
employees."[60] By 1937, the Junior League's executive secretary, Katherine R.
Van Slyck, corrected herself for talking about "servants" instead of "household
employees." And, finally, in 1941, the league's magazine printed a three-part
series on needs for standards[61] and began to join legislative coalitions.

By the mid-1930s, workers organized to balance employers' reluctance
to grant better working conditions. Sometimes organization took the form of
a labor union affiliating with the AFL or, after 1935, the newly formed CIO.

Workers at the biennial YWCA Industrial Assemblies of 1934 and 1936 voted
to pursue voluntary contracts as an educational device but also to appeal to
the American Federation of Labor, to "experiment" with unions, and to promote legislation.[62] As one worker representative argued, "A voluntary agreement is much the same as a company union with the employer dictating rather
than having a satisfactory agreement between employer and employee."[63]

Union organization was the norm for self-respecting workers during
the 1930s. After the Wagner Labor Relations Act of 1935 explicitly excluded
domestic workers from its protections for workers organizing for collective
bargaining, journalist and American Newspaper Guild organizer Heywood
Broun advocated labor unions for this most oppressed group of workers and
ridiculed employers who feared intrusion in their homes. "The necessary
first step," Broun said, "would be to change the name to 'houseworkers,'" to
counter the "unconscious assumption that a houseworker is a serf or bound
servant."[64]

Black civil rights groups also supported organizing for presentation of
workers' demands. The National Negro Congress applauded the YWCA's
efforts but asked for more emphasis on organizing workers. The National Urban League's Workers' Council issued a pamphlet in 1936 that commended
YWCA and NCHE efforts at educating employers but observed that such
groups did not reach "the socially dangerous majority [of employers] who are
concerned only with paying domestics as little as possible for as much work
as possible." The council applauded incipient unionization in Jackson, Philadelphia, and Chicago, as well as the creation of groups in Atlanta, Memphis,
St. Louis, Richmond, and Seattle in conjunction with local Negro Workers'
Councils.[65]

Most workers' groups took the form of clubs and not unions. White
workers in Milwaukee, like black workers in Jackson and mixed-race groups
in Kansas City and San Diego, found labor unions unable or unwilling to recognize the special needs of domestic workers. A San Diego workers' group
affiliated with the Building Service Employees International Union (BSEIU)
of the AFL briefly during 1933 but gave up the charter when the union expected domestic workers to pay the same dues as locals of better-paid
workers.[66]

By the late 1930s, three locals of the AFL–affiliated BSEIU were in
place in New York City. These, however, had initially been formed with the
help of the national YWCA office as mixed unions of hotel chambermaids and
domestics. When the chambermaids joined the hotel local in 1935, the union
had to create separate locals for domestic workers. These locals, consisting
mainly of black workers, sought to place workers at standard wages and
hours and to act as intermediary with recalcitrant employers who refused to
pay the money owing workers or "unjustly accused [them] of stealing."[67]

After 1935, the CIO accepted requests to affiliate from groups in Oakland, Baltimore, and Washington. These groups also had difficulty meeting

the financial demands of the union. They attempted to control the labor supply by establishing skill and wage grades, but workers could not halt the influx of needy women. The ultimate union resort—strike or sit-in—was not feasible.[68] Domestic work, poorly paid and with hours that left little time for meetings, was not a high priority for unions. One expert reported the informal comment of "one well-known labor leader [that] the organization of house hold workers will come about as a sort of 'mopping up' process when we have the bulk of other women in unions."[69]

The promise of NRA codes, which benefited so many other workers, "aroused a wave of interest and indignation from [domestics] because they were left out."[70] Exclusion from the Economic Security Act of 1935 (the Social Security Act) intensified household employees' interest in sharing entiltlements that other workers were gaining through legislative action. When the NRA determined that domestic workers could be covered only by state hours and wages legislation, domestic workers turned their attention to state actions, focusing only on Social Security coverage at the national level.

Domestic workers were more effective in organizing for legislative campaigns for government regulation than for trade union recognition. This strategy, moreover, linked workers with reformers and women's clubs, who focused on law as a counterbalance to the economic power of employers. The organizer of the short-lived San Diego union, Gene Nicholson, turned from the AFL to the YWCA as a base for organizing a statewide federation of domestic workers' clubs in San Diego, Long Beach, Los Angeles, Oakland, San Francisco, and Pasadena to push for a 10-hour law in the 1935 legislative session. Though she argued that it was important to maintain a base independent of the mixed-class YWCA, she also believed in maintaining good relations with employers, who could be "educate[d] to the need for a change in the methods of running the home so as to liberate the domestic workers to a larger and more full life."[71]

Without cooperation from employers, hour and wage regulations were difficult to enforce. With legislation, the prospects seemed better for two reasons. First, as one commentator said, the simple existence of a law publicized a community moral standard for employers. Second, a state law enabled govenment employment offices to turn down calls for domestic servants that offered substandard working conditions. State employment offices, organized in a network by the U.S. Employment Service, were supposed to match available workers with jobs offered, even when the order was suspect or insulting. The order taker might inform the employer that the job would be difficult to fill at such low wages and long hours, but the agency could not refuse to post the notice; where there were no state laws to uphold, the Employment Service had to send a worker to any prospective employer who offered a job.

From 1933, when the USES was reactivated by the Wagner-Peyser Act to carry on the tradition of public labor exchanges begun during World War I,

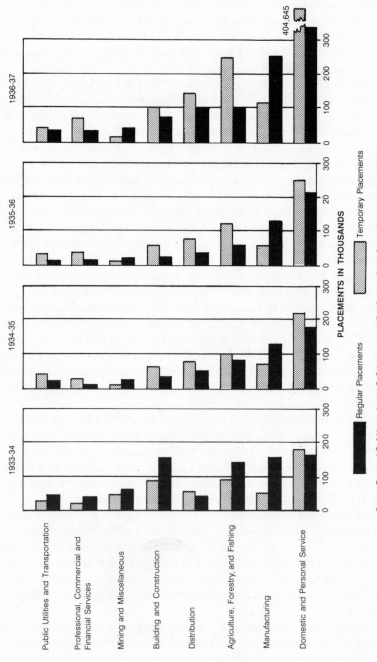

PLACEMENTS IN THOUSANDS

Regular Placements   Temporary Placements

1933-34   1934-35   1935-36   1936-37

Public Utilities and Transportation

Professional, Commercial and Financial Services

Mining and Miscellaneous

Building and Construction

Distribution

Agriculture, Forestry, and Fishing

Manufacturing

Domestic and Personal Service

404,645

Source: Raymond C. Atkinson, Louise C. Odencrantz, and Ben Deming, *Public Service Employment in the United States* (Chicago: Public Administrative Service for the Committee on Public Administration of the Social Science Research Council, 1940), 34-35, and table 5.

the system grew from "300 small and meagerly financed public employment offices [to a] network of more than 1,400 with a staff of over 18,000 persons" by 1938.[72] With responsibilities that ranged from locating workers for massive New Deal public works projects to serving the smallest local employer, the offices took hiring orders from the federal government and from the local housewife seeking a half-day worker. Of the placements with private employers, the largest category in every year from 1933 to 1938 was domestic and personal service, as seen in Figure 2.[73]

As a primary placement source, the USES could assist domestic workers and housewives. Although the Employment Service was financed mainly through congressional appropriations (it became wholly federally funded in 1941), it was administered by state officials with minimal federal supervision.

The state offices enforced local notions of protocol and of appropriate job assignments and conditions. When the war caused labor shortages in the early 1940s, some states stopped placing domestic workers. "In Baltimore, by contrast, local employment officials continued to refer black women for service jobs despite the persistent female labor shortage and the complaints from black women regarding this form of discrimination."[74]

The first state (and the only state by 1945) to cover domestics was Wisconsin, where the Industrial Commission had issued wage regulations for women and minors in domestic service in 1932. Local surveys soon found widespread disregard of the order. Only through the intervention of local clubs such as the YWCA, the League of Women Voters, and the Jewish Council, publicity by a prominent local minister, and accounts in local newspapers were housewives shamed into paying the legal minimum.[75] In general, state legislation limiting hours and setting a floor for wages introduced during the 1930s carried the customary exclusion of domestic and agricultural workers.[76]

Two fights illustrate the limits of domestic workers' success: the legislative battles over maximum hours in Washington State and California. In 1935–1936, the Seattle YWCA conducted a study that had the predictable result of revealing "cases of girls working 14 to 16 hours a day. While many other conditions needed improvement, hours were the employees' chief grievance." The Industrial Girls' Club of the Seattle Y decided to push for state legislation and received help from the League of Women Voters and the Federation of Women's Clubs for introducing a 60-hour bill in the 1937 session. The bill passed, though only after a provision for double pay for overtime was dropped. Indeed, an "emergency" clause enabled employers to escape fines if an emergency had required keeping the worker more than 60 hours.

Even with the bill's passage, it was easier to educate aspirants to domestic work in high school vocational education classes and NYA and WPA training programs than to reach housewives. Seattle, however, got star treatment because Anna Roosevelt Boettiger was a local journalist. When Elea-

nor Roosevelt visited in 1938, her daughter and others arranged a large public meeting with a speech by the first lady and dramatic skits to demonstrate to
housewives how to behave appropriately as managers, since, in Boettiger's
opinion, "not enough is being done to educate and help the employer."[77]

Inclusion of domestic workers in the California maximum hours bill
had been attempted in 1920 and 1934. In 1939, a renewed effort came from
the Household Employee's Alliance of the Bay Area composed of YWCA-
based clubs in San Francisco and Oakland. After three years' work on legislation and support bills for other groups, the alliance introduced a maximum
54-hour-week bill in the 1939 session. The group worked with the local labor
committee to get endorsement from the "Building Trades Councils, the
C.I.O., the A.F. of L., Railway Brotherhoods and Labor's Non-Partisan
League of Northern California. The doing of this has broadened the knowledge of all members of the club and had led to much more active interest in
community life." The northern California group was backed by the Second
Annual Household Employee's Conference in Pasadena, which attracted
workers from six southern California YWCA groups.[78] The bill, nevertheless,
failed.

Though strenuously pushed by the New York Women's Trade Union
League, three bills introduced into the New York State legislature in the
1939 session to require a maximum 60-hour week for domestic service, inclusion in the state's minimum wage law, and workmen's compensation coverage for disability in homes with two or more workers[79] failed to pass, as did
a maximum hours law in Illinois. Reviewing the failure of state efforts to gain
basic hours and wages coverage, some scholars lay the blame on middle-class
women's groups, which "have supported other types of labor legislation, [but]
are loath to back proposals that would apply to them and their workers."
Housewives had, as another commentator concluded, "the false idea that
such laws would interfere with the way they want to manage their homes."[80]
Legislative action on hours accomplished no more than voluntary contracts.

The final struggle to ensure that domestics received some of the gains
won by labor during the 1930s came with the Social Security Act amendments of 1939. Less controversial than reducing hours of work was guaran-
teeing security in old age and during unemployment. Passed in 1935, the
Social Security Act guaranteed economic security for different groups of
needy Americans through four different provisions. Older Americans would
receive help in their retirement years through either Old Age Assistance, a
means-tested grant administered by state governments, or Old Age Insurance, paid as an entitlement out of payroll taxes collected by the federal government. Children in families bereft of a father would be supported through
Aid to Dependent Children (ADC), which gave a grant to the child and to
the widowed mother as caretaker. Families of workers whose jobs were lost
would receive Unemployment Compensation to tide them over until the
family wage earner, usually the father, found another job.

Domestic workers and agricultural workers were explicitly excluded from coverage under the retirement and unemployment provisions. Black civil rights groups immediately protested exemptions that would exclude "more than fifty per cent of gainfully employed Negroes [who] came under these headings."[81] Secretary of the Treasury Henry Morgenthau responded to NAACP Secretary Walter White that "whether collections for the contributory system are made from these [agricultural and domestic] classes of workers, there is no proposal to exclude them from the benefits of the non-contributory system."[82]

As civil rights groups knew, however, the difference between the contributory and noncontributory provisions was significant. Old Age Assistance and ADC were federally subsidized payments administered by state authorities. Retirement and survivor benefits and unemployment compensation were entitlements supposedly paid for by the worker like insurance, with eligibility set by Congress and payments "earned" according to workers' contributions. Though the federal government paid half of Old Age Assistance benefits up to $30 a month, the benefit level depended on the state's contribution, and state-appointed boards determined individuals' need and benefit. In 1937, the NAACP reaffirmed that "the Act which was designed to aid the people farthest down and most dependent . . . makes no provision whatsoever for three-fifths of all Negro workers [who work as agricultural, domestic and casual laborers] in its old age benefit and unemployment compensation provisions, [but leaves them] subject to the arbitrary action of the States."[83] (Research in Social Security data in the late 1930s found, indeed, a large overrepresentation of aged domestics on public assistance.[84])

The architects of Social Security, especially the first chair of the Social Security Board, Arthur Altmeyer, advocated linking benefits to contributions so as to counter political pressure to pay all older Americans a standard monthly benefit, a notion that gathered considerable political support in the movement inspired and led by Dr. Francis Townsend, a California physician. Altmeyer expected Old Age Insurance payments to be large and universal enough to scuttle Townsend's appeal.

Even though Old Age Insurance was a tax imposed on employers and workers and held in a special fund to pay retirement benefits, calling it insurance and linking a worker's earnings to the benefits he or she received entailed different record-keeping requirements from straightforward taxation.[85] Only large businesses with payrolls or regularly employed workers were presumed to be able to keep records and collect the taxes necessary to conform to an insurance model. The original 1935 design, therefore, included a small percentage of American workers, most of them white men; the initial payback (scheduled for 1942) was small relative to welfare, needs-based benefits for workers eligible for Old Age Assistance in the years before it began to pay off.

As welfare paid out more benefits and gained public support, social insurance planners, according to historian Jerry Cates, felt compelled to speed up and enlarge payouts. By 1939, the Social Security Board, seconded by President Roosevelt, presented Congress with substantial amendments, most notably to pay survivor benefits to "aged widows and younger widows with dependent children" until the children reach 16 years of age, or 18 "while they are regularly attending school." The 1935 act awarded a modest lump sum to the estate of a deceased employee.[86]

Survivor payments had the additional advantage of moving deserving widows off ADC needs-based, state-directed rolls and onto the federally funded and administered insurance scheme. The American Association of Social Workers, the League of Women Voters, and the American Home Economics Association supported such a change, because the federal–state match had been set lower than the match for Old Age Assistance (up to $18 for one child, $12 for a second, in comparison to $30 for an Old Age Assistance recipient). States also had to match a larger percentage of the children's grant ($\frac{2}{3}$ rather than $\frac{1}{2}$), so they were accepting fewer children on the aid rolls.[87] It was assumed that the old age system would not have to pay out substantially more than it took in, because many widows would have worked at least part of their lives in covered employment during which they would have contributed some of the funds that would now come back to them as survivors of male workers.[88]

Grounding social welfare in employment-connected insurance required including as many workers as possible, the Social Security Board concluded. Though four years' experience indicated that many more workers than anticipated would move in and out of covered employment and, therefore, gain benefit entitlements, the board recommended including domestic and agricultural workers in the retirement provisions and domestic workers in the unemployment system.[89]

For black workers having to appeal to local southern white authorities for old age, work relief, or ADC assistance, inclusion could mean freedom from racial oppression. Many southern authorities refused to certify black domestic workers for direct relief, especially ADC, on the ground that domestics were employable because jobs were available and domestics could rely on their mothers or other female relatives, generically called "aunts," to care for preschool children while mothers worked.[90] Relief agencies, moreover, often would not certify them as employable on government-subsidized relief projects, so they remained dependent on the racially segregated and low-wage local economy. Julia Kirk Blackwelder recounts as typical the story of one black woman, mother of three, in San Antonio, who was told by the local relief office to take a weekly housecleaning job or be "cut off from everything all together." The anxious woman reported that

> I told her I was afraid to accept the job in the private home because I registered for a government job and when it opens up I want to take it.

She said she was taking people off the relief and I have to take the job in the private home or none.[91]

A panoply of women's organizations favoring labor legislation mobilized testimony and letters for House Ways and Means Committee hearings on the amendments in February and March 1939, as did the National Negro Congress.[92] But they organized too late; the committee voted in a March 17 mark-up session to delete coverage for agricultural and domestic workers, as well as employees of charitable and nonprofit organizations. Apparently swayed by opposition from minsters and from college fraternities and so-rorities, and loath to expand taxation on businesses during a mild economic upturn, the committee decided to make no extensions in coverage.[93] Leaving out poor workers who obviously merited protection was rationalized because of the difficulty of administering collections and wage records for domestic workers.

Responding almost immediately, Amey Watson and a revitalized NCHE saw a use for research. The NCHE raised funds for a German refugee scholar, Erna Magnus, who had worked for the International Labor Organization in Geneva during the mid-1930s, to undertake a survey of all writings about domestic workers and Social Security and then to compile and analyze employment records of domestic workers. Assisted by the Social Security Board, which had seen its recommendation rebuffed by Congress, Magnus collected data to prove that domestic workers would not receive Social Security entitlements except through coverage of domestic work and indicated various systems already tested in Europe for domestics' contributions and records.

Magnus found that the majority of domestic workers would not receive retirement benefits through their spouses because many were divorced or single (34 percent among white domestics in the upper age brackets). Husbands of married domestics, entitled after 1939 to survivors' benefits, often worked in noncovered employment. Also, women would not be covered through working in covered jobs, because they did not move out of housework but rather moved in and out of a variety of service jobs, including domestic work. Finally, a large percentage of domestics had children dependent on their incomes and needed coverage for unemployment and survivors' benefits for their dependents (37 percent of Baltimore domestics in 1940, for instance.)[94]

The War Years

The threat of World War II, which sparked defense employment and improved workers' chances of bargaining for legislation and wages, increased efforts for domestic coverage. After the failure to win inclusion of domestic workers in the 1939 Social Security amendments, the YWCA and Women's Bureau began an information campaign to support amendments introduced by Senator Robert Wagner in 1940 and 1941. The YWCA issued a booklet of information for workers and a plan for lobbying that included creating women's group, labor, and interracial coalitions.[95]

A similarly diverse liberal committee formed in New York to push for inclusion of domestics in workmen's compensation. With committee members including Mrs. Irving Berlin and Mrs. Corliss Lamont, and Mrs. Benjamin Spock and Fannie Hurst as officers, the committee worked under the auspices of the Women's Trade Union League to sway the New York State legislature toward proper social responsibility. Domestic employment had come of age as a trendy social issue.[96]

The war brought higher wages but not shorter hours. And workers felt more connected to an outer world in which legal rights were a legitimate expectation for all workers. Interracial activity became more normal among younger women in southern as well as western and midwestern YWCAs. The war seemed to offer an opportunity that would not last long and should be seized. CIO affiliates of domestic workers organized in Baltimore and Washington.

At the end of the war all the legislative struggles remained unfulfilled: for Social Security coverage, reduction of hours, raising of wages, unemployment, and workmen's compensation. And once again, housewives would not attack the problem of the organization of household work but would seek, instead, a labor force with no choice but to acquiesce. Black women remained domestics in the South until civil rights activism made their job demands political issues. Puerto Rican women were imported to the mainland to fill up slots left by native-born white women. Women who could quit housework for other employment did so, and more women took up the pattern previously reserved for household workers, doing a day's (or half-day's) paid work and then cleaning, laundering for, and feeding men and children in their own homes.

On numerous occasions between 1920 and 1945, domestics formed associations, wrote to public officials, spoke out at meetings, and lobbied legislatures. Especially after Roosevelt's election in 1932 and growing public support for government regulation of the terms of labor—hours, wages, collective bargaining, retirement security—they sought inclusion in such laws: not only legal recourse for poor treatment but also the moral authority gained from public recognition of them as workers.

The reasons domestic servants failed to gain endorsement of their rights reveal the fault lines separating women's interests as housewives and as service workers. Domestic workers cleaned houses, cooked, and cared for children so that middle-class women could improve life for themselves, their families, and their communities. Reformers sought decent conditions for domestics but did not challenge notions of the home as a 24-hour center of emotional support and physical nurturance. Especially in organizations like the interracial, cross-class YWCA, reformers unwilling or unable to choose one value over another compromised efforts for legislative action with education campaigns for voluntary contracts.

Domestic workers, as a concentration of old, young, nonwhite, and low-wage women, were not able to counterbalance the powerful images of domesticity with a vision of the home as workplace. Domestic work remained outside the protection of the law.

Seven

Dirt and Divisions Among Women

A doll I can carry,
The girl that I marry
Must be.
—*Annie Get Your Gun*, 1946

When the musical comedy heroine Annie Oakley heard Frank Butler sing "The Girl That I Marry," she became desperate at the distance between his image of an ideal mate and her evident unsuitability: she was a sharp-shooter wearing buckskin and boots, rather than satins and laces. Annie and Frank finally united, but the message was clear. If a woman wanted matrimony, she had better learn to clothe herself in the paraphernalia of femininity. The woman about to embark on keeping house had better look and smell as if she never saw a dirty dish or dirty floor, much less scrubbed one.

As we saw in Chapter Two, the housewife who was unable to disguise the labor involved in housework and whisk away dirt from her own appearance as well as from the house risked offending a husband's delicate sentiments—his ideal of angelic womanhood. Successful housekeeping kept intact an image of pure women residing in pristine homes as well as making homes pleasant. Making housework look like something other than work was a job requirement; making accomplishment appear effortless, a measure of proficiency.

To succeed in this role, the model wife needed another woman to do the hard and dirty physical labor. She needed a woman different from herself, one whose work and very identity confirmed the housewife's daintiness and perfection.

The equation between the "good" housewife and the "good" (doll-like) woman is the core of the theoretical insights I hope to develop. Historians have often noted the cultural distinctions between "good" women and "bad" women based on sexual standards of purity and licentiousness, and the issue of sexual propriety continues to simmer in feminist scholarship.[1] The home has been reified as the setting for good women, virtuous wives and mothers. Its work has been haloed with maternal imagery. Yet the work carried on in the home is unconsciously identified with dirt and decay, which threaten to taint the character of the woman who does it. A wife's association with physical dirt contaminates her character in much the same way as her association with illicit sex. In the Western unconscious of the past two centuries, indeed, dirt and sex live in close association, and women who clean up things associated with bodies find themselves mysteriously deemed sexual and powerful regardless of their actual social status.

The theory that underlies this book is that sex, dirt, housework, and badness in women are linked in Western unconsciousnesses and that white middle-class women sought to transcend these associations by demonstrating their sexual purity and their pristine domesticity. To achieve this image, MCHs created and passed on a vision of being white, middle-class, and female that required an exquisite home setting for its fulfillment. They sought not only material well-being, though that was certainly one advantage, but mental comfort, the comfort of being a good woman. Their ease required not only service but contrast with a woman who represented the bad in woman, a woman who does housework and also embodies physical and emotional qualities that distinguish her from the housewife. Through creating a proper home and through contrast with a servant, the MCH found her identity as a good woman. It was this desire to differentiate herself and to sustain a compelling, though limited, image of womanhood that led white middle-class women to devalue housework, to deny their connection with it, and to act in ways that maintained other groups of women in domestic service and related occupations.

These concepts of moral and sexual purity have rarely been linked with a wife's housework. One explanation may be that housework has historically been regarded as refined in relation to the "lower" and harsher grades of discomfort and drudgery. Working-class women, whose alternatives were factory regimen and sweated labor or care of a little cottage supported by a workingman's salary, dreamed of securing a reliable husband. Even in plantation slavery the woman field hand was regarded as a rougher creature than the house slave, who also felt relatively inferior to the mistress. (The images of wifely comforts at home have always had a reverse side—of the servant as sexual prey for men of the house, which I shall discuss momentarily.) Housework, then, was seen as easy and pleasant work compared to other jobs open to women.

But the working-class image of keeping a comfortable little house was not adequate for middle-class women whose husbands worked at professional, mental, clean jobs. For this woman, beginning in the nineteenth century, her efforts to be a worthy partner for her husband, to be pure and genteel, required not soiling her hands. She had to have a servant to do the heaviest labor and to free her time for other, more pleasant tasks of the bourgeois home.

In brief, then, I think that white middle-class women sought to avoid housework for the same reasons they avoided flamboyant behavior; both were connected with bad women and inferior morality. When MCHs could no longer avoid doing housework, as happened progressively during the period covered by this book, they needed to exert even greater control over their own suspect bodies and to escape the home. This is an unusual assertion, and I believe that connections developed between sex, dirt, housework, and women in the nineteenth century, and that they are related to the dirt aversion evident in housework design between 1920 and 1945. Changes taking place during this period threatened white middle-class women with loss of their servants and, consequently, their detachment from manual labor and their feeling of distinctiveness from other women.

Dirt

In our culture, we tend to believe that attitudes toward dirt and hygiene result from the logical unfolding of precise scientific knowledge about cleanliness and health. One might assume that the high national consumption of tobacco, alcohol, and sugar would dispel such confidence in human rationality. We remain firmly committed, nonetheless, to the belief that our customs are based on enlightened, progressively improving knowledge and that practices different from ours are backward and superstitious.

On the contrary, the concept of "dirty," like other emotionally significant abstractions with which it is connected—sex, birth, nourishment, death—has a history inextricably linked with changes in family life, in cultural representations of bodies and regulation of sex, and in organization of work. Dirt is not a scientific fact but a principal means to arrange cultures, a point that has been made most effectively by anthropologist Mary Douglas.[2] Historians are just beginning to study Americans' changing standards of dirt, an essential complement to understanding housewives' sanitary standards.[3]

Other historical studies about images of socially despised groups provide useful insights, however, when viewed through Douglas's purity–taboo bifocals. "Dirtiness" appears always in a constellation of the suspect qualities that, along with sexuality, immorality, laziness, and ignorance, justify social rankings of race, class, and gender. The "slut," initially a shorthand for "slattern" or kitchen maid, captures all these personifications in a way unimaginable in a male persona.

Numerous studies suggest that, beginning at least in the late eighteenth century the designation *dirty* was regularly applied to women, to working-class men and women, and to women and men seen as racially different from the dominant group. Winthrop D. Jordan's fine study of the development of black slavery and racism in the United States, *White Over Black*, demonstrates the unconscious equations between dirt, black skin, sensuality, and physical strength held by dominant white men. Though white plantation owners feared black men's anger and fantasized about their sexual prowess, their most vivid fantasies focused on black women, the temptresses who threatened white men's reason and self-control.[4]

Though there are many explanations for how humans divide up the world into dirty and clean, pure and taboo, the ones I find most informative about Western culture of the past two centuries come from the greatest student of the nineteenth-century Western mind, Sigmund Freud, and analysts who have followed him. Freud linked fears of dirt with infantile experiences of a pleasurable body that had to be regulated to conform to adult demands. Infants took as natural and enjoyed their various body fluids and excrement and had to internalize their parents' perceptions that these portions of the self and the uncontrolled body they represented were "dirty" and "bad." As they showed interest in their physically pleasurable genitals, they also found that these displays were forbidden by parents and came to distrust their sensuality and sexual impulses. But they never lost the infantile memory of pleasure, and they carried into adult lives hostility to, and fascination with, those things linked unconsciously in the mind: feces, money, gift, baby, and penis, according to Freud.[5] In this view, the Victorian man's ambivalent obsession with money, "filthy lucre," becomes understandable as a passion for, and reaction against, infantile pleasure in filth. For women, Freud believed that maternity allowed a purifying physical release of tension.

Freud's analysis of the mistrust of the body may not be universally true, but it certainly described the psyche of his world, the bourgeois world of nineteenth-century Europe. To be shaped into civilized beings capable of reason and planning, which became preeminently valuable qualities in the capitalist and imperialist expansionism of the nineteenth century, humans had to repress or sublimate psychological pressures to pursue physical desire.[6] But neither Freud nor subsequent analysts worried about the effects on women's minds of injunctions to self-discipline that were not acted out within the cash nexus of the marketplace.

Freud's understanding of sexual repression was also limited by his view of physical impulses as innate drives necessarily stymied by civilization's standards and by his focus on the father. For Freud, the male child incorporated his "lessons" about physical restraint only in the Oedipal phase, when, turning his phallic desires toward the mother, he faced the threat of castration by the father. Accepting the father's superiority and the promise that he would someday be allowed a woman just like his mother, the male child incorporated his father's rule (and that of all the fathers embedded in law) and accepted the restraints of civilization. He gained a superego–conscience. Women, however, already without a penis and "castrated," had an incomplete incorporation of society's laws, internalized a less firm superego, and tempted men away from the work of building and refining "civilization."[7] Certainly women did not have access to any of the socially approved forms of sublimation for men: scientific research, exploration, commercial and industrial development, scholarship. Only religion and motherhood offered compensations, and these were not so engrossing as those available to men.

Late twentieth-century feminist accounts grounded in one of Freudianism's successors, object-relations psychology, have focused on the importance of the mother in the infant's mental life. This approach has clarified the connection between women's natural and social role as mothers and their association with dirt and sex in the West during the past two centuries. Unlike Freud, who thought women were associated with sex because of their psychic inadequacies, Dorothy Dinnerstein, Jane Flax, and Nancy Chodorow have laid out a compelling picture of infantile mental life that shows how the infant learns to connect mother and body in the unconscious. Though this account has been told in the works of these and other authors, it is still so unfamiliar and alien to our antipsychoanalytic society that I repeat the developmental story that helps explain men's and women's fear of women and mental associations of the female with the polluted and unclean.[8]

Infants in our society experience mothers and the other women who are caretaking substitutes as both nurturing and withholding nurturance, sometimes against the infant's often compelling desires and at the age when the infant is completely dependent on adults for survival. The mother or surrogate lives on in adult minds as the creature always connected in infant experience with food, warmth, tending the body, and giving it comfort. Mothers cuddle and respond to the child's demands, but they also abandon it to respond to the demands of other children and adults. Faced with a creature (almost always female) who is both necessary and infuriating, powerful and terrifying, the child splits beloved and sensually adored and offending mother in two, loving the "good" mother and those aspects unconsciously connected with goodness and hating the "bad" mother and those things unconsciously equated with badness.

According to the object-relations theory, however, crucial links between one's sense of self and the female come in a pre-Oedipal phase when the child is learning to be a separate and individuated being, to control its body and to do so in relations with beloved *objects*, the awkward psychoanalytic term for persons who elicit emotional–psychic attachments. In this phase, the tasks of devlopment are to learn to accept and to reconcile both autonomy and nurturance—to be, in the simplest terms, both separate– individuated and attached to others. The fear is that if one is too indepen- dent and autonomous, one will not be connected with a loving and nurturant other. And if one is too loved, nurtured, and connected to someone else, one will lack independent and autonomous action. Moreover, the child carries out the process of separation–individuation in relation to the infant care- taker, the woman felt as both good and bad, who in the infant's fantasy may both nurture and obliterate.

Little boys and girls resolve this stage somewhat differently. Boys learn fairly easily that they can be separate from the mother, indeed, that they are supposed to be different from her. But they also learn that nurturance comes from women and that they do not carry the capacity inside themselves. With fear of abandonment and fear of being overwhelmed by the mother, boys split their responses to women, who may offer nurturance and comfort, but only if they lack power that will threaten male autonomy. Despising, or con- straining, the creatures on whom one's physical and psychic satisfactions de- pend becomes a protection against loss of self.

For girls, separating from the nurturant mother is more difficult be- cause they are told by cultural messages that they are like her. Little girls are less encouraged by mothers to be autonomous and have a harder time sepa- rating psychologically from the mother and the overwhelming as well as reas- suring aspects of her nurturance. As a consequence, girls remain less certain of their capacities for autonomous action, more afraid that independent ac- tivity will result in an obliteration of nurturance and of self. They also, how- ever, incorporate the mother into their identities and experience themselves as repositories of female power, which is both good and bad, nurturant and destructive.

What feminist analysts have added to Freud, then, is the recognition that infantile physical feelings about body and dirt, sex and punishment, per- vade feelings about independence and caring. Experiencing sex and dirt re- calls unconscious infant joys that were banished by superego constraints on pleasure; they also resonate with being nurtured and fearing that the nur- turer will destroy toddlers' efforts at independence.

No wonder, then, that individual children solve the problem of anger at the mother or intense desire for her by splitting female images. They deny their anger and love and her power and instead depict her as all-loving and radiantly beneficent. They also carry the unconscious fears, however, that she has aroused responses so great that they feel as if they might obliterate her through the hostility of anger or the merging of passion and that the powerful mother will reciprocate; thus the result of the child's strong feelings is fear of obliteration by the mother. In households in which a mother nur- tures and tends to her own children, the child may act on one or the other of these feelings and holds them in tension. In much of the middle class for much of the nineteenth and early twentieth centuries, however, it was possible to split feelings and to project them onto two distinct women—mother and servant.

In Western culture of the past two centuries, with servants often acting as mother substitutes to children of the middle class, the split between adored good, nonthreatening mother and bad women who could be despised because of their class and race was overlaid onto other social relations that defined goodness and badness for women. Even when children adored the nurturant mother surrogate, they learned early that she was not the good mother and to shift their allegiances.[9]

Images of good and bad women, then, have such salience because they are linked in the Western unconscious with feelings about mothers and our infant bodies and selves. For men, these splits may cause confusion in dealing with women and pain as they seek to recover the original nurturance that was lost to them when they lost the infant connection with the mother. It helps to explain the fear and hostility to women as eliciting feelings of internal anarchy and potentially overwhelming power. But men have been able to escape these self-doubts and fears through control of households, businesses, government, and military enterprises in which they sublimate aggressive energies and gain connection with sensual pleasure through association with bad women and nurturance through socially regulated sex in marriage with good, safe women.

Women, however, had to sublimate and repress physical impulses and guilt without being able to control institutions. For women, also, the physical self always made persistent and shaming demands. Women inhabited less easily regulated bodies than men, bodies that it seemed less possible to deny and to transcend. Women from the age of about fifteen to about fifty reliably appeared unclean in menstruation. In the centuries before indoor bathrooms and manufactured tampons and douches, it must often have been difficult for women to disguise this periodic "uncleanness," which evidently aroused fear and disgust in men. Psychoanalyst Clara Thompson reported that some female patients in the 1940s felt menstruation a sign of incompetence because it was a body product that, unlike feces and urine, could not be controlled by a sphincter and, therefore, represented a moral failure. Other women felt unclean because of genital odors. One woman feared marriage "because she would not be able to keep her body clean at every moment in the presence of her husband."[10]

More than white middle-class men, who could project sensuality onto women, dark-skinned people, and workers, middle-class women find the sensual in themselves and in other women. Dominant men split feelings about good and bad women and project them onto different groups of women. Women, however, experience these split feelings within themselves.[11]

This division of self has occurred in a society that has split the images of offending and valued women and projected them onto other salient social divisions of class and race. The badness of women of darker skins and lower incomes has functioned on many levels to sustain the material and psychic comfort of good women and the men who are their fathers, husbands, and sons. Working-class women and women of color have been the repositories for images of sexuality and moral inferiority; they have been depicted as legitimate sexual outlets for men, as loose women who also are so powerless that they pose no threat to men's authority and autonomy; their presence enabled good women to be missionaries for social purity, and they performed the labor that enabled good women to appear dainty and clean. These social and cultural divisions and their long history have expanded the mental associations we carry about good and bad women.

For women more than men, this division offered a precarious confidence. Men could never become so polluted as women, and there was no danger, no matter how degraded they became, that they would become female. For women, however, confidence in self-image depended upon differentiation from other women, who confirmed the good woman's elevation from dirt and shame. During the nineteenth and early twentieth centuries, the existence of sharp class and race divisions guaranteed a labor force to serve the good woman and also constant signals in sexual and social behavior that the angelic wife of a middle-class household was unique among women.

Sex

Numerous historians of Victorian America and England have examined men's dual images of women—Madonna/Magdalen, virgin/whore, angel/devil—and some have linked them explicitly with class and race divisions. Men sought sexual outlet with women who posed no social or political threat and simultaneously denied the sexual prowess of their female peers and partners—the "respectable" white women who became their wives.[12] In England, where class constituted the primary social division, the likeliest candidates for the sexual pleasures of well-to-do men were "domestic servants, girls from the working or lower classes, and prostitutes of varying degrees of expensiveness."[13] In the United States, black slavery provided white masters easy access to women perceived as sexually enticing and nurturant. In sex with them, white men found full dominion over the desired and dominating "mother" and appeasement of their fear of her power. Though their wives also had the basic sensual impulses found in all women, they, men believed, had become good through sheltered ignorance and must be kept that way.[14]

Taking sexual pleasure with impoverished women and slaves freed middle-class men from doubts about the purity of their wives and from fears of proper women's innate, though restrained, sensuality. In a century in which men felt a terror of the sexuality represented by the female,[15] they used religion, medicine, and marriage to contain and control female power and usually sought sexual expression with powerless women.[16]

Wives came to represent other sensual pleasures, those of a comfortable house filled with lavish furnishings, ample food, and pleasing garments. Domesticity "offered subtle erotic inducements" to the development of bourgeois feelings. Material comfort measured success, but it also gratified infantile longings for physical pleasure split from sexual shame.[17]

Why men accepted the split between good and bad women, sex with inferiors and comfort with their wives, is not difficult to comprehend. Why their female peers accepted the contraints of "goodness" is less obvious. Nevertheless, these women rapidly adopted the new sexual standards and wrapped themselves in their angelic imagery. Perhaps semiconsciously, women welcomed an ethic of "passionlessness" as a defense against husbands' sexual demands and ensuing pregnancies and men's general depreciation of female morality. Certainly, the ethic provided a new justification for women's influence: moral superiority grounded in chaste sexuality.[18]

Women gained a step in the climb to attain full humanity grounded in reason and mental effort. Accepting sexual restraint enabled women to appear more like men, who embodied the standard of human achievement.[19] It freed them from fears of their own unruly demands. And in societies increasingly fractured along race and class lines, it guaranteed respect and material comfort to some women that were denied to many other women. No wonder that the woman of elevated class, race, and family chose to develop those impulses that accorded with images of good women rather than impulses that led to self-judgments and social consequences of bad women. All classes of women sought respectability, but slave women had little power to fend off white men's sexual demands, and working-class women had low wages to augment, most easily by selling sexual favors.

Home

The proper environment for the sexually chaste woman was the marital household, the home that became a staple of popular imagery and aspiration. Like feelings about women, however, those about the home were split into good and bad components, which were the domains of different women. In domestic work, images of sexuality and dirt joined with the reality of housework to create emotionally powerful images.

Links between housework and psyche depend on the home as the center for intimate and sensual existence. Housework took care of those things that society found most unappealing, embarrassing, and tainted: the visible needs and evidences of fallible bodies. Housewives, or their domestic alter egos, prepared the food to sustain bodies (transforming other living things into dead forms for people to ingest) and cleaned up the detritus left from meals: boiling babies' diapers, toilet-training children, removing bed pans for the sick, clearing away evidence of human excrement. They washed clothes and bedclothes soiled by sweat, odors, hair, and dead skin thrown off by bodies. And they straightened up and ordered the objects in homes and removed all intrusions—soot, sand, mud, polluted air, dust, grease, body odors—that were disapproved.

The nineteenth century witnessed important changes in the standards for these tasks, their organization in homes, and who performed them. First, middle-rank families could afford servants to take the heaviest physical labor off the housewife; one of the most basic effects of bourgeois life was that wives enjoyed comforts as much as husbands. Second, and perhaps related, the cleaning standards set for these servants were noticeably raised, and sites of household work were clearly divided from spaces for living. American house plan books designated numerous specialized rooms, dividing public spaces from private, adult spaces from children's, women's from men's, and keeping "the service aspects of the house hidden from the eyes of visitors."[20] In England, "Victorian architectural writers [were] obsessed with the fear of cooking smells pervading the halls or living-rooms in any way and [went] to elaborate ends to prevent this intrusion."[21] Third, the work of women was much more clearly divided along race and class lines, with the darker-skinned and poorer cleaning up the physical detritus of the lighter-skinned and better off.[22] Western Europe's imperial experiences produced racial hierarchies similar to those in the United States. Settlers, colonial administrators, and military families had black servants and servants in quantity, and the images of that life were brought home to Europe.

The United States received the ethos of female fragility from Europe, especially England, and added its own unique system of gender differentiation developed in the institution of black slavery. In Europe, peasant girls became servants to the urban bourgeoisie. In America, Irish immigrant "Bridgets" continued the pattern of rural women doing housework for urban ones and were often stigmatized in racial terms as slovenly, licentious, and dark.[23] The dominant image of the servant, however, was fixed as a black slave woman whose purpose in life was to serve white ladies (regardless of the actual shade of skin, which was much more varied than indicated by this neat dichotomy).[24] In Britain and the American Northeast, the contours of class were visible in the clothing, manners, and carriage that distinguished the mistress from her maid; in the American South, skin hue intensified the sense of physical difference. Ladies looked like, or were perceived as, delicate, pure creatures, almost too pure to be sullied by the exigencies of living. Servants looked like, or were perceived as, physically strong, linked to animals by their power and by their labor. At the simplest, ladies were *clean* and servants were *dirty*.

The division between whose body was clean and tended accordingly, and whose body became relatively unclean in the process, was more firmly drawn in the nineteenth century than previously. The capacity to be clean and sweet-smelling became a visible sign of the mental and moral capacities believed to characterize the bourgeoisie and their homes tended by angelic wives and daughters. Bourgeois women could attain this preciousness because working-class domestics scrubbed floors and stoops on their knees, emptied chamber pots, cooked every meal, scoured pots and pans, and laundered the family's clothing weekly. The wife's cleanliness was made possible by the domestic's dirtiness. Images of good and bad women were easily projected onto middle-class and working-class women.

The class and race divisions between mistresses and servants visibly heightened the emotional attributions of the division of household labor. The work of cleaning up the "bad" body was given to "bad" women, and this work distribution confirmed the dominant beliefs that class and race differences were due to the moral superiority of middle-class white women and the moral degradation of working-class and black women.

Home, Sex, and Work in the 1920s and 1930s

I began this work asking how notions of bourgeois gentility were sustained when in the twentieth century most women came to do the work of their homes and feelings about women's contamination could no longer be split between the housewife and the domestic. How did middle-class women make this transition—in actual work and in self-image? How was the home as an unconsciously dirty place connected most deeply with our despised physical fallibilities made emotionally habitable when there was no despised domestic to deflect feelings of dirtiness from wives and mothers?

I have offered three answers in this book, and I would like to speculate about a fourth. First, I have concluded that until almost midcentury, servants continued to take the greatest burden from middle-class women and to be the primary women associated with dirt. By having an "other" in her home, the middle-class woman not only got work done, but also her pristine identity affirmed. By emphasizing her difference from women domestics, the housewife upheld her position as a pure woman and as a person almost as detached from concern for the physical needs of life as her husband, almost as unsullied as he. The price, of course, was separation from the interests of other women, exploitation of the labor of other women, and continued denial of her own power and responsibility.

Second, middle-class households continued the pattern of finding sensual satisfactions in consumer goods, while simultaneously making life cleaner and less erotic. Encouraged by rising consumer standards and advertisements, MCHs gained ever higher ideals of furnishings to own, accoutrements for meals, child-developing toys to purchase, and personal attractiveness to tend and pamper.

The increase in consumer pleasures required, however, a matched increase in hygiene and order. Despite important changes in household sanitation, most obviously the spread of fully equipped bathrooms, home washing machines, and "clean" gas and electric fuels, continuous work was required to keep households up to magazine standards of presentability and wives up to advertising and movie norms of beauty. Meal preparation and cleanup and cleaning rooms and soiled clothes remained constant preoccupations.

Both kitchens and bathrooms were obsessively cleaned, according to the reports of housewives and servants. Weekly cleaning of stoves and daily cleaning of dishes, counters, and floors indicated the need to remove food odors and remnants from sight. Refrigeration slowed down natural decay and enabled a housewife to keep leftovers, but she then had additional work to disguise these as fresh food, incorporated into new dishes and not simply warmed up.

Daily scrubbing of bathrooms and provision of clean towels removed remainders of the physical needs of excretion and of body cleansing. Tidying living rooms, changing bed linens and airing mattresses, straightening curtains and placing pillows and window shades at even angles, all worked to make the home an ordered and perfect place that looked as if it had not been disturbed by human life.

Clothing standards rose with the advent of commercial laundries and home washing machines. The fastidiousness of perfect clothes heightened distinctions between those able to hire such equipment and those unable to do so. Hygienic distinctions between servants and mistresses remained intact, though now wives also wanted their servants to be fresh-smelling and not to disturb the atmosphere even when the servant sweated to put out the labor necessary to maintain the domestic aura. When servants could not meet criteria of personal hygiene, the wife's superiority was demonstrated; when they could, it was also proof of the wife's virtue, since she, or women like her, had trained the servant to civilized manners and demeanor.

Third, the MCH defined her own housework job to resemble the rationalized, sublimated work world of her husband. Instead of envisioning radical reforms of household-based service, middle-class American women sought to remove the stigma from the occupation that defined daily work for most women by masculinizing it. They postulated a male standard of worthy endeavor and likened housework to men's production work instead of to women's service work. Men had no associations with the infant experience of physical weakness and sensual pleasure. To adopt the model of men's work was to emulate rational, abstract work.[25] Housewives could portray their work as managerial and economic—analogous to their husbands'—and deflect images of manual tending to physical needs onto the women who cooked, laundered, and cleaned for wages.

Home economics as a college-based, research-defined field promised to elevate housework from manual labor to a profession like engineering. It enabled women's culture of homemaking to be more widely recognized and undoubtedly raised women's self-confidence and ability to care for families. Simultaneously, it accepted masculine standards of value and rationality and based good homemaking on commercial consumption. And, at the same time that the discipline helped to define minimum standards of household well-being, it also showed women how to organize their housework in conformity to income and race status. Beneficial though systemizing household information was, it left intact the devaluation of housework in the middle class and in popular culture.

Working-class women, however, could not reject the work on which their incomes as servants depended and the activities in which they spent hours of their lives and in which they felt pride of accomplishment. Domestics saw the possibility of their occupations being treated like other work, with hours and wages regulated like industrial jobs and with health, retirement, and unemployment benefits like other employment. These conceptions depended upon seeing housework as work and not as an invisible set of services performed out of sight of husbands and the public world. Servants had a notion of housework as a job, like a factory job, and not, since it was not their own home, the place connected with sensuality and repression. Their conception led to transforming service work into a business and caring for food, people, and laundry in commercial enterprises, a shift that would accelerate after World War II.

When servants vanished, hygienic standards for work increased, and MCHs found they had no one's work to manage but their own and that they could no longer live at home as angels. My speculation is that the fourth change that occurred was that middle-class housewives lost the ability to split womanhood into two groups, with themselves on the good side. Instead, increasingly, the split between good and bad became internalized, and women engaged in heightened efforts to control and to deny the power and dirt of their bodies.

As women became more directly linked to the dirty work of the home, they spent more time purifying their own bodies and eradicating their physical shame. Even more than in the nineteenth century, a woman's virtue exhibited itself in the ordered and exquisite use of purchased objects and in the maintenance of a body that exhibited no dissolution—a youthful, perfumed, fit body.

In the care of their bodies, as well as their domestic space, wives exercised greater fastidiousness as they became more solely identified with the home. Restraints on the sensual self shifted, but they did not erode. Women could be sexy for their husbands but not for other men. The MCH's relationship to her husband often exhibited maternal qualities; she overlooked his boyish high spirits and thoughtlessness, and she put away household cares to play with him when he came home from work. In brief, she was a good mother, who kept at bay signs of her domestic work, her own physical aging, and her sexual power. The witty, sexy, youthful wife of the 1920s and 1930s was on her way to being the "playmate" of the 1950s, a fantasy of sexiness without sexuality, of "sanitized" and nonthreatening sex.

By 1945, the American home and the American housewife had achieved the position they would enjoy in the post–World War II era as the loveliest, best-smelling, most sanitary houses and women in the world. Almost magically, the homes were spotless without marring the beauty of the women responsible for them. Such magic was sure to be short lived.

Dualisms Between and Within Women

Feminist theorists of the past two decades have emphasized the pervasiveness of images of women that link them to an untrustworthy mortal body and how these images are contrasted with the image of men as thinking beings who master their bodies as well as all else in the natural world. Standard cultural oppositions between reason and emotion, asceticism and sensuality, pain and pleasure, purity and impurity, cleanliness and dirt have been linked with the fundamental male–female dualism.[26] These theorists have usually assumed that *all* women suffer equally from identification with the elements unconsciously associated with the fact of being a woman. They have not examined the effects on women of another dichotomy we know to be true, that between good and bad women, between virgin–seductress, angel–whore, and Madonna–Magdalen, a dualism that divides women from each other but that also divides a woman within herself, since no woman can escape completely the fear that she carries bad impulses within her.

This book rests on the proposition that Western culture depicts all women as potential seductresses and monsters but that white middle-class women have been given the hope that they can squelch social suspicion and self-doubt through two means: restricting themselves to housework and to marital sex and distinguishing themselves from women of color and working-class women. The obliteration of personal fears, however, requires constant new assertions of purity and, ironically, inhibition of other forms of self-assertion. These inhibitions are notable in political decisions like requiring white clothing for suffrage marches in the 1910s and for Equal Rights Amendment rallies in the 1970s. White is visually dramatic, but as the bride's color, it also conveys messages of virginity, nonsexuality, physical purity, and fragility.

White middle-class women of the 1920s and 1930s, like women of the 1980s, did not claim sexuality as an act of self-development outside acceptable social contraints. Although overt sexual behavior became more acceptable and good sexual relations came to be seen as the cement holding marriages together, a double standard persisted. Young women had to take care to be sexy enough to be normal and yet to mete out sexual availability with great care to avoid "the onus of 'bad girl' status."[27] Ultimately, sexuality had to be sanctified by marriage and wedded to housewifely duties.

This dualism has persisted throughout the twentieth century. Black women have emphasized how white women continue to enjoy the benefits and to suffer the limitations of acting like ladies. They remain "nice girls," as black poet Doris Davenport has noted:

> [White women] cling to their myth of being privileged, powerful and less oppressed . . . than black wimmin. Why? Because that is all they have. . . . Somewhere deep down (denied and almost killed) in the psyche of racist white feminists there is some perception of their real position: powerless, spineless, and invisible. . . . The "white suprema-cist" syndrome, especially in white feminists, is the result of a real in-feriority complex, or lack of self-identity.[28]

It is not only white skin, itself a socially defined perception, that keeps white women's privileges intact; it is white middle-class women's acceptance of and complicity in a hierarchy of female goodness that imputes moral superiority to some women's life patterns and immorality to others'.

Women are still aspiring to be good, even when that means confine-ment and self-restraint. Despite current fashions of clothing that reveal women's legs, hips, and breasts, the emphasis on women's controlling their sexuality or channeling it into motherhood (with its Madonna associations) remains. Women's obsessions with fashion and cosmetics and shaping their bodies to wear fashionable apparel may even be seen as a denial of physi-cality, as women seek to shape and to disguise their universally deficient bodies to fit a narrow ideal of the beautiful.[29] Girls are still reading romances that teach them that sex is justified if one is in love and that marriage culmi-nates and cleanses sexual activity.[30] Young women students imagine a full professional life as well as having children, unwilling to imagine their lives tainted by the care infants need.[31]

This book has been intended to show how myriad women shaped their individual existences within cultural notions of good and bad women and within economic and racial realities of privilege and need. The systems harmed all women, though in different ways. I hope that I have clarified the ways in which it harmed white middle-class women and the women on whom they relied to perform stigmatized and exploited labor so that we can all begin to attack those profound internal images of femininity and good-ness/badness that inhibit and drain us and that keep us fearful of and sepa-rated from other women.

Afterword

In concluding, I want to glance at what happened to domestic service and housework between 1945 and 1980 from the perspective of the late 1980s, to assess how household work is done now, and to offer a vision of what housework might become. I hope to clarify how the issues of the book remain alive for us to confront.

As the end of World War II approached, middle-class housewives around the United States began to hope that women workers would leave industrial jobs for domestic service. Peace, they wistfully assumed, would bring domestics back into the home as well as the boys back from overseas. Through local private community organizations and public employment offices and schools, MCHs sought to attract and persuade domestic workers to return to service.

Some MCHs expected servants to return to live-in status, but most recognized, as Katherine Davis, chair from 1940 to 1945 of the National Committee on Household Employment, put it, that "household servants are gone forever." Instead, housewives should expect to do more of their own housework (which they had leaned to do during the war) and to hire live-out, part-time, or specialized domestic services. Even if a housewife got a full-time worker, she would, said Katherine Davis, work only "an 8-hour shift [so] she won't be there at both ends of the day—to get [the] husband's breakfast and see the children off to school and to serve dinner and wash up afterwards." Most likely, the worker would come part-time, three days a week, or every morning or afternoon to do such tasks as cleaning, making beds, and preparing evening meals.[1]

The U.S. Women's Bureau began planning before the war's end for conversion of women's jobs, including the issue of how to keep the improved wages and working conditions gained by domestics during the war. "Bettering conditions in this field [was] definitely women's responsibility—with women constituting most of the workers and most of the employers." In March 1946, the bureau held a conference on household employment and initiated a survey of community actions. Once again, the bureau encouraged local groups and the U.S. Employment Service to propagandize for voluntary compliance with set wages and hours.[2]

Across the South, where black women workers had few options, public schools persisted in matching federal funds to pay for evening courses in vocational fields relevant to women employed in domestic service. Though the great majority of these school programs were for black workers, a few schools for working-class whites in the Midwest and around the employment magnet of New York City offered courses in housework and home management for women employed in domestic service.[3] Puerto Rican women also had limited job opportunites and responded to employment agencies in Chicago and New York, which recruited them in 1945.

In some large cities, where domestic workers had typically been most in demand, local employer committees combined with the YWCA, the National Urban League, and the state Employment Services to "call back" the domestic, as the St. Louis project put it. Public meetings were held in which MCHs spelled out their goals and domestics and their representatives laid out their demands.

In a remarkable exchange in St. Louis, housewives listened to a session called "Worker Speaks," in which domestics

> described their dissatisfaction, such as the lack of respect implied in the employer's use of their given name; they wanted to be addressed by their surname. . . . They wanted a regular time schedule, such as other workers enjoyed, so that they too would be able to plan lives of their own. They pointed out that they also had families and outside interests. They did not want to be referred to as "servants" or "maids," nor should they be expected to use the "back door" entrance, especially at night.

Employers wanted the women to work, but some were annoyed at "the question of front or back door entrance as 'mere quibbling' and said it was straining a point to attempt to choose a name for a 'domestic'"[4]

Despite employers' lack of empathy, economic and social circumstances favored the reduced number of domestics. Down to 9.5 percent of all women workers by 1944, this group could hope that committees of employers would work to reduce hours and raise wages. Local committees set standards for live-in domestics, but they also adopted wage scales for daily and hourly work.

Presbyterian church women issued a pamphlet, *Martha in the Modern Age* (1945), to encourage followers to pay "either the minimum rate set up by the Federal Fair Labor Standards Act or 'prevailing wages paid in other occupations which require an equal amount of training or skill,'—whichever is the higher and overtime pay in excess of 40 . . . hours."[5] The National Board of the YWCA agreed to have its local committees cooperate with offices of the U.S. Employment Service to match up Y workers and employers and to survey and report local conditions. Community boards in many cities formulated voluntary codes for their membership and colluded with employment services to inform the general public about them. In Akron, Ohio, for instance, though the USES could not specify hours and wages, it "permit[ed] the USES representative to explain to the prospective employer the existing labor market situation, including comparative wages, hours, and other working conditions [that competed for worker placement]."[6]

Efforts to get workers into Social Security and for their inclusion under state wage, hour, and workmen's compensation laws intensified. Economic circumstances that moved household workers into day work at better than minimum wage rates rendered wage and hour limits moot. Old age and retirement insurance remained an issue, however, until the 1950 amendments (effective January 1951) to the Social Security Act. Even this coverage was effective only for women working regular part-time hours, "employed by a single employer for at least 24 days in a calendar quarter [at least twice a week] with cash wages of at least $50 for service in the quarter."[7] Similar limitations were placed on workmen's compensation, which applied to employers with more than one worker and hiring workers for regular, full-time jobs.

In proposing the 1939 amendments, the Social Security Advisory Board unsuccessfully recommended that domestic workers be covered by unemployment insurance. New York State covered workers in households with four or more workers in 1936, but, except for Hawaii, until the 1970s, all other states followed the federal guidelines in excluding domestic workers. In 1965, New York State dropped the four-person rule and covered any household with a "cash payroll of $500 or more in a calendar quarter," which brought about one-fourth of New York's domestic workers into the system. By 1976, only Arkansas and the District of Columbia had added domestic workers to unemployment coverage. In that year, Congress approved amendments that added an estimated 308,000 out of approximately 1.4 million domestic workers through a federal requirement that states cover employers with a payroll of $600 or more in a calendar quarter. This most recent reform was designed to leave out the majority of domestic workers because the dollar amount "was arrived at as a means of excluding from coverage the householder who employed primarily one person for 1 day a week."[8] In 1988, day workers remained unprotected against unemployment.

Efforts to improve their legal status during the 1940s and 1950s did not enhance the social standing of domestics, as was symbolized in the failure to change the occupation's name. Though the YWCA had used the term *house-hold worker* throughout the 1930s and the Women's Bureau used *household employment* by the end of 1940s *maid* had become the popular name, used even in USES documents. Though avoiding painful associations with ser-vitude, *maid* nevertheless retained images of immaturity, inferiority, and somewhat laborious service. Only in the 1960s, after pressure from the civil rights movement and renewed organization of domestic workers in a new version of the National Committee on Household Employment did *maid* give way to *general houseworker* and *cleaning woman.*

Housewives were unwilling to raise the status of maids but continued to postulate a world in which they were plentiful. In the postwar era of high expectations for home life and of larger families, families sought "help to aid the hard-pressed mother of young children, or to assist with the care of in-valid or aged members, or to release the homemaker for some other type of work which she can fruitfully do in her community." As married women con-tinued to move into paid employment, albeit primarily in part-time work, they needed help with chores that could not be turned over to machines. Even "power laundries and 'dydee wash' [diaper service went] just so far, but [left] much to be done to keep clothes and linens clean. [And] eating all meals out or from containers sent into the home [was] a possibility for some but not a probability for all families."[9]

Despite need and some local efforts, women with any job alternatives left domestic work. By the 1950 census, only 8.4 percent of the female labor force remained in the occupation. Only when middle-class housewives them-selves had to do most of the work did they begin to perceive the design of housework as an isolating and hard job.

In the fifteen years after World War II during which households in-creased in size, became more isolated from each other and from outside ser-vices in suburban developments, and lost access to domestics in a decreas-ingly segregated labor market, MCHs struggled to meet the standards that had developed earlier in the twentieth century. Badgered to produce three, four, or even five children and berated by magazines and commentators about their duties as housekeepers and as wives and mothers, many women struggled through the 1950s. The houses got cleaned, the children were fer-ried to their doctor appoinments and music lessons, and husbands were pro-vided with spotlessly clean shirts. But the tinder was being laid for the fiery outburst proclaimed in *The Feminine Mystique* (1963) and for its rapid spread through the eager hands of suburban housewife readers.

When Betty Friedan described in the book the "problem that has no name" of the educated, suburban housewife as boredom, isolation, and waste of intellect, she appeared to suggest that the complaint was not with housework but with the class of women expected to do it. Housework, Friedan implied, was dreary stuff that might best be done by working-class women (or men) with low job expectations; as an occupation for talented women, it was insufferable. The time had come, she asserted, for sophisticated women to give up the pretense that domestic tasks were sufficiently congenial and absorbing to fill up an adult existence.

Paradoxically, the other critique to emerge from the 1950s was a recognition of how demanding housework was, an analysis middle-class women discovered when they, like working-class women earlier in the century, began to take care of homes *and* to hold paid jobs. Not many of these women responded with political protest. But like their predecessors, they used their superior economic position to hire day workers to do part of the household labor. For some such women in the 1950s and 1960s, decreasing employment discrimination made it possible to remain responsible for housework while escaping suburban isolation. Their incomes were large enough to buy services and household work or to negotiate with husbands to help with part of the work.

The women's liberation movement of the 1970s spawned numerous analyses of how privatized, female-centered housework functioned to maintain women's isolation and men's power in the public arena. A generation of women tried to resocialize men to share burdens of child care, cooking, and cleaning. Experiments to shift the work's locus and gender were short-lived, however, and many women radicals resumed responsibilities for child care and housework.[10] By the end of the 1970s, analysts focused on the "double day," which, not surprisingly, weighed more heavily on working-class than on middle-class women.

The conservative reaction of the 1980s, institutionalized through the election of Ronald Reagan to the presidency, sought the revitalization of housewifery as a main objective.[11] Marriage and motherhood were women's primary roles, according to such conservative spokesmen as George Gilder and some of the contibutors to the monthly magazine *Commentary;* only devoted women could adequately care for children, the elderly, and hardworking men. The resurgence of family motifs in popular and academic culture affected even the political Left, which sought to recapture working-class images of supportive, extended families for the support of socialists and the Democratic Party's left wing (seen on national television in Mario Cuomo's "The Party Is a Family, the Nation Is a Family" speech at the 1984 San Francisco convention).[12]

Despite various suggestions for reform, in the 1980s housework remains the primary responsibility of adult women. Working-class women find that their housework is no easier and their paid jobs, often in the service sector, are low paid. Middle-class women remain responsible for their housework and use substantial parts of their paychecks to cover dependent care, cooking, cleaning, and laundry.

Many of the services women now buy are performed commercially. Child care centers, nursing homes, home health aid providers for the disabled and elderly, fast food restaurants, caterers, and cleaning companies offer these specialized services for prices sufficient to attract large corporations into these businesses. Office spaces where adults spend most of their lives are cleaned by crews directed by large companies. Only among rich families or the well-to-do with two income earners do households expect to hire someone to take over some of the wife's household responsibilities. Most of the work except housecleaning is done outside the home and by crews of workers.

What has not changed in these services is the compensation and character of the labor force. The majority of workers in these industries are female; the labor force is heavily immigrant and nonwhite; and, though a tight labor market keeps wages well above the federal minimum wage (itself in decline relative to average wages), benefits and protections are lacking. The same picture holds in private household employment. Day workers essentially work on a contract to perform certain tasks, usually to standards they set themselves—and often without supervision because the employer is at her paid job. Sociologist Mary Romero has described this process in detail and concludes that contemporary household workers (who do "housekeeping" and not "maid's" work) have restructured the job from wage work to a petty bourgeois craft job; they have improved their daily work routine but not its benefits.[13] They rarely get Social Security, paid vacations, or annual raises; nor do they have health insurance, which U.S. health policy ties to regular employment in large companies.

Coupled with the continued low value of housework and its related tasks is the resurgence of nostalgia for home life of the 1950s.[14] One response to a growing sense that Americans do not eat well—because of environmentally polluted food, ingestion of excessive cholesterol, teenage anxiety, and busy family schedules that disrupt meals—are calls for a return to home-prepared meals to salvage Americans' physical and emotional health. Daily newspapers carry food sections. In a long *Washington Post* article, "The Late, Great Art of Cooking" (June 1, 1988), a nutritionist insisted on the connection between home cooking and nurturance: "When people reject food preparation, they lose an opportunity to nurture others": "It's an inherent part of women to be nurturers. I think that they need this nurturing to maintain their humanity." Nurturance, in this account, requires spending a great deal of time on food shopping, preparation, and serving.

Instead of attributing responsibility to farmers, food processors, manufacturers, and advertisers—all of whom profit from food—experts demand that women oversee their families' well-being by finding healthy food products, preparing food so that nutrition is not lost, and serving food in such a way that family members feel neither undernourished nor overstuffed and do not "assuage bad feelings [with the] tremendous amount of high calorie food readily available."[15] In this scenario, women's task is to maintain a healthy household against assaults from large and well-financed businesses. One favorite example is supermarkets in which one check-out gate out of eleven self-righteously proclaims that it does not feature candy so as to protect adults from importunate, advertiser-prompted children's demands. Such a solution makes full sense only in a culture with fantasies of perfectly run, clean, and cosseted homes, in which mothers are believed to be so powerful that they can guard families against external contamination.

Similar attempts to recenter responsibility on overworked women can be seen in proposals concerning child care and dependent care. Since these services are expensive to hire, other proposals would give families financial incentives to keep someone out of the labor force to provide care within the home. (Women are never specified as the "someone," but they nearly always are.) As a presidential candidate in 1988, George Bush suggested a plan that would credit families with preschool children through the tax system. Households would not necessarily have to hire child care; they could simply claim the money to "pay" the mother for staying home. These solutions carry the same problems for housewife–workers that domestics have always remarked: they isolate women, require long hours of work, and include no security for retirement (or divorce, which is a form of unemployment for the full-time housewife). They make sense only in light of nostalgic versions of the twentieth-century history of wives' household responsibilities, which, in reality, inevitably entailed exploitation of the wife or a servant.

What is to be done? Can we care for people without condemning women to isolating, low-status work, whether performed for love or for wages?

A first step is to accept that taking care of one's physical needs, except for the chronically disabled, is a basic adult responsibility not to be foisted onto others. Mahatma Gandhi realized that the idea that no man is too great to clean up after himself is revolutionary. Since much of the feeling of greatness (of power) comes from being served, giving up this elixir requires humans to find other sources of self-worth. For men, it may mean confronting bodily realities—dirt, decay, imperfection—that can usually be kept at bay and projected onto women. For women, whose escape from body has always been less successful than men's, it may mean finding a self-image other than that of the perfect housekeeper, mother, and wife.

To expect all adults to do the work still centered in homes—cleaning, laundry, meal production, and dependent care—would require organizing our days differently. Long hours increasingly demanded by professional life and expected from hourly production workers racking up overtime make sense only in a society that assumes that the toilers have someone else to take care of their basic physical needs. Otherwise, the burden becomes intolerable. Our prevailing assumption is that those able to earn good incomes, whether paid workers, wives, or other household members, go to good jobs, and those with less earning power take care of the daily vicissitudes of life. Demanding that each adult accept some of these chores would go a long way to changing attitudes about life, I suspect, as many protected adults find what unremitting work it takes to sustain and to protect life. A similar lesson was learned by MCHs during World War II, when they had to take over housework and discovered how hard it was when done every day.

Relying on others through purchasing some services is not necessarily exploitation, but consumers must make certain that workers are covered by benefits taken for granted in a civilized society; service work can no longer be treated as domestic employment was before World War II. People who work in service industry jobs in child care, home health visiting, nursing homes, office cleaning crews, and catering and restaurants deserve retirement and health benefits and unemployment insurance. Often female, immigrant, and nonwhite, these workers suffer from the devaluation of their labor and the fact that our regulations were designed for full-time industrial employment.

Everybody was dependent as a child and will become so again in old age; any of us may suffer disability or a harsh illness. Caring for dependent people cannot be simply a female, domestic responsibility. As medical costs of illness have risen, we have moved as a society to cover catastrophic health expenses. Chronic nursing home and in-home care are also being recognized as expensive and essential costs that few families can sustain, either financially or physically. When a family does care for its elderly members, this is usually done by an adult woman, who gives up her job and risks her own retirement well-being. By dint of numbers of votes and their lobbyists, elder Americans are making certain that society in general takes over a larger share of their catatrosphic and chronic care. Admirable in its intent, legislation authorizing this care should, nevertheless, include measures to protect workers who will be paid for supplying hospital and home care.

Child care is a growing problem, and not just because of the increase in the numbers of working mothers. Caring for children has gotten harder, not just because families have to synchronize schedules to get everyone to work, to school, to day care, and back home but because children's environment has become more hazardous. Certainly, Michael Dukakis's proposals for state-supported child care centers that meet standards of excellence is valid in not putting all responsibility on mothers.

Even more important is a belief that society at large is responsible for safe streets for children to play in, high-quality libraries and schools for them to learn to read in, and nutritious food merchandised to children. In poor neighborhoods of cities like Washington, D.C., even the best of mothers cannot protect children from the stray bullets of drug dealers; that requires taxes for adequate police and employment programs to offer drug users a different way to live.

When we remember the 1950s only as the era of "Father Knows Best" and "Leave It to Beaver," and attribute their happy childhoods to their mothers' presence in kitchens cooking good food, we forget that other children suffered deprivation from racial discrimination and poverty—misfortunes that were eased, but not erased, by mothers' nurturance.

Black domestic workers, for instance, could only ward off some blows society struck against their children during the 1940s and 1950s. In his speech to the 1988 Democratic Convention, Jesse Jackson concluded with an image of his mother going to her housework job with runs in her stockings so that he and his brother could attend school in new socks without holes in them. His mother's attentiveness spared him some embarrassment but did not ease the shame of her sacrifice.

Children are a national asset and need to be treated as such. So long as we hold unquestioningly and absolutely to the legend of mothers' magical powers to cleanse, nourish, and protect, however, we are likely to adopt programs that leave the private household as the unsupported and overstrained guarantor of health and development. And because no single adult can provide all the advantages and care needed, in our cultural unconscious "good mothers" will continue to be those whose class, race, and education enable them to hire the labor of poorer, less powerful women.

During the era between world wars, images of well-educated, beautiful women who, with blithe enthusiasm, devoted their whole intelligence and energy to making life comfortable dominated the culture. These images, however, in themselves somewhat illusory, hid the reality of exploitation of other women, less powerful and unable to create counterimages of their work and lives. These conditions are being replicated today, as a large group of service workers take over those tasks that better-off women can hire out. It is time to recognize the underside of the nation's domestic past and to build a future in which no work is hidden and no labor invisible.

Notes

Abbreviations

Bethune Museum–Archives National Archives for Black Women's History, Bethune Museum and Archives, Washington, D.C.

LC Library of Congress

NA RG National Archives, Record Group:
RG 9, National Recovery Administration (NRA)
RG 12, Office of Education
RG 69, Federal Emergency Relief Administration and Works Progress Administration (WPA)
RG 86, Women's Bureau
RG 119, National Youth Administration (NYA)
RG 257, Bureau of Labor Statistics

NAACP MSS National Association for the Advancement of Colored People MSS, Library of Congress

NCHE MSS National Committee on Household Employment MSS, Labor Management Documention Center, School of Industrial and Labor Relations, Cornell University, Ithaca, New York

NSPIE MSS National Society for the Promotion of Industrial Education MSS, Library of Congress

NWTUL MSS National Women's Trade Union League MSS, Arthur M. and Elizabeth Bancroft Schlesinger

Library and Archives for Women's History,
Radcliffe College, Cambridge, Massachusetts

Schlesinger Archives   Arthur M. and Elizabeth Bancroft Schlesinger
Library and Archives for Women's History,
Radcliffe College, Cambridge, Massachusetts

YWCA MSS   Young Women's Christian Association National
Board MSS, Sophia Smith Collection, Smith
College, Northampton, Massachusetts

YWCA National Board MSS   Archives, YWCA National Headquarters, 726
Broadway, New York City, New York 10003

One

1.   Socially, sexually, politically, and domestically, middle-class women inhabited a conservative environment after 1920. Nancy F. Cott's *The Grounding of Modern Feminism* (New Haven: Yale University Press, 1987) describes how vibrant, multi-focused pre–World War I feminism narrowed to demands for equal rights in the public sphere and educated women's entitlement to professional jobs. Women lost their sense of grievance as a group excluded from public life and were divided between speaking as a subordinated class and achieving as individuals. In Carroll Smith Rosenberg's *Disorderly Conduct: Visions of Gender in Victorian America* (New York: Oxford University Press, 1985), the concluding chapter, "The New Woman as Androgyne: Social Disorder and Gender Crisis, 1870–1936," depicts the conservatism of post-1920 attitudes toward the "New Woman," including even the sexual liberation that was supposed to result from women's winning equality in public life with suffrage; homosexuality was attacked as a psychological problem, and "Boston marriages" and lesbian relationships of the presuffrage years succumbed to the pressures to limit sexual experimentation within heterosexual bounds. Dolores Hayden, *The Grand Domestic Revolution: A History of Feminist Designs for American Homes, Neighborhoods, and Cities* (Cambridge, Mass.: MIT Press, 1981), shows (in chap. 13, "Madame Kollantai and Mrs. Consumer") how women gave up advocating cooperative kitchens for shared housework and accepted consumption of goods and services in private homes as symbolic opposition to Russian collectivism, denoted in this instance by Alexandra Kollantai, head of the women's division of the Soviet Central Committee Secretariat. J. Stanley Lemons, *The Woman Citizen: Social Feminism in the 1920s* (Urbana: University of Illinois Press, 1975), documents right-wing attacks on women's groups and feminism, which, in the wake of the Bolshevik Revolution, were seen as communistic. Women's organizations moderated their public stances accordingly.

2.   Hayden, in *The Grand Domestic Revolution*, recounts housewives' efforts to replace private domestic work ("Homes Without Kitchens and Towns Without Housework," chap. 11), or to attempt to find older women to relieve younger women from some child care and cooking for part-time professional employment ("Coordinating Women's Interests," chap. 12).

3.   Even though more married women were employed, they could not claim work

as a human right. Winifred D. Wandersee, *Women's Work and Family Values, 1920–1940* (Cambridge, Mass.: Harvard University Press, 1981), argues that "the growing flexibility in their tendency to work reflected changing attitudes toward family roles as well as an unshaken commitment to family responsibilities" (p. 3). Earning income for the family did not entitle a woman to slough off her job of taking care of home and children, even though she presumably bought many services to help with house care. Lois Scharf's *To Work and to Wed: Female Employment, Feminism, and the Great Depression*, Contributions in Women's Studies, 15 (Westport, Conn.: Greenwood Press, 1980) puts this story in perspective by showing how educated women enunciated aspirations to apply their training in professions outside the home during the 1920s but shifted their rationale for employment to family "need" during the Depression. Most married women of the middle class did not take paid work after marriage, but if they did, they apologized for not having time for their proper roles as charity workers and social leaders.

4. Karen Anderson, *Wartime Women: Sex Roles, Family Relations, and the Status of Women During World War II*, Contributions in Women's Studies, 20 (Westport, Conn.: Greenwood Press, 1981), documents the myriad responsibilities women had for maintaining civilian life when most resources were going to military activities and offers reasons why the war contributed to a postwar "feminine mystique": women's war work was countered by injunctions to be feminine; a shortage of men encouraged traditional feminine behavior and early marriages; women had to mediate amid material shortages and emotional hardships; and the war heightened images of men as warriors protecting domesticated women. D'Ann Campbell, *Women at War with America: Private Lives in a Patriotic Era* (Cambridge, Mass.: Harvard University Press, 1984), concludes in chapter 6, "Heroines of the Homefront," with the judgment that housewives "tried to make a warm home life in flimsy trailers, crowded apartments, and overpriced houses. They repaired, mended, and conserved. They stood in long lines, lugged home their purchases and children, and devised ways to keep their families clothed, healthy and well fed" (p. 185). Susan M. Hartmann, *The Home Front and Beyond: American Women in the 1940s* (Boston: Twayne, 1982), clarifies material circumstances as well as cultural messages that would encourage women to accept "intensified emphasis on home and family" (p. 25).

5. Ruth Schwartz Cowan, *More Work for Mother: The Ironies of Household Technology from the Open Hearth to the Microwave* (New York: Basic Books, 1983), and Susan Strasser, *Never Done: A History of American Housework* (New York: Pantheon, 1982), though with different political views on technology's impact, agree that its promise to shorten the housewife's workday was delusory.

6. Barbara Ehrenreich and Deirdre English, *For Her Own Good: 150 Years of the Experts' Advice to Women* (Garden City, N.Y.: Anchor Press/Doubleday, 1979), focus on medical experts and the shift from religious authorities' to scientists' and physicians' regulation of housework, child care, and women's lives.

7. Roland Marchand, *Advertising the American Dream: Making Way for Modernity, 1920–1940* (Berkeley and Los Angeles: University of California Press, 1985), in a section titled "Modern Maids and Atavistic Ambitions," assumes that even most middle-class and a large number of upper-middle-class households did not have regular servant help by the 1930s, even though (or perhaps as a consequence) advertisers displayed household products in settings "enriched . . . by dominion over attractive and attentive personal servants" (p. 205).

8.   See note 1 for post-1920 conservatism and feminism's self-limitation, especially
Cott's *Grounding of Modern Feminism.*

9.   Judith Rollins, *Between Women: Domestics and Their Employers* (Philadelphia: Temple University Press, 1985), chap. 5, "Deference and Maternalism."
Rollins's book was important for my clarification of the connection between systems
that define some women as "good" and "clean" and others as "dirty" and "bad" and
the maintenance of social relations of domination and subordination.

10.   Barbara Welter, "The Cult of True Womanhood, 1820–1860," in *Dimity Convictions: The American Woman in the Nineteenth Century* (Athens: Ohio University
Press, 1976), 21.

11.   Witold Rybczynski, *Home: A Short History of an Idea* (New York: Viking Penguin, 1986), esp. chap. 4, "Commodity and Delight," points up the oddity of speaking of "comfort as an idea," since we have learned to take it for granted as a physical
condition. The idea developed in northern Europe during the eighteenth century
and became one of the quintessential elements, along with privacy and domestic inti-
macy, of the bourgeois household.

12.   Faye E. Dudden, *Serving Women: Household Service in Nineteenth-Century
America* (Middletown, Conn.: Wesleyan University Press, 1983), argues that a shift
in nineteenth-century terminology for hired household workers from "help" to "servant" reflected basic changes in the work of the home and the role of the housewife.
The shift from task-oriented hiring, with the hired woman giving help on particular
jobs, to hiring a servant to take over the significant tasks of household work is the
major cultural–economic shift that preceded the mistress–servant relationship of the
1920s and 1930s. Her argument that housework has a history that she has recovered
for the nineteenth-century North and West of the United States, and that this history
is of differential experiences of privilege and oppression, offered encouragement for
my work about a later period. Likewise, her conclusion that domestic service enabled
the middle-class woman, freed from the need to earn income or to care for her own
house, to become a feminist and a leader in the social reform and social welfare move-
ments of the second half of the nineteenth century only because of the involuntary
support of the domestic echoes my disquiet about the unequal relations between employers and employees in the 1920s and 1930s.

13.   Catherine Clinton, *The Plantation Mistress: Woman's World in the Old South*
(New York: Pantheon, 1982), calls the plantation mistress the "slave of slaves" because of her heavy responsibilities to care for everyone, including slaves. Clinton is
describing production of clothing, medicines, and food, however, and not acts of service, which distinguish the servant's work from her mistress's.

14.   Daniel E. Sutherland, *Americans and Their Servants: Domestic Service in the
United States from 1800 to 1920* (Baton Rouge: Louisiana State University Press,
1981), argues that "the American experience with Negroes and immigrants . . .
firmly entrenched the social stigma [of domestic service]. Negroes supplied the most
odium" (p. 4). From the eighteenth century on, the connection between Negroes and
service meant that racial prejudice amplified disrespect for domestic work; in the
nineteenth century, xenophobia joined race prejudice to degrade immigrants entering domestic work.

15.   Helen Lefkowitz Horowitz, *Alma Mater: Design and Experience in the
Women's Colleges from Their Nineteenth-Century Beginnings to the 1930s* (New
York: Knopf, 1984), reports that Wellesley College ended student domestic work in
1896; Mount Holyoke College, where, in 1837, Mary Lyon had initiated the scheme

of students doing their own domestic work to keep down costs for women's higher education, followed shortly thereafter (p. 205).

16.   Elaine Tyler May, *Great Expectations: Marriage and Divorce in Post-Victorian America* (Chicago: University of Chicago Press, 1980), part 2, "Matrimony Unveiled in the Early Twentieth Century."

17.   Steven Mintz and Susan Kellogg, *Domestic Revolutions: A Social History of American Family Life* (New York: Free Press, 1988), in chap. 6, "The Rise of the Companionate Family, 1900–1930," note that *companionate marriage* was originally used by Denver Judge Ben B. Lindsay in *Revolt of Modern Youth* (1925) to refer to childless marriages contracted simply to legitimize sexual relations. By the mid-1920s, however, the term was already coming to mean "marriage unions held together not by rigid social pressures . . . but by mutual affection, sexual attraction, and equal rights" (p. 115). I use the term with this connotation.

18.   Clifford Edward Clark, Jr., *The American Family Home, 1800–1960* (Chapel Hill: University of North Carolina Press, 1986), chap. 5, "Modernizing the House and Family," recounts the Progressive-era shift to smaller homes, though they were built at a prodigious pace so that in some American cities roughly one-quarter to one-half of the population between 1880 and 1920 owned homes. Homes designed without quarters for live-in servants were not meant to require extra work from housewives. Ideally, simplifying tasks and reducing the amount of space to clean would offer housewives more freedom and greater opportunities for self-development in creative and social–political activities. The average number of persons per family declined from 4.6 in 1900 to 4.25 in 1920, 4.01 in 1930, and 3.67 in 1940, according to George J. Stigler, *Domestic Servants in the United States, 1900–1940,* Occasional Paper 24 (New York: National Bureau of Economic Research, 1946), 21, table 11.

19.   Bettina Berch, *The Endless Day: The Political Economy of Women and Work* (New York: Harcourt Brace Jovanovich, 1982). "The Leading 10 Occupations of Women Workers, 1870–1970," table 1-3, was compiled from U.S. Department of Labor, Bureau of the Census, and decennial census reports (pp. 12–13). "Participation in the Labor Force: 16 Years of Age and Older," table 1-1, was compiled from Employment and Training Report of the President, 1979, and the 1979–1980 Bureau of Labor Statistics Report, 611 (p. 5).

20.   Stigler, *Domestic Servants,* 2–3.

21.   Amey E. Watson, "Employer-Employee Relationships in the Home," *Annals of the American Academy of Political and Social Science* 143 (May 1929): 49–60, in a special issue titled "Women in the Modern World," gives the 5 percent figure.

22.   Using Stigler's family and servant totals in *Domestic Servants* yields slightly higher percentages, as follows:

	1900	1910	1920	1930	1940
Servants (1,000s), incl. laundry, trained nurses, cooks, other	1,509	1,867	1,484	2,025	2,098
Families (1,000s)	15,964	20,053	24,201	29,905	34,949
Servants: families	9.4%	9.3%	6.1%	6.8%	6.0%

Calculated from tables 1 and 11, pp. 3, 21. Stigler included practical nurses, though their occupation fell outside the usual definition of domestic servants, because the work was similar, and to offset his exclusion of "housekeeper," which he thought inaccurate because of enumerators listing as housekeepers women doing housework in their own homes. Appendix A, "The Number of Servants," explains numerous problems with obtaining a count of servants. Only in 1940 was there a category of "domestic servant," and this number had to be compared to various classifications used in earlier censuses. The ostensible decline in domestics in 1920 was ignored because it probably reflected an undercount resulting from the census's abandoning "the emphatic 1910 instruction to ascertain the occupation of every person" (p. 39).

23.   Cowan, *More Work for Mother,* 175, citing "Time Costs of Homemaking: A Study of 1,500 Rural and Urban Households," U.S. Department of Agriculture, Agricultural Research Administration, Bureau of Human Nutrition and Home Economics (mimeographed, 1944), and *Household Management and Kitchens,* Report of the President's Conference on Home Building and Home Ownership, vol. 9 (Washington, D.C., 1932). Cowan considers these numbers low by contrast with previous decades. I interpret them as high by contrast with succeeding decades.

24.   Anne Byrd Kennon, "College Wives Who Work," *Journal of the American Association of University Women,* 20 (June 1927):100–106, and Virginia MacMakin Collier, *Marriages and Careers: A Study of One Hundred Women Who Are Wives, Mothers, Homemakers and Professional Workers* (New York: Bureau of Vocational Information, 1926), both cited in Cott, *Grounding of Modern Feminism.* Well over half of these college-educated, middle-class, employed women were not doing the bulk of their housework, even though they accepted an image of themselves as homemakers.

25.   Campbell, *Women at War,* 284, n. 16. citing Roper-*Fortune* poll, October 1937, in Hadley Cantril and Mildred Strunk, *Public Opinion, 1935–1946* (Princeton: Princeton University Press, 1951), 791.

26.   Maurice Leven, Harold G. Moulton, and Clark Warburton, *America's Capacity to Consume* (Washington, D.C.: Brookings Institution, 1934), 58–62, 222, table 36. Appendix A, VI, "Incomes of Families," explains that the Brookings economists calculated household income as an extrapolation from rents paid because rent and not household income was reported on the 1930 census. Appendix B, "The Utilization of Income," I, lists the categories for a number of cost-of-living studies conducted between 1924 and 1934. A 1929 study of the expenditures of federal employees includes "servant hire" under "home maintenance." A 1932 study of maintenance-of-way road workers had no mention of servant hire (p. 241). The questionnaire's design indicated what surveyers expected to find in houses of different classes: servants for upper-level clerks but not for manual laborers.

27.   Stigler, *Domestic Servants,* 30, 24, 26, 36.

28.   Bureau of Labor Statistics, "Family Disbursements of Wage Earners and Salaried Workers, 1934–1936," NA RG 257, contains many consumer and cost-of-living surveys, the major nationwide ones in addition to the 1934–1936 Family Disbursements survey being the 1918–1919 "Cost of Living Schedules for Urban Families" and the 1935–1937 "Study of Consumer Purchases." After consultation with Jerry Hess of the National Archives and Erik W. Austin, who is directing computerization of the 1935–1937 data for the Inter-University Consortium for Political and Social Research, I decided to draw a sample from the 1934–1936 survey. The 1934 data are easier to use because household demography and expenses are on the same interview schedule, whereas the 1935 schedules are filed separately from the demographic data, and its class limitations were not expanded in the 1935 data. Although only

middle-income earners were sampled in the 1934 study, many of the wealthy included in the 1935–1937 sample refused to cooperate with interviewers, whom, according to Erik Austin, they viewed as hirelings of the New Deal. The 1934 study overrepresents workers with stable jobs in good-sized firms. Major employers in the cities surveyed were asked to supply a list of regularly employed workers, and from this list the Bureau of Labor Statistics drew its sample for collecting wage and expenditure data. I relied on Lorna Forster, a George Washington University doctoral candidate in sociology, for sampling techniques and data analysis; on Jennifer Watson, George Washington University Master's candidate in women's studies, for data collection and entry; and on my patient colleague Joe Gastwirth, professor of statistics, for sensible and inventive advice as to how to interpret findings. A chi-square statistic was used to analyze nominal-level data, and a Pearson's product moment correlation coefficient to analyze interval-level data to determine significant variables, which were then used in a logistic regression model of the factors involved in hiring laundry or domestic work. The data are available in a file at the George Washington University Academic Computing Center.

29.   Maurice Leven, *The Income Structure of the United States* (Washington, D.C.: Brookings Institution, 1938), 145, table 1, citing Leven, Moulton, and Warburton, *America's Capacity to Consume.*

30.   Thanks to the astute advice of my colleague James O. Horton, Departments of History and American Studies, we assigned a different identifying number to each occupation, instead of categorizing and clustering them. The result of almost nine hundred occupations for workers in sixteen hundred households provides a rich picture of wage earning in the 1930s and makes more striking the cluster of occupations that emerged as those of families likely to hire laundry work and a slightly different profile of those hiring domestic service.

31.   Sophonisba P. Breckenridge, *Women in the Twentieth Century: A Study of Their Political, Social and Economic Activities* (New York: McGraw-Hill, 1933), 126.

32.   Allyson Sherman Grossman, "Women in Domestic Work: Yesterday and Today," *Monthly Labor Review*, August 1980, pp. 17–21, table 1, p. 18. Grossman relies on Alba Edwards's *Sixteenth Census of the United States: 1940, Population Comparative Occupation Statistics for the United States, 1870–1940* (Washington, D.C.: U.S. Bureau of the Census, 1943) and does not seem to distinguish between "domestic and personal service" and "domestic work, private household." The numbers from which she calculates percentages are lower than those cited by Stigler, *Domestic Servants,* and she does not seem to be aware of the probable undercount in the 1920 census, which is analyzed at length by Stigler. Despite these problems, one can still assert that the occupation remained significant for women wage earners.

33.   David M. Katzman, *Seven Days a Week: Women and Domestic Service in Industrializing America* (1978; rpt. Urbana: University of Illinois Press, 1981), 292, table A-11.

34.   Mary Romero, "Sisterhood and Domestic Service: Race, Class and Gender in the Mistress/Maid Relationship," paper presented at the 1987 Society for the Study of Social Problems meeting in Chicago, cites Albert Camarillo, *Chicanos in a Changing Society* (Cambridge, Mass.: Harvard University Press, 1979), and Mario Barrera, *Race and Class in the Southwest: A Theory of Racial Inequality* (South Bend: University of Notre Dame Press, 1980). Sarah Deutsch, "Women and Intercultural Relations: The Case of Hispanic New Mexico and Colorado," *Signs* 12 (Summer 1987),

also citing Barrera, states that in the 1930 census, "41.6 percent of gainfully employed 'Mexicans' were listed under domestic service" (p. 734, n. 50). I am indebted to Mary Romero for sharing her papers with me and for helping to fill a significant gap in my East-Coast-biased data.

35.   Evelyn Nakano Glenn, *Issei, Nisei, War Bride: Three Generations of Japanese American Women in Domestic Service* (Philadelphia: Temple University Press, 1986), 72–73, table 2. Domestic employment varied directly in relation to the availability of alternative jobs. Glenn points out that 50 percent of Issei women in San Francisco were in domestic work, but only 6.4 percent in Los Angeles and 3.3 percent in Seattle, which she attributes to opportunities for small entrepreneurs in Seattle, at least (p. 77, table 3).

36.   Breckenridge, *Women in the Twentieth Century*, 114, table 6.

37.   Mary Elizabeth Pidgeon, *Changes in Women's Employment During the War*, Women's Bureau Special Bulletin 20 (Washington, D.C.: U.S. Government Printing Office, 1944), cited in Hartmann, *Home Front and Beyond*, 86.

38.   "War and Post-War Trends in Employment of Negroes," *Monthly Labor Review* 60 (January 1945): 3, cited in Hartmann, *Home Front and Beyond*, 90.

39.   E. P. Thompson, *The Making of the English Working Class* (New York: Vintage Books, 1963), brought the relational concept inherent in Marxian theory into widespread use by American historians. I agree with Thompson's statement in the preface: "The notion of class entails the notion of historical relationship. Like any other relationship, it is a fluency which evades analysis if we attempt to stop it dead at any given moment and anatomise its structure. . . . We cannot have two distinct classes, each with an independent being, and then bring them *into* relationship with each other. . . . Class happens when some men, as a result of common experiences (inherited or shared), feel and articulate the identity of their interests as between themselves, and as against other men whose interests are different from (and usually opposed to) theirs. The class experience is largely determined by the productive relations into which men are born" (p. 9). Domestic work, I am assuming, is one of the productive relations that characterizes women's experience of class relations.

40.   I had investigated racial differences in the construction of gender in Phyllis Marynick Palmer. "White Women/Black Women: The Dualism of Female Identity and Experience in the United States," *Feminist Studies* 9 (Spring 1983): 151–70. My goal was to understand how white women defined themselves *in relation to* black women. I did not clarify that whiteness is a racial category that needs study and explanation as much as blackness until I read, in Gisela Bock's "Racism and Sexism in Nazi Germany: Motherhood, Compulsory Sterilization, and the State," *Signs* 8 (Spring 1983): 400–421, about how "Nazi pronatalism for 'desirable' births and its antinatalism for 'undesirable' ones were tightly connected." Racism and sexism intertwined to define which women were good and what their social duties were. Good women learned to bear children, to maintain houses, and to accept economic dependency "not so much from the continuous positive propaganda about 'valuable motherhood,' but precisely from the opposite: the negative propaganda that barred unwelcome, poor, and deviant women from procreation and marriage" (p. 419). I was trained out of thinking of dualisms as innate or inevitable by Jane Flax, whose early statement about the historically shifting nature of social categories in "Postmodernism and Gender Relations in Feminist Theory," *Signs* 12 (Summer 1987): 621–43, has been expanded in her book, *Thinking Fragments: Psychoanalysis, Feminism, and Post-Modernism in the Contemporary West* (Berkeley and Los Angeles: University

of California Press, 1989). A classic statement of how gender, race, and class were socially created in the Reconstruction South and maintained in the early twentieth-century New South is Lillian Smith, *Killers of the Dream* (New York: Norton, 1964). Many Afro-American scholars in literature and history now call for "racializing" thinking about white women, notably Hazel Carby at the session on "Working from the Margin; Displacing the Center: The Politics of Our Scholarship," at the American Studies Association Conference, Miami Beach, Florida, October 1988.

Two

1.   I use the acronym MCH for middle-class housewives in imitation of Christopher Morley's invention of WCG in the novel *Kitty Foyle*. WCG stands for "White-Collar Girl," the ubiquitous unmarried young woman of the 1930s making her independent way in a clerical or sales job, the undesirable alternative to being an MCH.

2.   Elaine Tyler May, *Great Expectations: Marriage and Divorce in Post-Victorian America* (Chicago: University of Chicago Press, 1980), 158.

3.   Glenna Matthews, *"Just a Housewife": The Rise and Fall of Domesticity in America* (New York: Oxford University Press, 1987), 193–94. Matthews answers the question of why women consented to the deskilling of the home and loss of self-respecting housewifery by saying that women resisted commodification by, for instance, baking their own bread long after commercial bakeries made doing so unnecessary. This is, as she says, only a partial answer.

4.   Barbara Welter, "The Cult of True Womanhood: 1820–1860," in *Dimity Convictions: The American Woman in the Nineteenth Century* (Athens: Ohio University Press, 1976), 21. According to Welter, through the four virtues of womanhood, "piety, purity, domesticity and obedience," women countered the masculine business practices of cutthroat competition. Women's self-restraint enabled the United States to accept economic development grounded in principles at odds with religious beliefs and community norms of charity. Though the 1920s and 1930s offer a considerably more complex trade-off between masculine values in the marketplace and feminine values in the home, women's acceptance of housewifely duties was essential to the revolutionary transition from a production economy built on moral values of self-denial and saving to a consumption economy built on values of self-fulfillment through spending. The realization that these periods were not so contradictory as they have seemed grew as I read Daniel Horowitz's provocative study, *The Morality of Spending: Attitudes Toward the Consumer Society in America, 1875–1940* (Baltimore: Johns Hopkins University Press, 1985), which concludes that "the differences between traditional and modern moralism are fundamental but there are also important similarities" (p. 166). Twentieth-century commentators on standards of living feared that the middle class sought "transitory happiness" through consumption rather than intellectual and aesthetic cultivation, just as nineteenth-century commentators feared the working class's intemperance, social rowdiness, and pursuit of leisure.

5.   Phyllis Rose, *Parallel Lives: Five Victorian Marriages* (London: Chatto & Windus, 1983), 5–6, 16.

6.   Anna Garlin Spencer, *The Family and Its Members* (Philadelphia: Lippincott Family Life Series, 1923), 43. Spencer was a special lecturer in social science at

Teachers College of Columbia University, where she met Benjamin Andrews, the editor of the Lippincott series.

7. Ernest R. Groves and Gladys Hoagland Groves, *Wholesome Marriage* (Boston: Houghton Mifflin, 1927), 140. Ernest R. Groves, professor of social science at the University of North Carolina, is described by Christopher Lasch in *Haven in a Heartless World: The Family Besieged* (New York: Basic Books, 1977) as "one of the leading advocates of training for marriage" (p. 37).

8. Sinclair Lewis, *Main Street* (1920; rpt. New York: Signet Classics, 1961), 33.

9. Ibid., 432. Marcus Cunliffe, *The Literature of the United States*, 4th ed. (New York: Viking Penguin, 1986), points out how unusual Lewis's ending is, having his heroine choose the ridiculed small town, "a solution he can make plausible only by suggesting that, after all, her husband is a sturdy, honest person, while Carol has been weak and self-centered" (p. 330). Her foray into the larger world has taught her how to be stronger and more resolute in the effort to cultivate Gopher Prairie, a moral many women must have found apropos.

10. Lewis, *Main Street*, 422–23.

11. Nancy F. Cott, *The Grounding of Modern Feminism* (New Haven: Yale University Press, 1987). Chapter 5, "Modern Times," concludes that in marriage advice literature of the 1920s "feminist intents and rhetoric were not ignored but appropriated" (p. 174).

12. Anna M. Galbraith, *The Family and the New Democracy: A Study in Social Hygiene* (Philadelphia: Saunders, 1920), 315.

13. Mildred Weigley Woods, Ruth Lindquist, and Lucy Studley, *Managing the Home* (Boston: Houghton Mifflin, 1932), 9. Woods was director of adult education in homemaking, Phoenix, Arizona, Lindquist was associate professor of home economics at Ohio State University, and Studley was assistant professor of home economics at the University of Minnesota.

14. Mary Hinman Abel, *Successful Family Life on the Moderate Income*, 2d ed. (Philadelphia: Lippincott, Family Life Series, 1927), 22.

15. Henrietta Ripperger, *A Home of Your Own and How to Run It* (New York: Simon and Schuster, 1940), xviii.

16. Woods, Lindquist, and Studley, *Managing the Home*, 10.

17. Kathy Peiss's *Cheap Amusements: Working Women and Leisure in Turn-of-the-Century New York* (Philadelphia: Temple University Press, 1986) provides interesting data about working women's support for the developing urban, commercial, nonfamily entertainments of movies, dance halls, and amusement parks. Horowitz, *Morality of Spending*, chap. 8, recounts how professional families chose to spend relatively more money on household space and home-based entertainments such as reading magazines and giving dinner parties compared to working-class families of the same era, who spent more of their income on movies.

18. Ida Bailey Allen, *Home Partners, or Seeing the Family Through* (N.p.: Privately printed, 1924), 12–15. Mrs. Allen was the author of cookbooks and, during the 1920s, presented Monday morning chats about cooking with Crisco on a Radio Homemakers Club sponsored by Proctor and Gamble, according to Alfred Lief in "*It Floats*": The Story of Proctor and Gamble* (New York: Rinehart & Co., 1958), 152.

19. Kathleen Norris, *Barberry Bush* (Garden City, N.Y.: Doubleday, Page, 1927), 55.

20. Ibid., 123–24.

21. Ibid., 298.

22.   Horowitz, *Morality of Spending*, 141–43, describing Jessica Peixotto's 1923 study of faculty households at the University of California, Berkeley, published in 1927 as *Getting and Spending at the Professional Standard of Living.*

23.   *French's Cream Salad Mustard Makes Salads, Salad Dressings, Sandwiches, Savories* (Rochester: R. T. French Company, 1925) offered recipes selected and tested by M. Jean Marie Bernillon, chef at the Ritz-Carlton in Philadelphia. *Everyday Recipes* (New Orleans: Wesson Oil People, 1929) has main dishes identified as "tea room style." I am indebted for these examples of companies' recipe-advertisement booklets to my George Washington University English Department colleague and sister scholar of American domestic life, Ann Romines.

24.   Bertha Streeter, *Home Making Simplified: A Book for the Bride as Well as for the Experienced Housekeeper Who Is Still Confronted with Unsolved Problems* (New York: Harper & Brothers, 1922), 215–16.

25.   Galbraith, *Family and the New Democracy*, 302.

26.   Ripperger, *A Home of Your Own and How to Run It*, xv.

27.   Woods, Lindquist, and Studley, *Managing the Home*, 1.

28.   Della Thompson Lutes, *A Home of Your Own* (Indianapolis: Bobbs-Merrill, 1925), 330.

29.   Hazel Kyrk, *Economic Problems of the Family* (New York: Harper & Brothers, 1933), 85, citing Jessica B. Peixotto, *Getting and Spending at the Professional Standard of Living* (New York, 1927), and Yandell Henderson and Maurice R. Davie, *Incomes and Living Costs of a University Faculty* (New Haven: Yale University Press, 1928).

30.   Christine Frederick, *The Ignoramus Book of Housekeeping* (New York: Sears, 1932), 6.

31.   Charlotte Adams, *The Run of the House* (New York: Macmillan, 1942), 15–16. Adams's discussion of the "brave" young wife echoes military language and implies that the young wife keeping up appearances compares to the young man going off to war—surely an unintentional comparison written before the United States entry into World War II.

32.   Emily Newall Blair, *The Creation of a Home: A Mother Advises a Daughter* (New York: Farrar & Rinehart, 1930), 2. Blair was vice-chairman of the Democratic National Committee from 1921 to 1928 and president of the Woman's National Democratic Club. One assumes that she perceived giving household advice as a plus for her political career.

33.   Fannie Hurst, *Lummox* (New York: Harper & Brothers, 1923). My thanks to talented assessor of American women writers and friend Michele Slung for telling me to read this novel. Hurst delivered a talk titled "The Lady of the House," which called on housewives to honor their servants' merit with fair treatment and wages, at a symposium on household employment, sponsored by the YWCA and the Federal Council of Churches, in New York City, November 28, 1939 (YWCA MSS, Reel 98).

34.   Lutes, *A Home of Your Own*, 44.

35.   Lewis, *Main Street*, 167.

36.   Galbraith, *The Family and the New Democracy*, 300.

37.   Streeter, *Home Making Simplified*, 29–30.

38.   Samuel S. Paquin, ed., *Her Book: A Treasure of Household Lore* (New York: R. M. Travis Corporation, 1932), 203.

39.   Florence LaGanke Harris, *Everywoman's Complete Guide to Homemaking* (Boston: Little, Brown, 1936), 129.

40.   Wood, Lindquist, and Studley, *Managing the Home*, 8.

41.   Lillian M. Gilbreth, *The Home-Maker and Her Job* (New York: D. Appleton, 1927), 15.

42.   Lutes, *A Home of Your Own*, 376–77.

43.   Enid Wells, *Living for Two: A Guide to Homemaking* (New York: David Kemp, 1939), 401.

44.   Lita Price and Harriet Bonnet, *How to Manage Without a Maid* (Indianapolis: Bobbs-Merrill, 1942), 75.

45.   Fannie Hurst, *Imitation of Life* (New York: Harper & Brothers, 1933), 152.

46.   Vesta J. Farnsworth, *The Real Home* (Mountain View, Calif.: Pacific Press Publishing Association, 1923), 82.

47.   Cott, *Grounding of Modern Feminism*, 165–66.

48.   Elizabeth Bussing, "Marriage Makes the Money Go," in *The Good Housekeeping Marriage Book: Twelve Ways to a Happy Marriage* (New York: Prentice-Hall, 1938), 77.

49.   Lewis, *Main Street*, 381.

50.   Streeter, *Home Making Simplified*, 21–23.

51.   Helen Mougey Jordan, M. Louisa Ziller, and John Franklin Brown, *Home and Family* (New York: Macmillan, 1935), 188–89.

52.   Lutes, *A Home of Your Own*, 333.

53.   Ripperger, *A Home of Your Own and How to Run It*, 117. The drawing of the elegantly clad housewife at work contrasts strikingly with line drawings of servants, who are shown as old and fat, implying that a housewife looks very different from a servant even though both may do the same work.

54.   Gilbreth, *Home-Maker and Her Job*, 12.

55.   Susan Glaspell, *Ambrose Holt and Family* (New York: Frederick A. Stokes, 1931), 314–15. Blossom begins to confront her differences with her wealthy and beloved father when her husband Lincoln tells her of his sadness that Atwood is cutting down a woods in which Lincoln had made penny whistles and daydreamed during his childhood. Lincoln respects his father-in-law's business acumen and accepts the argument of business necessity at the same time as he despises its consequences. Blossom, however, is ready to fight: "Perhaps I know nothing about business, but I know something about woods." Though she does not save the woods, Blossom conserves and links love of nature, poetry, life, and family as domestic values; a woman's love can make up for environmental depredations.

56.   Ibid., 16.

57.   Ibid., 10.

58.   Christopher Morley, *Kitty Foyle* (New York: Grosset & Dunlap, 1939), 336–39.

59.   Simone de Beauvoir's *The Second Sex* (1952; rpt. New York: Vintage Books, 1974) captures the quality of male desire for care by an independent woman, a woman, as de Beauvoir says, "who freely accepts [man's] domination, who does not accept his ideas without discussion, but who yields to his arguments, who resists him intelligently and ends by being convinced" (p. 208). Even though nature seems disquieting (with its threats of deaths and the end of immanence), "it becomes beneficial when woman, too docile to threaten man's works, limits herself to enriching them and softening their too rugged outlines" (p. 204). De Beauvoir is describing this concept as timeless, which it may be, but I have found it a particularly evident attitude in the popular culture of the 1930s and 1940s.

60. Harris, *Everywoman's Complete Guide*, 281.
61. Paquin, ed., *Her Book*, 213.
62. Cott, *Grounding of Modern Feminism*, 157.
63. Hurst, *Lummox*, 15.
64. Groves and Groves, *Wholesome Marriage*, 141–42.
65. Beth L. Bailey, *From Front Porch to Back Seat: Courtship in Twentieth-Century America* (Baltimore: Johns Hopkins University Press, 1988), esp. chap. 4 and 5, "The Worth of a Date" and "Sex Control."
66. Ibid., 81, quoting Gay Head, "Boy Dates Girl Jam Session," *Senior Scholastic*, December 1943, p. 45.
67. Bailey, *From Front Porch to Back Seat*, 90.
68. Anne Fisher, *Live with a Man and Love It!* (New York: Dodd, Mead, 1937), 17.
69. Wells, *Living for Two*, 404–5.
70. Morley, *Kitty Foyle*, 18.

Three

1. Hilary Rose, "Hand, Brain, and Heart: A Feminist Epistemology for the Natural Sciences," *Signs* 9 (Autumn 1983): 73–90, provides an excellent analysis of the difference between industrial and service production: "The production of people is . . . qualitatively different from the production of things. It requires caring labor— the labor of love" (p. 83).
2. Laura Shapiro, *Perfection Salad: Women and Cooking at the Turn of the Century* (New York: Farrar, Straus and Giroux, 1986), makes the point that "one of the chief differences between housekeeping and homemaking was that, in the course of the latter, women were free to acknowledge that drudgery was drudgery. . . . Once housework had been recognized as neither a science nor a mission, but simply an unalterable element of woman's fate, other aspects of domesticity ballooned" (p. 225).
3. Alfred D. Chandler, Jr., *The Visible Hand: Managerial Revolution in American Business* (Cambridge, Mass.: Belknap Press of Harvard University Press, 1977), 469–76.
4. Glenna Matthews, *"Just a Housewife": The Rise and Fall of Domesticity in America* (New York: Oxford University Press, 1987), describes Carol Kennicott's envy of her former maid Bea Sorenson, happily occupied in caring for her husband, child, and home. As Matthews says, "[Sinclair] Lewis seems to indicate that domesticity would not be so obnoxious were it coupled with sexual symmetry" (p. 177).
5. Robert S. Lynd and Helen Merrill Lynd, *Middletown: A Study in Contemporary American Culture* (New York: Harcourt, Brace, 1929), used the term *business class* to describe the men who earn a living by working with people, working with their tongues, selling or promoting things and ideas, and using nonmaterial institutional devices; the class also includes professionals not in business. This group contrasts with working-class households in which livings are earned by working with things, working with hands, making things, and using material tools (p. 22). By 1925, when the Lynds conducted their survey, they found that working-class households in Muncie, Indiana, accepted that a wife might work at some times; the rest of her activity was to be spent on housework. For a business-class wife, taking a paid job shamed her husband; she was not, however, to drudge at housework so as to have no time for charitable work and evening social life. I have used the term *businessman's*

wife in the same spirit as the Lynds, because it captures the social norms for the class of women most likely to want freedom from housework but without the income to hire full-time, live-in servants—that large, influential social group between the wealthy and the working class. When the Lynds returned to Muncie (Middletown) in 1935, they found that more business-class wives were holding paid jobs even as norms for filling up time without paid employment had strengthened. See *Middletown in Transition: A Study in Cultural Conflicts* (New York: Harcourt, Brace, 1937), 180–86.

6.   Theodora Penny Martin, *The Sound of Their Own Voices* (Boston: Beacon Press, 1987).

7.   Charlotte Adams, *The Run of the House* (New York: Macmillan, 1942), 17.

8.   Dorothy Dinnerstein, *The Mermaid and the Minotaur: Sexual Arrangements and Human Malaise* (New York: Harper Colophon Books, 1976), offers the clearest explication of how the unconscious minds of men and women in the twentieth-century West link infantile experiences of boundless care with feelings that adult women should give such care. At the same time, these caregivers are linked with infantile feelings of powerlessness against the mother's removal of care, punishment, or simply limitation of giving. Consequently, the desire for service from adult women coexists with a desire for these women to have less power than the person being served. Dinnerstein speculates that women have less need to be served because, as females, they identify with the maternal figures of their infancy and experience vicarious gratification from the service they give to men and children. This psychoanalytic view of domestic work is developed more fully in Chapter Seven below.

9.   "The Servant Problem," *Fortune* 77 (March 1938): 81–85, 114–18. This article is the source for the following paragraphs.

10.   The *Fortune* story illustrates the mediating function of the home, in which consumerist fantasies of infant pleasure are transformed into realistic experiences, at least for high-income husbands and, to a lesser degree, their children. Would consumption be so intoxicating if the service element were removed? Did post–World War II men scramble for consumerist satisfactions, as recounted in Barbara Ehrenreich's *The Hearts of Men: American Dreams and the Flight from Commitment* (Garden City, N.Y.: Anchor Books, 1983), because the level of household service was dropping and they were searching for compensatory satisfactions?

11.   Records of the Cambridge mothers' clubs are in the Schlesinger Archives. Similar records presumably could be found in other cities. Four generations of clubs are documented in the Schlesinger collections: Mothers' Club of Cambridge, 1881–1942; Mothers' Discussion Club, 1889–1973; Mothers' Study Club, 1911–1962; and Mothers' Thursday Club, 1920–1968. See "Written and read to the Mothers Discussion Club on the occasion of the Golden Anniversary, Dec. 6, 1949, by Frances H. Elliot," typescript, Mothers' Discussion Club, Box 2, Folder 13; "Some Subjects That Have Interested Mothers' Clubs, 1878–1940," typescript, Mothers' Study Club, Box 1, Folder 9; "Winfred Whiting paper at 30th Anniversary of the Mothers Study Club, Dec. '44," typescript, Box 1, Folder 6; typescript of talk "given at a Mothers Club Meeting, January 26, 1931," no author, Box 1, Folder 5; and diary of club meetings, Mothers' Thursday Club, vol. 2, p. 15.

12.   Ethel P. Howes, Foreword, in Esther H. Stocks, *A Community Home Assistants Experiment* (Northampton, Mass.: Smith College, 1928).

13.   Mothers' Thursday Club, vol. 2, p. 15, n.d., Schlesinger Archives.

14. Agnes Durham, "The Educational Work [in home economics]," n.d., typescript, Bureau of Vocational Information (1919–1926), Box 7, Folder 115, Schlesinger Archives.

15. My account of the feelings of middle-class wives is drawn from letters to the Roosevelts and to the Women's Bureau, questionnaire responses to YWCA surveys, magazine surveys, Women's Bureau studies, and published accounts of housewives' meetings. Letters to the Women's Bureau are quoted in this and the succeeding chapter and identified in the text by place and date of correspondence. These letters are from NA RG 86, Box 923, Correspondence Household (Domestic), 1943–1947; Box 924, Correspondence Household (Domestic), 1941; Box 925, Correspondence Household (Domestic), 1936–1940; and Box 926, Correspondence Household (Domestic), 1933–1935. Popular articles collected in the files of the YWCA, National Committee on Household Employment, and Women's Bureau indicate journalistic notions of what housewives were thinking or wanted to read. Advice books on how to do housework were produced by educated middle-class women and often made the point that the writer was recounting her own experiences. I have used this prescriptive material cautiously.

16. Benjamin R. Andrews, *Economics of the Household: Its Administration and Finance* (New York: Macmillan, 1923), 412.

17. Adams, *Run of the House*, 32–34.

18. Christine Frederick, *Household Engineering: Scientific Management in the Home* (Chicago: American School of Home Economics, 1920), 391.

19. Elizabeth Ross Haynes, "Negroes in Domestic Service in the United States," *Journal of Negro History* 8 (October 1923): 431, cites an Indianapolis, Indiana, survey of 1922, which showed that 91.6 percent of households hiring domestic workers had electric irons.

20. Dorothy P. Wells and Carol Biba, eds., *Fair and Clear in the Home* (New York: Women's Press, 1936), 42, describe a home that had been observed and reported as a model among YWCA housewives who employed servants.

21. Lydia Ray Balderston, from whose book, *"Housewifery": A Textbook of Practical Housekeeping* 5th ed. (Chicago: Lippincott, 1936), Figure 1 was adapted, was identified as a former instructor in Housewifery and Laundering at Teachers College, Columbia University. Her book was regularly recommended for courses and in bibliographies, as its numerous editions suggest.

22. Marion Hurst, *Household Employees Handbook* (Oklahoma City: Dewing Publishing Company, 1939), 22. This text was recommended in Women's Bureau publications and other bibliographies for its clear and detailed instructions.

23. Adams, *Run of the House*, 23.

24. Edith M. Barber, *Speaking of Servants: How to Hire, Train and Manage Household Employees* (New York: McGraw-Hill, 1940), 91.

25. Allison Gordon, *What Shall We Do About Household Employment?* (Washington, D.C.: American Association of University Women, 1940), Appendix I.

26. Instructions for stain removal and thorough cleaning abound. This particular list comes from "Detailed Unit Plans for a Course in Household Service," Kansas State College Department of Education, Summer 1938, NCHE MSS, Box 4.

27. Andrews, *Economics of the Household* (1923), 441–47, reported on a 1917 survey of commercial laundries by the New York City Department of Public Health. Andrews concluded that "the absence in the average steam laundry of proper sorting

rooms for the clean linen and the consequent contact with soiled linen may result in a possible reinfection of the clean clothes." Guarding her home against contact with external pollution was a major part of the housewife's job.

28.   O. E. Schoeffler and William Gale, *Esquire's Encyclopedia of 20th Century Men's Fashions* (New York: McGraw-Hill, 1973), 198–202. The authors connected the nineteenth-century invention of the detached collar with women's housework. "A Mrs. Hannah Montague of Troy, New York," they said, "is credited with creating the detached collar, which . . . was 'to hold the world by the neck for one brief, shining century.' Legend has it that one day in 1820, to reduce the drudgery of producing a fresh shirt every day for her blacksmith husband, Mrs. Montague simply snipped off the collar and washed it. Thus was born the first detachable collar" (p. 199). I thank Shay Cunliffe for directing me to this valuable source.

29.   This laundry routine is a composite drawn from Jean Littlejohn Aaberg, *Don't Phone Mother* (Philadelphia: Penn Publishing Company, 1940), 33–35, and Hurst, *Household Employees Handbook*, 102–6.

30.   Aaberg, *Don't Phone Mother*, 33.

31.   Ibid., 36, 37.

32.   Adams, *Run of the House*, 60.

33.   Harvey Levenstein, *Revolution at the Table: The Transformation of the American Diet* (New York: Oxford University Press, 1988), describes the development of new nutrition by home economists working in food laboratories and then the addition of the newer nutrition, which was spawned by commercial companies seeking to sell products infused with newly discovered "protective" vitamins and minerals to prevent illness. Andrews, *Economics of the Household* (1923), concluded, on the basis of collegiate laboratory experiments, that "the work connected with food preparation (exclusive of time at table) [is] the largest single task in housekeeping" (p. 403). By food preparation, he means preparing food, setting the table, and washing dishes after the meals.

34.   Hazel Young, *The Working Girl Must Eat* (Boston: Little, Brown, 1944). This is the eighth printing of a recipe book originally published in 1938. My English Department colleagues Gail Paster, Judith Plotz, and Ann Romines spotted the imperative in the phrase "preparations for the future," which appears in every day's dinner plan.

35.   Helen Drusilla Lockwood, Professor of Literature, Vassar College, "A Democratic Concept of Household Employment," delivered at Symposium on Household Employment, November 28, 1939, p. 20, YWCA National Board MSS, Reel 98.

36.   "The Time It Takes to Keep House: A Thursdays-off-and-on Time Project for Employers," *Woman's Press* 34 (January 1940): 20.

37.   Benjamin R. Andrews, *Economics of the Household: Its Administration and Finance*, rev. ed. (New York: Macmillan, 1935), 297.

38.   "All in the Family," *Woman's Press* 22 (February 1928): 82–85, quote on p. 84.

39.   Frederick, *Household Engineering*, 396–97.

40.   Hurst, *Household Employees Handbook*, 60–61. Numerous books taught appropriate serving. Lucy G. Allen's *Table Service* (Boston: Little, Brown, 1937) was first printed in 1915, with second and third editions in 1924 and 1933. By 1937 the book had gone through five printings.

41.   B. Eleanor Johnson, *Household Employment in Chicago*, Women's Bureau Bulletin 106 (Washington, D.C.: U.S. Department of Labor, 1933), 22. Sally Buck

(Mrs. Paul H. Buck), "Concerning the Early Days of Cambridge Home Information Center," n.d., typescript, Cambridge Home Information Center MSS, Box 1, Folder 1, Schlesinger Archives, describes the organization's formation during World War I to plan food conservation activities, which led to canning projects and "the first successful demand for labeling of ingredients in canned goods."

42.   Alice Bradley, *Electric Refrigerator Menus and Recipes* (Cleveland: General Electric Company, 1927), was dedicated to "the Modern American Homemaker" and tells how "not only fresh food supplies but left-overs are kept from spoiling" (p. 11) Bradley is identified as "Principal of Miss Farmer's School of Cookery" and "Cooking Editor of Woman's Home Companion." Levenstein, *Revolution at the Table*, 156; his chapters 12 and 13 are good on the proliferation of canned and frozen products.

43.   Young, *The Working Girl Must Eat*, 22.

44.   Bradley, *Electric Refrigerator Menus*, 57–59, for cold soups and aspic jelly, and 97–100, for "Twenty-Seven Flavors for Frozen Desserts."

45.   Lita Price and Harriet Bonnet, *How to Manage Without a Maid* (Indianapolis: Bobbs-Merrill, 1942), 77.

46.   Frederick, *Household Engineering*, 396. Frederick considered a servantless house one without a live-in, full-time servant.

47.   Andrews, *Economics of the Household* (1935), 442, citing data collected by the Bureau of Home Economics, U.S. Department of Agriculture, which were presented in *Household Management and Kitchens*, vol. 9 (Washington, D.C.: President's Conference on Home Building and Home Ownership, 1932), 27–28, 36.

48.   Johnson, *Household Employment in Chicago*, 21.

49.   Amey E. Watson, *Household Employment in Philadelphia*, Women's Bureau Bulletin 93 (Washington, D.C.: U.S. Department of Labor, 1932).

50.   Levenstein, *Revolution at the Table*, 162.

51.   Shapiro, *Perfection Salad*, concludes that by the 1930s "cookery could be seen, in the light of technology, as a brief and impersonal relation with food. And food itself could be understood as a simple necessity, one that ought to be manipulated and brought under control as quickly and neatly as bodily functions were handled by modern plumbing" (p. 228). As a reminder of life and of humans' connection with nature, both through eating food and experiencing its natural course through the body into excrement, food is charged with significances of goodness and badness learned in infancy. Although I take Levenstein's and Shapiro's point that food is a cultural norm, which changes regularly, I find that the changes of the 1920s make sense as the underside of consumerism. As people buy "goodies," they also turn on their "bad" bodies and ignore their own physical realities, a topic more fully discussed in Chapter Seven. They substitute the satisfactions of "clean" purchases for sensual gratifications of their "bad" bodies.

52.   Rima D. Apple, "The Commercialization of Scientific Motherhood in the United States, 1880–1950," paper delivered at the Seventh Berkshire Conference on the History of Women, June 1987, describes how advertisers made scientific claims for products for infants and simultaneously used emotional appeals to mothers, who were expected to evaluate products.

53.   Topics listed are found in records from the four Cambridge Mothers' Clubs, note 11 above.

54.   "Some Subjects That Have Interested Mothers' Clubs, 1878–1940," p. 11, typescript, Mothers' Study Club, Box 1, Folder 9, Schlesinger Archives.

55.   "Written and Read to the Mothers Discussion Club on the Occasion of the Golden Anniversary, Dec. 6, 1949, by Frances H. Eliot," p. 6, typescript, Mothers' Discussion Club, Box 2, Folder 13, ibid.
56.   "We Illiterate Alumnae," n.d., Women's Education and Industrial Union MSS, Box 9, Folder 77, ibid.
57.   Bulletin of the Bureau of Part-Time Work, 105 West 40th Street, New York City, n.d., ibid., Folder 72. The bulletin noted that the bureau was established because "many women with specialized training and valuable experience are available for regular employment on this part-time basis, that is, mornings or afternoons, nearly a full day, or two or three full days a week, etc."
58.   "Labor and Democracy in the Home," 24. Hilda Worthington Smith MSS, Box 15, File 254, Schlesinger Archives.
59.   Quoted by Eunice Fuller Barnard, "Calls for a Kitchen Code Now Resound," New York Times Magazine, October 14, 1934.
60.   Catherine Hackett, "A Code for Housewives," Forum 91 (April 1934): 238–42.
61.   Gordon, What Shall We Do About Household Employment? Appendix I, reporting on an American Association of University Women survey in Bethlehem, Pennsylvania, gives the modal answer to the question "What daily duties does the hostess [employer] assume?" as "They made the beds and kept the bedrooms in order except for cleaning and did the marketing, took care of the children and did the cooking." Two questions later, however, the survey reports, "In every case the employers said they expected the children to obey the maid when left with her—and in no case did the maids object to children," which implies that the maids also did child care.
62.   "Statements of Household Problems Presented to a Meeting Sponsored by the National Committee on Employer-Employee Relationships in the Home," n.d., typescript, NA RG 86, Box 928.
63.   Andrews, Economics of the Household (1923), chap. 12, "Household Operation—Housework," 402. By the 1935 edition, time in baby care had gone up to 5 hours, 41 minutes per day (p. 445).
64.   The typescript, "Labor and Democracy in the Home," tells of the encounter between household workers meeting at the Hudson Shore Labor School and of "employers of household workers attending the Vassar Summer Institute at Vassar College," meeting under the supervision of Caroline Ware. See section 5, "Budgeting for Household Service," 29–35.
65.   Leisa Bronson, Claremont, California, to Miss McGrew, December 6, 1938, YWCA MSS, Box 43, Sophia Smith Collection.
66.   Dorothy Wells, national office, to Mrs. F. W. Meier, New Orleans YWCA Employment Secretary, November 9, 1933, YWCA MSS, Reel 98.2, Household Employment—Local Surveys.
67.   "Wages, Hours and Working Conditions of Domestic Employees in Connecticut," Monthly Labor Review 43 (December 1936): 1508–13, reporting a study conducted by the Connecticut Department of Labor and Factory Inspection.
68.   Dorothy Dunbar Bromley, "Are Servants People?" Scribner's December 1933, pp. 377–79.
69.   Lucy Randolph Mason, General Secretary of the National Consumers' League, "The Perfect Treasure," Junior League Magazine, February 1934, p. 36, NAACP MSS, Box C322, File Labor General, 1/12–6/14. "The perfect treasure" seems to have been a customary way to describe good servants, as if they were buried treasure

that one could unearth and, of course, get for free. Employers talked of such a woman as their hiring goal, according to Katherine Davis, who found when she was president of the National Committee on Household Employment and spoke to employer groups about contracts and better conditions for servants that they were disappointed she was not, instead, lecturing about how to find "the perfect treasure" (Interview with Davis, June 11, 1988).

70.   Grace Robinson, "My Maid—Impossible Female: A Search for the Perfect Servant," *Liberty* 71 (March 22, 1930), 59.

71.   "A Supplementary Article on Domestic Service Workers," by the president of the Domestic Efficiency Association, 4, NA RG 86, Box 4, Correspondence Relating to Women's Bureau Bulletin 39, *Domestic Workers in Baltimore* (1923) based on the Records of the Domestic Efficiency Association. This letter protesting the conclusions Women's Bureau staff drew from the association's records reveals the differences between reformers treating the servant problem as an issue of labor rights and housewives seeing it as an issue of household management. The anger and frustration of these harassed Baltimore matrons appears in their remark that "the very people who contend that domestic service ought to be performed on the 8 hour day principle, are found to be themselves luxuriating in the old-fashioned almost feudal service" (p. 5).

72.   Hurst, *Household Employees Handbook*, 7–8.

73.   Helen C. Wright, *Sunset's Household Handbook* (San Francisco: Lane, 1941), 116.

74.   Gordon, *What Shall We Do About Household Equipment?* Appendix I.

75.   Mrs. M. H. Stearne, Birmingham, Alabama, "The Case for the Household Employer," in "Labor and Democracy in the Home," Hilda Worthington Smith MSS, Box 15, File 254, Schlesinger Archives.

76.   Wells and Biba, eds., *Fair and Clear in the Home*, 52–53.

77.   Ibid., 53.

78.   Ibid., 34.

Four

1.   Frances E. Olsen, "The Family and the Market: A Study of Ideology and Legal Reform," *Harvard Law Review* 96 (May 1983): 1497–1578, is a cogent description of the mentality of dichotomized household–marketplace thought. Previous historical work documenting how the dichotomy grew as household work and its organization diverged from production work and its organization is found in Nancy F. Cott, *The Bonds of Womanhood: "Woman's Sphere" in New England, 1780–1835* (New Haven: Yale University Press, 1977), 58–62.

2.   The insight that housewives and domestics had different religious observances and values came as a result of questions raised by Richard Strassberg, director of the Labor Management Documentation Center, Cornell University, and historian of American religion. Once aware of religious differences between housewives and servants, one notes substantial evidence, as in Evelyn Nakano Glenn's account of Japanese women serving whites, that cultural differences exacerbated work tensions. Elizabeth Clark-Lewis, "'This Work Had a End': African-American Domestic Workers in Washington, D.C., 1910–1940," in Carol Groneman and Mary Beth Norton, eds., *"To Toil the Livelong Day": America's Women at Work, 1780–1980* (Ithaca: Cornell University Press, 1984), argues that a major impetus for black women's seeking day work was to participate in church associations unavailable to the domestic with only Thursday and Sunday afternoons (after church services) free. Child rearing

was another arena for culturally based disagreements. Historians of family practices, notably Jacques Donzelot in *The Policing of Families* (New York: Pantheon Books, 1979), have pointed out that in the eighteenth century striking divergences in working-class and middle-class child-rearing notions became evident. Working-class children were more constricted and physically punished and middle-class children were allowed free movement and punished emotionally by withdrawl of approval. How divergent values were negotiated by the working-class domestic caring for middle-class children has not been studied, as is pointed out by anthropologist Shellee Colen in her presentation "Stratified Reproduction: West Indian Child Care and Domestic Workers in New York City" on the panel "The Intersection of Class, Gender and Race: North American Women of Color in Domestic Service," National Women's Studies Association Conference, Spelman College, June 1987.

3.   Grace Robinson, "My Maid—Impossible Female: A Search for the Perfect Servant," *Liberty* 71 (March 22, 1930): 52–53; "The Servant in the Home," *Fortune* 4 (December 1931) reports the "heterogeneous aspect" of domestic workers on the Pacific coast, by which the author means that the usual black worker was joined by Scandinavian women, Chinese men, and Indian schoolgirls (p. 46).

4.   Lois Rita Helmbold, "Making Choices, Making Do: Black and White Working Women's Lives and Work During the Great Depression" (Ph.D. dissertation, Stanford University, 1982), concludes that "working in exchange for a place to live was the single most common Depression strategy which unattached women used to provide themselves with housing when they could not find the money to rent or own a home" (p. 87). My reading of the data is that this strategy was much more available to white working-class women than to nonwhite women because more white women became resident workers than did black women. Lois Rita Helmbold, "Beyond the Family Economy: Black and White Working-Class Women During the Great Depression," *Feminist Studies* 13 (Fall 1987): 629–55, agrees, on the basis of her sample of northeastern and midwestern cities, that "white women replaced black women [in various occupations] by moving down the occupational ladder of desirability. For black women already on the bottom rung, there was no lower step, and they were effectively pushed out of the labor force" (p. 636).

5.   "Changing Proportion of Negroes in Population of North and South," *Monthly Labor Review* 18 (March 1924): 10–12. Mary Anderson, "The Employment and Unemployment of Negro Women," July 1934, p. 3, typescript, NA RG 86, Box 1601; George J. Stigler, *Domestic Servants, in the United States, 1900–1940* (New York: National Bureau of Economic Research Occasional Paper 24, 1946), 9:

Female Negro Servants (thousands)

	1900	1910	1920	1930	1940
5 southern states	189	264	226	319	326
5 northern states	58	89	99	174	166

Southern states = Alabama, Mississippi, Georgia, South Carolina, Louisiana
Northern states = New York, Massachusetts, Pennsylvania, Ohio, Illinois

6.   Their own racial isolation may have led African-American domestics to isolate Jewish employers as the one distinct "racial" group among white middle-class employers. Black and white domestic workers spoke of Jewish employers as unreasonable in their service demands and cheap in payment. A partial reason seems to have been Jewish employers' keeping kosher households. St. Clair Drake and Horace R.

Cayton speculated, in *Black Metropolis: A Study of Negro Life in a Northern City* (New York: Harcourt, Brace, 1945), "The statements of Negro servants about middle-class Jewish employers reflect all the derogatory anti-Semitic stereotypes which exist among white people. Yet, many of these same servants will praise Jewish employers for being 'less prejudiced' than other white employers. At least two-thirds of some 150 domestic servants [in Chicago] who spoke of Jews thought that they treated Negroes 'more like equals' than other employers but 'paid less'" (p. 244).

7.   Jacqueline Jones, *Labor of Love, Labor of Sorrow: Black Women, Work and the Family, from Slavery to the Present* (New York: Vintage Books, 1986), 182.

8.   Clark S. Hobbs, "The Whip Changes Hands," *Baltimore Evening Sun*, May 16, 1941, p. 30, reported that in Baltimore "the supply of domestic servants is closely related to the payroll of Bethlehem Steel Company, the largest single employer of Negro men in this locality. A layoff there has always sent hundreds of women scurrying out in search of jobs, and the resumption of activity has always had a contrary effect" (Series 13, Box 1, Bethune Museum-Archives). My analysis of the Jackson, Mississippi, data from the 1934–1936 Family Disbursements survey of the Bureau of Labor Statistics disclosed a similar pattern; see Chapter One, above, at note 28.

9.   Erna Magnus, "Domestic Workers in Philadelphia: Summary and Conclusions," 1940, pp. 1, 5, typescript, NCHE MSS, Box 5.

10.   Julia Kirk Blackwelder, *Women of the Depression: Caste and Culture in San Antonio, 1929–1939* (College Station: Texas A & M University Press, 1984), 62.

11.   B. Eleanor Johnson, *Household Employment in Chicago*, Women's Bureau Bulletin 106 (Washington, D.C.: U.S. Department of Labor, 1933), 43.

12.   Clark-Lewis, "'This Work Had a End,'" makes the point forcefully that black women domestics were "active forces in history" (p. 212) as they left secure resident jobs for day work, formed clubs of working women who gained influence in black churches and neighborhoods, and opened savings accounts (p. 208).

13.   Elizabeth Ross Haynes, "Negroes in Domestic Service in the United States," *Journal of Negro History* 8 (October 1923): 425.

14.   Ibid., 422, cites the following statistics:

Average Daily and Weekly Wage of Negro Domestic Workers
by Occupation for Selected Cities, 1923

	Day work	Gen'l housework	Cooks	Maids	Part-time workers	Mothers' helpers
New York	$3.80	$13.85	$16.50	$13.00	$8.00	$11.00
Philadelphia	2.75	12.50	13.50	9.50	7.50	8.25
Baltimore	2.75	9.50	11.00	8.50	6.00	5.00
Washington	2.00	9.25	10.75	8.50	7.50	8.00
Detroit	3.35	9.50	11.00	9.00	9.50	9.50
Indianapolis	2.25	10.00	13.50	9.00		8.00
Boston	3.00	12.00	12.50	10.50		
Los Angeles	3.80		15.00	11.50		
Montgomery	1.75	7.00		6.50		
Nashville	1.75	7.00		6.50		

15.   Christine Frederick, *Household Engineering: Scientific Management in the Home* (Chicago: American School of Home Economics, 1920), section "The Servantless Household," 400.

16.   Haynes, "Negroes in Domestic Service," 427.
17.   Ibid., 433. Clark-Lewis, "'This Work Had a End,'" recounts how one of her interviewees assessed the employers' hypocrisy about Sundays: "They'd get up and go out to Sunday morning church. . . . He'd act like Sunday was such a holy day around there. He made it clear Sundays was a day of rest. But us? We'd work like dogs just the same. We didn't get no rest on that day" (p. 210).
18.   Robinson, "My Maid."
19.   Frederick, *Household Engineering*, 409. Frederick included various part-time and day-work arrangements under the category of "The Servantless Household." Her terminology indicates that housewives did not think that day work was the same as service.
20.   Haynes, "Negroes in Domestic Service," 391–92.
21.   Johnson, *Household Employment in Chicago*, "Character of the Employee Group," 44, 32. A 1923 Women's Bureau survey of the records of the Baltimore Domestic Efficiency Association likewise found cooking a favorite task for black women, following closely after "maid's work." For white women, "maid's work" was also the preference, with nursing as a second choice. Neither group of women wanted to do "general work," arguably the most all-encompassing and hard of the domestic categories.
22.   "An Evaluation of Household Employment as an Occupation," by 125 household employees, summarized by Stella Paula Manor for the Industrial Branch, National Board, YWCA, typescript in NCHE MSS, Box 4, Folder 8.
23.   See Chapter Three, note 15, for the full citations to correspondence in the Women's Bureau files in the National Archives, RG 86. In conversation with Evelyn Glenn, I realized I had seen no letters from Mexican-American, Japanese-American, Philippine, or Indian women. Letters were from native-born, ethnically unidentified white and African-American women and from women identified as Scandinavian, German, and French Canadian. For the women's stories to be documented in public records, Glenn suggested, they had to know English.
24.   Lois Bailey, "Slave Markets," 1939, typescript, SF Employment—Domestics (2), Schlesinger Archives; "Minutes of Sub-Committee Meeting of the Committee on Street Corner Markets, August 20, 1941," organized by the New York Women's Trade Union League, typescript, NCHE MSS, Box 3, Folder 20. The Harlem office of the New York State Employment Service reported that domestic workers preferred part-time work because "two part time jobs usually bring $15 per week and [car]fare, with much shorter hours. . . . Through cooperative efforts of Domestic Service in all offices, the scale rate for morning and afternoon domestic part time has increased. A standard rate has been accepted for days' work" (Annual report, Box 322, File "Labor General," 1/29–3/24 1937, NAACP MSS).
25.   Bettina Berch, "'The Sphinx in the Household': A New Look at the History of Household Workers," *Review of Radical Political Economics* 16, no. 1 (Spring 1984): 105–21, points out that middle-class reformers and housewives thought they could increase the supply of domestics by raising the status of housework. The best way to raise status was by providing workers more training. The low status of the job presumably derived from its irregular training and recruitment. Reformers had taken this conclusion from Lucy Salmon's classic and oft-cited *Domestic Service* (1893). The "Salmon solution," as I call it, dominated middle-class discussions during the 1930s. Workers often agreed that they could use more training and would like to learn how

to do parts of the work better. But they always returned to labor laws as an equally essential and more direct means of gaining respect.

26. Erna Magnus, "The Social, Economic, and Legal Conditions of Domestic Servants: II," *International Labor Review* 30 (September 1934): 336–64, examined the legal status of domestic service and concluded that it had generally been unregulated and construed as legally different from other work, so that the domestic had less legal recourse than virtually any other class of worker. Magnus's expertise, gained as a German economist working for the International Labor Organization (ILO), was useful to housework reform groups when she was forced to immigrate to the United States in 1938. She became affiliated with the National Committee on Household Employment and, with its backing, was funded by the Social Security Board to study the possibility of including domestic workers under the retirement and unemployment provisions of the Social Security Act.

27. The YWCA surveyed employment offices in 1933 to assess the impact of the Depression on workers hired through YWCA employment offices. Some were found to offer no pay at all, but only room and board. Others sought to raise hours: "Some employers offer work for every other day in the week, paying part-time wages and crowding in a whole week's work." Survey results were reported by Margaret T. Applegarth, "Is the Lady-of-the-House at Home?" *Woman's Press* 28 (November 1933): 472–74, 490. For black women whose ancestors experienced slavery in the American South, the irregular relations of domestic work seemed more like a return to enslavement than it did to women of racial and ethnic groups that had not experienced slavery. Other groups used the label but without the same historical meaning. I realized this difference after hearing a penetrating commentary by Barbara Omolade at the Feminism and Legal Theory Conference, Madison, Wisconsin, June 1986. I thank Professor Martha Fineman, University of Wisconsin Law School, for this informative occasion.

28. Perla Kerosec-Serfaty, "Experience and the Use of the Dwelling," in Irwin Altman and Carol M. Werner, eds., *Home Environments* (New York: Plenum, 1985), 65–86. Kerosec-Serfaty, a French phenomenologist, observes, "In any dwelling, there exists a particular way of establishing the relationship between the 'hidden' and the 'shown' *whatever the nature of this hidden may be,* for example, women, servants and their hall, or the body" (pp. 73–74). She examines the impact of burglary and concludes, "The loss of mastery over the visible/hidden distinction goes together with a feeling of disgust due to a gross, arrogant, imposed contact. . . . This emphasizes one's . . . vulnerability" (p. 78). My George Washington University American Studies colleague Clarence Mondale recommended this fascinating article.

29. Erna Magnus, "The Social, Economic, and Legal Conditions of Domestic Servants: I," *International Labor Review* 30 (August 1934): 193, describes this phenomenon and notes that in 1928, 28 percent of Swedish domestics were aliens, a pattern Magnus attributes to the shortage of workers, which necessitated importing them. I am suggesting that the reverse may also be true—that employers sought workers different from themselves and thus preferred foreign-born to native-born workers.

30. BC 321, 1/6–12/16 1931, NAACP MSS.

31. "Labor and Democracy in the Home," 20. Hilda Worthington Smith MSS, Box 15, File 254, Schlesinger Archives.

32. Virginia McGregor, "A Study of the Wages of Household Employees in the Y.W.C.A.'s of Thirteen Illinois Communities" (1939), NCHE MSS, Box 5.

33.   Mary Heiner, University of Chicago, "Regulating Hours Through the Use of
Time Schedules," typescript of conference paper, February 1929, NWTUL MSS,
Box 2, File 24, Schlesinger Archives.
34.   Anonymous letter to Marie Carrel (Women's Bureau researcher), n.d., NA RG
86, Box 926.
35.   Community Council of St. Louis, "Study of Household Employment in St.
Louis," April 1935, typescript in YWCA National Board MSS, Reel 98, Household
Employment—Studies.
36.   Applegarth, "Is the Lady-of-the-House at Home?" 474.
37.   "Labor and Democracy in the Home," 11.
38.   Household Employees News 1 (February 1942), NCHE MSS, Box 3, Folder 12.
The newsletter was published in San Francisco by the Sutter Street YWCA.
39.   "Labor and Democracy in the Home," 25.
40.   Household Employees News 1 (February 1942): 6, NCHE MSS, Box 3, Folder 12.
41.   Community Council of St. Louis, "Study of Household Employment in St.
Louis," April 1935, YWCA National Board MSS, Reel 98.
42.   Domestic Employees Club, Inc., flyer "Would you Tolerate Domestic Slavery?" printed in Milwaukee, Wisconsin, 1935, NCHE MSS, Box 4.
43.   "Labor and Democracy in the Home," 10.
44.   Box C-322, File "Labor—General June 16–December 12, 1934," NAACP
MSS. A number of child "horror" stories are in the odd collection put together by the
Chicago YWCA's committee on Household Employment, The Women in the House:
Stories of Household Employment, ed. Ruth Sergel (New York: Woman's Press,
1938). All the chapters have case studies, vignettes that illustrate domestic workers'
thinking and housewives' interpretation of disagreements about policies for doing
particular jobs and about the etiquette of housewife–domestic relations. Chapter 9 is
"The Child in the House." The book illustrates the YWCA's effort to mediate between housewife and the domestic, and the cases are evenly divided in demonstrating domestics' stupidity or backwardness and housewives' stupidity and arrogance. In
general, domestics perceived that parents took the child's side whenever the domestic and child disagreed.
45.   Gene Nicholson, secretary and organizer, Domestic Employees Union, San
Diego, California, to Mrs. Franklin D. Roosevelt, November 24, 1933, in which she
outlines a model code adopted by organized domestic workers (NA RG 86, Box 926).
46.   Marion Hurst, Household Employees Handbook (Oklahoma City: Dewing
Publishing Company, 1939), 26. Margaret T. Mettert, Injuries to Women in Personal
Service Occupations in Ohio, Women's Bureau Bulletin 151 (Washington, D.C.: U.S.
Government Printing Office, 1937), gave data of injury claims from an Ohio law that
covered employers with three or more employees. Most injuries to female domestic
workers in these households with large staffs and, therefore, presumably not the
worst working conditions, were cuts and lacerations, burns and scalds, usually of
hands and fingers. Though these might be seen as minor injuries, 40 percent of the
1933 claimants had over 7 days' disability (pp. 2–3).
47.   The Household Worker in New York State, 1948 (Albany: New York State Department of Labor, Division of Reasearch and Statistics, 1948), 32.
48.   Applegarth, "Is the Lady-of-the-House at Home?" 473.
49.   NA RG 86, Box 923.

50.   Irene Colwell, Special Agent, United States Employment Service, to Mary
Anderson, March 12, 1932, NA RG 86, Box 273.
51.   Julietta K. Arthur, *Bridget Goes to the Doctor* (American Medical Association,
1941), NA RG 86, Box 923.
52.   *Household Employees News* 1 (September 1941), NCHE MSS, Box 3, Folder 12.
53.   *Household Work in New York State, 1948,* 23
54.   Mary Viola Robinson, *Old-Age Insurance of Household Workers,* U.S. Women's
Bureau Bulletin, 220 (Washington, D.C.: U.S. Government Printing Office, November, 1945), 14–15, summarizing Mary Elizabeth Pidgeon, *The Employed Woman
Homemaker in the United States,* Women's Bureau Bulletin 148 (Washington, D.C.:
U.S. Government Printing Office, 1936), 6–7, 10–12.
55.   Erna Magnus, "Negro Domestic Workers in Private Homes in Baltimore," *Social Security Bulletin* 4, no. 10 (October 1941): 1–3; Erna Magnus, "Domestic Workers in Philadelphia Summary and Conclusions," typescript, NCHE MSS, Box 5.
56.   United States Employment Service, drafts of standards for housework jobs,
May 1945, Series 5, Folder 195, Bethune Museum–Archives.

Five

1.   Contemporary historians have debated the wisdom of women's seeking professional recognition through the development of segregated fields as opposed to inte-
grating themselves into men's professional schools and societies. Mary Roth Walsh,
*"Doctors Wanted: No Women Need Apply": Sexual Barriers in the Medical Profes-
sion, 1835–1975* (New Haven: Yale University Press, 1977), and Margaret W.
Rossiter, *Women Scientists of America: Struggles and Strategies to 1940* (Baltimore:
Johns Hopkins University Press, 1982), demonstrate that integration generally meant
official quotas and unofficial barriers to women's training and professional recognition.
The perils of segregation, on the other hand, were self-restriction and development
in the narrow channels that men left to women. In either situation, women took what
men let them have. When men decided that a field had promise, as happened in
home economics after World War II, they simply took over the structures created by
women. In this instance, the male influx was accompanied by a new name, human
ecology, that indicated the transformation of the discipline from home-centeredness
to human-centeredness, from female to male.
2.   Rossiter, *Women Scientists,* chap. 8, describes the employment of women scientists in government, with a significant group being in "feminized" programs such
as home economics. The director of the Bureau of Home Economics in the Department of Agriculture, Louise A. Stanley, was "the highest-ranking woman scientist in
the federal government" in 1938 (p. 229).
3.   Rossiter, *ibid.,* notes that when male-led scientific groups achieved professional standing, they raised requirements to force out the nondegreed, unpublished
science workers or to justify giving them a different and lesser status in the organization. By the beginning of the century, these groups had established that one test to
recognize a professional group was that it excluded amateurs: the amateur–
professional distinction supposedly measured competence or seriousness among
those who pursued the same work and research interests.

4.   Annegret S. Ogden, *The Great American Housewife: From Helpmate to Wage Earner, 1776–1986*, Contributions in Women's Studies 61 (Westport, Conn.: Greenwood Press, 1986), reviews influential prescriptive literature to demonstrate that this has been the dominant image of the good life for women and of the good woman throughout the entire national history.

5.   Mary Schenck Woolman, Chair of Women's Committee, to Cleo Murtland, Secretary of Women's Work, September 11, 1915, Container 31, NSPIE MSS, "Women's Discussions of Principles and Policies," Meeting of Women's Committee of the NSPIE, February 21, 1917, Container 21, ibid.

6.   Mary Schenck Woolman to Cleo Murtland, May 9, 1915; Woolman to Dodd, May 29, 1915; Woolman to Murtland, June 11, 1915, Container 31, ibid.

7.   David Snedden to H. E. Miles, February 9, 1920, Container 17, ibid.

8.   Charlotte Williams Conable, "Woman's Work in Woman's Place: An Analysis of the Home Economics Profession," unpublished paper, 1975, available from Women's Studies Program, George Washington University; Charlotte Williams Conable, *Women at Cornell: The Myth of Equal Education* (Ithaca: Cornell University Press, 1977), chap. 4, "The Education of Womanly Women and Manly Men, 1885–1960." Rossiter, *Women Scientists*, 199–202, describes how home economists fought for research facilities and the status of research faculty during the 1920s, even though the bulk of their university work was training teachers to staff high school home economics programs.

9.   Conable, *Women at Cornell*, 113–15; Geraldine Joncich Clifford, "'Marry, Stitch, Die, or Do Worse': Educating Women for Work," in Harvey Kantor and David Tyack, eds., *Work, Youth, and Schooling: Historical Perspectives on Vocationalism in American Education* (Stanford: Stanford University Press, 1982), 223–68.

10.   "1926–1928 Biennial Survey of Home Economics Education," NA RG 12, Box 107. Rossiter, *Women Scientists*, 258–59, describes "women scientists' greatest success in the 1920s and 1930s [as] the food and home products industry, which not only hired many of them, but, like home economics departments at universities and bureaus in government, even promoted some of them as well."

11.   Helen Pundt, *AHEA: A History of Excellence* (Washington, D.C.: American Home Economics Association, 1980), surveys reports in the *American Home Economics Journal* that show the association working from 1920 to 1926 for the Fess Amendmendment. The group finally desisted in the face of President Calvin Coolidge's hostility to bills requiring increased government expenditure (p. 56).

12.   Black Women Oral History Project, Interview with Flemmie P. Kittrell, OH-31, Schlesinger Archives.

13.   James D. Anderson, "The Historical Development of Black Vocational Education," in Kantor and Tyack, eds., *Work, Youth and Schooling*, 180–222, 186ff.; Linda Marie Fritschner, "The Rise and Fall of Home Economics" (Ph.D. dissertation, University of California, Davis, 1973), 65–68, 95; Alvin Dodd, NSPIE secretary, to Edward Trigg, Hampton Institute, February 23, 1915, explaining scholarship given by NSPIE to Trigg: "Many of the methods which we first worked out and improved upon at Hampton are now being put into operation for the benefit of white boys and girls so that you see in reality the negro has set an example for the kind of training which will be of great value and service to whites as well as blacks" (NSPIE MSS, Container 21).

14.   Anderson, "Black Vocational Education," 193, 186.
15.   Fritschner, "Rise and Fall of Home Economics," 65.
16.   Texas V. E. Plans, 1927–1932, NA RG 12, Container 80.
17.   American Home Economics Association press release on the Fess Home Economics Amendment (H.R. 21), n.d., NSPIE MSS, Container 5.
18.   "Pamphlet on the Fess Amendment," sponsored by American Home Economics Association, General Federation of Women's Clubs, Parent-Teachers Association, League of Women Voters, National Society for Vocational Education, American Association of University Women, National Grange, and the Women's Christian Temperance Union, ibid.
19.   California Report to U.S. Office of Education, 1930–1931, NA RG 12, Container 9, California Vocational Education F & S (Financial and Statistical) Reports, 1917–1935. Adelaide S. Baylor, Chief, Home Economics Education Service, U.S. Office of Education, to Lillian Peek, State Supervisor of Home Economics, State Board for Vocational Education, Austin, March 25, 1932, NA RG 12, Container 80, Texas V. E. Plans, 1922–1937.
20.   Texas F & S Reports, 1923–1924, 1927–1928, NA RG 12, Container 80. Though federal instructions required states to identify schools in which only "colored" students were enrolled, it did not require the indentification of Mexicans. The Texas school authorities, nevertheless, named such schools in El Paso and in the Rio Grande Valley in Pharr, Weslaco, and Cotulla.
21.   California State Board of Education, *Documents Relating to Vocational Education*, Bulletin 23-A (Sacramento: California State Printing Office, 1921), 42–43, in NA RG 12, Container 10, California V.E. Plans, 1921–1937.
22.   Board of Vocational Education, State of Illinois, *Statement of Plans and Policies, 1927–1932*, Bulletin 44 (Springfield, Ill.: N.p., n.d.), in NA RG 12, Container 21, Illinois V. E. Plans, 1917–1937.
23.   State of Ohio Department of Education, *Home Economics: Course of Study for High Schools in Vocational Home Economics Education* (Columbus: N.p., 1930) 14, 35.
24.   State of Georgia, Annual F & S Reports, 1917–1918, in NA RG 12, Container 16.
25.   Mary Romero, "Transcending or Reproducing Hierarchy Between Women? Chicana Private Household Workers' Relationships with Employers," paper presented at the 1988 National Association for Ethnic Studies Conference, Springfield, Mass., p. 17, and quoting Mario T. Garcia, *Desert Immigrants: The Mexicans of El Paso, 1880–1920* (New Haven: Yale University Press, 1981), 112.
26.   Texas F & S Report, 1927–1928, NA RG 12, Container 81.
27.   Evelyn C. Adams, *American Indian Education: Government Schools and Economic Progress* (Morningside Heights, N.Y.: King's Crown Press, 1946), 72.
28.   California V.E. F & S Report, 1930–1931, NA RG 12, Container 9.
29.   Illinois V.E. F & S Reports, 1928–1929, 1930–1931, Container 22, ibid.
30.   Virginia V.E. F & S, 1935–1936, Container 87, ibid.
31.   Carrie Lyford, *A Study of Home-Economics Education in Teacher-Training Institutions for Negroes*, Bulletin 79 (Washington, D.C.: U.S. Federal Board for Vocational Education, 1923), 5.
32.   Texas V.E. Plans, 1932–1937, NA RG 12, Container 80; Alabama V.E. Plans, 1917–1937, Container 23, ibid.; National Training School for Women and Girls catalog, ca. 1938, Carton 309, Nannie Helen Burroughs MSS, LC.

33.   Box 308, "National Association of Women Wage-Earners," and Scrapbook, Carton 345, Nannie Helen Burroughs MSS, LC. Evelyn Brooks Barnett, "Nannie Burroughs and the Education of Black Women," in Sharon Harley and Rosalyn Terborg-Penn, eds., *The Afro-American Woman: Struggles and Images* (Port Washington, N.Y.: Kennikat Press, 1978), 97–108, emphasizes Burroughs's commitment to the "puritan work ethic," to pride in black culture, and to the need for women's elevation within the race.

34.   Iris Prouty O'Leary, New Jersey home economist, to Lyman Abbott, NSPIE, January 1921, NSPIE MSS, Container 17. Typescript, "Editorial," (1924) illustrates the class and content confusion, with some questions for home economics teachers to ask themselves: "Have I over-emphasized training in technical skills and under-emphasized problems of management?. . . Have I established standards of living that are just a little better than those the girls are accustomed to in their homes (in general), but no better than they can hope to attain?" (ibid., Container 7).

35.   U.S. Advisory Committee on Education, *Vocational Education*, Staff Study 8 (Washington, D.C.: U.S. Government Printing Office, 1938), 141, citing U.S. Office of Education, *Standard of Policies* (1937), 61. Pundt, *AHEA*, summarizes the association's interests during the 1930s as moving from helping the housewife at home to monitoring advertising claims to protect housewives as consumers and teaching parents about new theories of child development and parental education "that had received impetus under the terms of the Laura Spelman Rockefeller Memorial grant" to the association (pp. 140–41).

36.   U.S. Advisory Committee on Education, *Vocational Education*, 141–43.

37.   My understanding of the character, motives, and strategies of the leaders who won relief funds for unemployed and poor women is heavily indebted to the work of Martha H. Swain, biographer of Ellen Woodward and author of "ER and Ellen Woodward: A Partnership for Women's Work Relief and Security," in Joan Hoff-Wilson and Marjorie Lightman, eds., *Without Precedent: The Life and Career of Eleanor Roosevelt* (Bloomington: Indiana University Press, 1984), and to Susan Wladaver-Morgan's excellent analysis of the politics of funding and cultural norms of projects in "Young Women and the New Deal: Camps and Resident Centers, 1933–1943" (Ph.D. dissertation, Indiana University, 1982).

38.   Ellen S. Woodward to Helen Swanson, Consultant Dietician, Texas Relief Commission, February 6, 1935, FERA State Series 453 "Texas," NA RG 69.

39.   Wladaver-Morgan, "Young Women and the New Deal," 138–39, 161–62, describes the more innovative aspects of FERA projects and the conservatism that appeared when projects focused only on jobs and possibly encouragement of women to enter the labor market. At that point, WPA programs ceased to encourage nontraditional work. WPA work projects limited the use of housekeeping aides, and newly passed Social Security legislation enabled local relief authorities to certify women heads of household with children under age sixteen for Aid for Dependent Children (ADC) payments rather than for jobs. Women with children would stay at home to do their own housework; women with housekeeping skills would find fewer relief jobs available. What Wladaver-Morgan misses, I think, is the racial effect of forcing black women, unlikely to be certified for ADC by southern officials and with only housekeeping job skills, into the domestic labor market.

40.   Wladaver-Morgan, "Young Women and the New Deal," 167, citing "Preliminary Report on Household Workers' Training Program," WPA General Subject Se-

ries, Entry 230, and WPA Division of Information, Information Service Primary File, Entry 824-B, News Release, March 22, 1938, both in NA RG 69.

41. Edward Lawson, "The WPA's 'Good Neighbors,'" *Service* 2 (March 1938): 8–10. Lowell F. James, former assistant project supervisor, New York City WPA Housekeeping Aides, to Walter White, NAACP, July 8, 1938, NAACP MSS, Box C418, File 7.2–8.5.

42. *Report: Division of Women's and Professional Projects, Works Progress Administration. Part Three. Accomplishments of Non-Federal Projects Accomplishments of Information Section*, July 1, 1935 to January 1, 1937, 299–300, 305, no shelf number, NA RG 69.

43. *Toledo* (Ohio) *Blade*, November 3, 1938; *Wilmington* (Delaware) *Journal Every Evening*, November 3, 1938, WPA Division of Information, Newspaper Clippings File, Entry 188, NA RG 69.

44. "Housekeepers Assigned to 67 Homes by WPA," *Syracuse* (New York) *Post Standard*, February 21, 1937, ibid., Entry 187, NA RG 69.

45. WPA in Ohio, District Four, "Program Script," for weekly broadcast, September 21, 1940, Station WGAR, Cleveland, Ohio, WPA Information Service Primary File, Entry 824-A, NA RG 69.

46. "Housekeeping Aides," October 9, 1940, Kansas, Entry 824-B, ibid.

47. WPA 1991, Map, "Female heads of families as % of all heads of families eligible for works program employment, as of January 15, 1936," in *An Analysis of Employment of Women on Works Progress Administration Projects, December 1935 through May 1936* (Washington, D.C.: U.S. Works Progress Administration, 1923), 13.

48. Margaret Batjer to Florence Kerr, Assistant Commissioner, WPA, August 28, 1939, reporting on inspection of Louisiana home economics projects, WPA General Subject Series 212.2, Box 487, NA RG 69. Batjer reported that not all southern cities misused the program, citing Memphis, San Antonio, and Dallas as "operating successful Housekeeping Aide projects according to national policies."

49. WPA of Louisiana, news release, October 24, 1940, to *Item Tribune* (New Orleans), WPA Information Service Primary File, Entry 824-A, ibid.

50. *Binghamton* (New York) *Press*, December 28, 1935, ibid., Entry 825-A.

51. "WPA Household Workers' Training and the U.S. Employment Service," prepared by Miss Price for Employment Service News, typescript in ibid., Entry 824-B; Ellen S. Woodward, "Household Employment and the W.P.A.," *Journal of Home Economics* 28 (September 1936): 440.

52. Ellen S. Woodward to Congresswoman Greenway, May 29, 1936, stated, "Though many of our women assigned to sewing and other projects were originally classified as domestic workers, actually most of them do not have the qualifications for this work." A penciled note at the top of the page explained, "This letter was written in order to reply to a charge that women could not obtain household help because workers of this type were all assigned to sewing projects" (WPA Information Service Primary File, Entry 824-A, NA RG 69). Susan Ware, *Beyond Suffrage: Women in the New Deal* (Cambridge, Mass.: Harvard University Press, 1981), 109, describes Woodward's heavy reliance on sewing projects to provide relief employment for tens of thousands of women. Sewing saved women from solitary domestic work and, as a relief job, generally paid higher wages.

53. Ellen S. Woodward, Director, Women's Work (FERA), to All State Emergency Relief Administrations, December 20, 1934, (NWTUL MSS), Box 3, Folder 25,

Schlesinger Archives; National Committee on Household Employment, Bulletin 5 (December 1936), quoting Anna Marie Driscoll, "Household Workers Training Program," WPA booklet, November 1936, NCHE MSS.

54. *Report: Division of Women's and Professional Projects, Works Progress Administration Part Three. Accomplishments of Non-Federal Projects Accomplishments of Information Section, July 1, 1935 to January 1, 1937,* February 17, 1937, WPA, 4 bound vols., no shelf number, NA RG 69.

55. Florence Kerr, "Training for Household Employment," *Journal of Home Economics* 32 (September 1940): 437.

56. "Meeting of the Household Employment Committee of the District of Columbia, April 2, 1937," File 212.2, Box 487, NA RG 69.

57. "WPA Demonstration Projects to Employ 'Domestic Workers,'" *Press Digest*, March 29, 1937, reporting "a local story in the Washington Star, Sunday, page A-4," n.d., ibid., Entry 825-A.

58. *Monthly Labor Review* 48 (January 1939): 114.

59. Florence Kerr, "Training," *Journal of Home Economics* 32 (September 1940): 438.

60. "Mrs. Pittsburgh in Hunt for Maid Finds Few Want Job; Employment Men Agree," *Pittsburgh Post Gazette,* May 2, 1936; George E. Sokolsky, "The Profession of Serving," *New York Herald Tribune,* May 25, 1936; "Housekeepers Assigned to 67 Homes by WPA," *Syracuse Post-Standard,* February 21, 1937, WPA Newspaper Clippings File, Entry 187, NA RG 69.

61. *Report: Division of Women's and Professional Projects, July 1, 1935 to January 1, 1937,* 356–57, NA RG 69.

62. "Final Report of the Philadelphia Institute on Household Occupations," 5, NWTUL MSS, Box 3.

63. "They Want WPA Jobs," *Toledo* (Ohio) *News-Bee,* July 15, 1937, WPA Newspaper Clippings File, Entry 187, NA RG 69. Jacqueline Jones, *Labor of Love, Labor of Sorrow: Black Women, Work and the Family, from Slavery to the Present* (New York: Vintage Books, 1986), reports that southern black women were dismissed from WPA jobs when crops needed harvesting; agricultural labor and domestic labor were the only jobs southern authorities would grant to black women (pp. 218–20).

64. "Home Service Classes," excerpt from Massachusetts Narrative Report 19, November 20, 1936, WPA Information Service Primary File, Entry 824-A, NA RG 69.

65. "Meeting of the Household Employment Committee of the District of Columbia, April 2, 1937," File 212.2, Box 487, NA RG 69.

66. *Jacksonville* (Florida) *Times Union,* September 22, 1936, WPA Newspaper Clippings File, Entry 187, NA RG 69.

67. "Home Service Training Project in Durham, N.C.," June 1938, WPA Information Service Primary File, Entry 824-A, ibid.

68. "Home Service Classes," excerpt from Massachusetts Narrative Report 19, November 20, 1936, ibid.

69. "Excerpt from Mississippi Narrative Report, November 1936," ibid.

70. Ellen S. Woodward to State Emergency Relief Administrators, "Working Procedure: Vocational Training for General Household Workers—E4.11," December 15, 1934, NWTUL MSS, Box 3.

71. "Project No. 7048 Entertains Visitors," *Baltimore Evening Sun,* March 18, 1938, WPA Newspaper Clippings File, Entry 187, NA RG 69.

72.   "Household Training Center Points Solution to Age-Old Maid Problem," *Hartford Times*, May 19, 1939, ibid., Entry 188.
73.   "Excerpt from New York City Press Release, November 17, 1937," WPA Information Service Primary File, Entry 824-A, ibid.
74.   Swain, "ER and Ellen Woodward," 145.
75.   Kentucky state reports, National Youth Administration, NA RG 119.
76.   WPA News Release to the *Houma, Louisiana Courier*, December 11, 1936, WPA Information Service Primary File, Entry 825-A, NA RG 69.
77.   Ora Brown Stokes to Mary McLeod Bethune and Mrs. Winthrop D. Lane, May 1942, Box 617, NA RG 119.
78.   Mary G. Shotwell to Lane, April 12–21, 1942, ibid.
79.   "WPA Training Refugee Women for Cook Jobs," *Chicago Times*, December 5, 1941, WPA Newspaper Clippings File, Entry 188, NA RG 69.
80.   Mrs. Jud Sullivan, Vice-Chair, San Francisco unit of American Women Voluntary Services, to Frieda Miller, Director, U.S. Women's Bureau, January 19, 1945, asked for help in getting federal Office of Education grants-in-aid to sponsor training schools for domestic workers to meet the anticipated postwar shortage. Mrs. Alfred Hess, American Women Voluntary Services, wrote Miller, May 28, 1945, asking her to sponsor a national meeting to discuss how to attract women leaving industry back to household work (Box 928, NA RG 86.)

Six

1.   *First Report of the Commission on Household Employment, to the Fifth National Convention of the Young Women's Christian Association, May 5 to 11, 1915* (New York: Commission on Household Employment, 1915), 33.
2.   Isabel Kimball Whiting, *The Beam in Our Own Eyes: One Homemaker's Experiment*, Bulletin 4 (New York: [YWCA] Committee on Household Employment, 1917), 8.
3.   Mary T. Waggaman, "Efforts to Standardize the Working Day for Domestic Service," *Monthly Labor Review* 9 (August 1919): 512.
4.   Genevieve Fox, "'Wanted: for General Housework,'" *Association Monthly* 13 (September 1919): 362. A report on the Y's cooperation with the U.S. Employment Service appeared in Waggaman, "Efforts to Standardize the Working Day," 509–15.
5.   "Resolutions No. 51 and 52," adopted by the Seventh Biennial Convention, NWTUL MSS, Box 2, Folder 24.
6.   Waggaman, "Efforts to Standardize the Working Day," 515.
7.   Judith A. Baer, *The Chains of Protection: The Judicial Response to Women's Labor Legislation*, Contributions to Women's Studies, 1 (Westport, Conn.: Greenwood Press, 1978), describes state supreme court and U.S. Supreme Court responses to proliferating state legislation regulating maximum hours of work and minimum wages (chaps. 2 and 3). Ronnie Steinberg, *Wages and Hours: Labor and Reform in Twentieth-Century America* (New Brunswick, N.J.: Rutgers University Press, 1982), chap. 3, "Early Labor Standards Legislation," concludes that a substantial minority of states had adopted maximum hour and night work laws by 1900, but that the legislation 'took off' between 1900 and 1920 (p. 62).
8.   Waggaman, "Efforts to Standardize the Working Day," 514.

9.   Philadelphia Council on Household Occupations, *Digest of Findings of the Philadelphia Study of Household Employment* (ca. 1930), findings committee chaired by Henrietta W. Calvin, chair of home economics education, Philadephia public schools, and research directed by Amey E. Watson, in Institute of Women's Professional Relations MSS, Box 2, Folder 20, Schlesinger Archives.

10.   Ibid, 5.

11.   "What One Home-maker Thinks," *Women's Press* 22 (February 1928): 83.

12.   Steinberg, *Wages and Hours*, 73, table 3.6.

13.   Organizations attending the 1928 conference may be divided into housewives' clubs—American Homemakers, Inc. (Boston), Bureau of Household Occupations (Providence, Boston, Hartford, Rochester), Housekeepers' Alliance (Washington, D.C.), Scientific Housekeeping, Inc. (New York City), General Federation of Women's Clubs, and Housewives' League of Chicago; home economics experts—American Home Economics Association, School of Practical Arts at Teachers College, Columbia University, American Taylor Society (represented by Lillian Gilbreth), Smith College Institute for the Coordination of Women's Interests, and Vassar Institute of Euthenics; and worker advocates—National Women's Trade Union League and the Women's Bureau, typescript, "Summary of the Work of Organizations" (NA RG 86, Box 927).

14.   Jean Collier Brown, *Concerns of Household Workers: Program with Household Workers in the Y.W.C.A.* (New York: Woman's Press, 1941), 7–15.

15.   Lucy Carner to Florence Thorne, American Federation of Labor, November 5, 1928, NCHE MSS, Box 2, Folder 7; "The Program of the National Committee on Employer–Employee Relationships in the Home," 1928, typescript, Institute of Women's Professional Relations MSS, Box 2, Folder 20, Schlesinger Archives.

16.   "Conference on Employer-Employee Relationships in the Home, Report of the Findings Committee," 17, Institute of Women's Professional Relations MSS, Box 2, Folder 20, Schlesinger Archives.

17.   Amey E. Watson to Mary Anderson, March 11, 1930, NA RG 86, Box 927.

18.   Reported in "Minutes of Seventh Meeting, October 2, 1930, of National Committee on Employer-Employee Relationships in the Home," NCHE MSS, Box 1, Folder 37. YWCA summer camps were of great importance to domestic workers because they were generally excluded from other summer schools for workers. Hilda Worthington Smith, founder of the Bryn Mawr Summer School and organizer of the Affiliated Summer Schools for Women Workers in Industry, reported to Amey Watson, in a letter of March 25, 1931, "Our present admissions policy is not to accept domestic workers unless they have previously worked in industry. Our faculty thinks the economics courses as taught in the school are not what the domestic workers need and that they should have a special course of their own. The Barnard Summer School is considering taking a group of domestic workers but nothing has been decided. . . . We are constantly receiving applications [from domestic workers] and believe that there is a special need for an educational program adapted to their own problems" (ibid., Box 2, Folder 17).

19.   Mary Anderson to Lucy P. Carner, November 18, 1930, ibid., Box 2, Folder 14.

20.   "National Committee on Employer-Employee Relationships in the Home, Summary of Second Conference, New York City, April 13 and 14, 1931," 8–9, typescript, NWTUL MSS, Box 2, Folder 24.

21.   Benjamin Andrews, *Household Employment Bulletin*, No. 1 (July 20, 1933), 12, NA RG 86, Box 927.

22.   Mrs. Philip LeBoutillier, New York City, to Lucy Carner, n.d., NCHE MSS, Box 2, Folder 19.

23.   Ann Corinne Hill, "Protection of Women Workers and the Courts: A Legal History," *Feminist Studies* 5 (Summer 1979): 247–73, offers these figures (p. 249) without specifying their source.

24.   Irving Bernstein, *A Caring Society: The New Deal, the Worker and the Great Depression* (Boston: Houghton Mifflin, 1985), chap. 5, "Fair Labor Standards," 118–19.

25.   Leonard Barcroft, Richmond, Virginia, to Hugh Johnson, October 6, 1933, NA RG 9, Entry 580–81, Box 247, File 1; "Low Wage Code for Negroes of Nation Planned by South," Press Service of the National Association for the Advancement of Colored People, n.d., and Lucy Mason Randolph, general secretary of the National Consumers' League, New York City, "Objections to Minimum Wage Discriminations Against Negro Workers," August 29, 1933, both in ibid., Harvard Sitkoff, *A New Deal for Blacks* (New York: Oxford University Press, 1978), notes that "eleven thousand of the thirteen thousand Negroes in Southern cotton mills were classified so as to exclude them from all NRA benefits" (p. 54).

26.   Bernstein, *Caring Society*, 295.

27.   Mary Anderson, "The Employment and Unemployment of Negro Women," July, 1934, typescript, p. 10, NA RG 86, Box 1601.

28.   Susan Ware, *Beyond Suffrage: Women in the New Deal* (Cambridge, Mass.: Harvard University Press, 1981), 91.

29.   Included with a memo of September 1, 1933, from Frances Williams to Henrietta Roelofs about coordinating actions "to get the Negro cause before the NRA." Weaver and the YWCA headquarters staff saw the NRA as an opportunity for interracial organizing because, as Weaver said, "Exclusion of domestic work from the NRA hurts those workers and also hurts regulated occupations, since, as in New Orleans, a commercial laundry can hire a domestic for less than $.20 an hour required by the code" for commercial laundries (YWCA National Board MSS, Reel 98.5).

30.   Grace L. Coyle, Executive, Laboratory Division, National Board, YWCA, to Mary Anderson, July 20, 1933, NA RG 86, Box 1717, "Codes, 1933–1936"; Grace L. Coyle to Henrietta Roelofs, July 21, 1933, asking for help with the letter campaign, exulted, "Sorry to disturb you on your vacation, but in these days when society is being made over one's personal affairs get somewhat interfered with" (YWCA National Board MSS, Reel 98).

31.   Bobbitt's letter to Johnson is dated September 1933. It appeared in "News Bulletin, Household Employment Project, National Industrial Council," n.d. ("11/2/33" in pencil). The bulletin also noted that the YWCA was cooperating with the Joint Committee: "Here is an instance where 'unity in industry' is very real, for Negro and white workers must stand together if standards are to be raised." Camp Gray Industrial Girls wrote to General Hugh Johnson, July 11, 1933, advocating wage rates for households, factory, and mercantile workers (YWCA National Board MSS, Reel 98.4).

32.   "Domestic Workers' Association," 1938, typescript, ibid., Reel 98.5.

33.   Thomas J. Hunt, President, Domestic Workers' Association, Philadelphia, to Franklin D. Roosevelt, December 31, 1934, NA RG 86, Box 926.

34.   Z. Elizabeth Moman, President, National Association for Domestic Workers, to "Dear Friend," NA RG 86, Box 1717, "Codes, 1933–1936."

35.   A. R. Forbush, Chief, Correspondence Division, to Eva J. Bulkely, Plainfield, New Jersey, January 31, 1934, NA RG 9, Metal File 622, Box 65.

36.   Mary Anderson, Director, to Z. Elizabeth Moman, National Association for Domestic Workers, December 14, 1934, NA RG 86, Box 926.
37.   Mrs. Allan K. Chalmers, Chair, Committee on Household Employment, to Household Employer Members, December 8, 1933, YWCA National Board MSS, Reel 97.
38.   My knowledge of the FLSA owes much to Eileen Boris and Vivien Hart, co-convenors with me of a panel celebrating the fiftieth anniversary of the FLSA at the Organization of American Historians Annual Meeting, Reno, Nevada, March 1988. Eileen Boris's book in progress on industrial home work and Vivien Hart's forthcoming book about the origins of minimum wage policies in the United Kingdom and the United States create a substantial portrait of this important and understudied piece of basic labor legislation. In addition to Ronnie Steinberg's important analytic account in *Wages and Hours*, a sparse historical account is given in Matthew Josephson's *Sidney Hillman: Statesman of American Labor* (Garden City, N.Y.: Doubleday, 1952). Chapter 19, "Lobbying: 1938," tells of Hillman's influence in achieving adoption of the FLSA.
39.   Phyllis Palmer, "Outside the Law," paper presented at the Organization of American Historians Annual Meeting, Reno, Nevada, March 1988.
40.   Steinberg, *Wages and Hours*, tables 4.8 and 4.9, 98–99.
41.   Baer, *Chains of Protection*, 89.
42.   Steinberg, *Wages and Hours*, provides the data for a state–federal, male–female comparison, even though she does not comment on the differential financial advantage of overtime over maximum hours regulations. Veronica Beechey, *Unequal Work* (London: Verso, 1987), chap. 9, "The Shape of the Workforce to Come," describes different preferences for overtime between contemporary men and women workers in the United Kingdom. Her findings that men like overtime as a way to increase their pay, while women want to be able to leave work earlier in the day, presumably because of the need to do house-related tasks, indicates that government pay and hour policies fit men's desires and patterns of work better than women's. Men want more pay on long hours; women want flexible hours and benefits across multiple jobs.
43.   Memo to the Presidents of Local Associations from Mrs. Kendall Emerson, Chairman of Public Affairs Committee, National Board, YWCA, October 23, 1933, YWCA MSS, Box 43, Sophia Smith Collection. A letter to Eleanor Roosevelt, November 1933, asking her to take even more visible leadership in publicizing a voluntary code, was signed by the NCHE; Brooklyn Catholic Big Sisters; Child Development Institute, Teachers College, Columbia University; Joint Committee on National Recovery Committee, Federal Council of Churches; National Association for the Advancement of Colored People; National Board, YWCA; National Consumers League; New Jersey Urban League; New York Consumers' League; New York State Employment Service; Philadelphia Council of Household Occupations; Women's Bureau, U.S. Department of Labor; and Women's Trade Union League (NA RG 86, Box 1717).
44.   Program Planning Committee, National Board, YWCA, minutes of meeting on household employment, November 26, 1940, noted that Jean Collier Brown had visited nine associations nationwide: "In one community the chairman of the board had been very much against her coming to speak to the girls but the girls had been so determined to hear her that she had gone anyway and been able to clarify the situation considerably before leaving" (YWCA National Board MSS, Reel 118.6).

45.   National Committee on Household Employment, *Bulletin* 4 (January 1936), NCHE MSS, Box 5.

46.   Reported by Jean Collier Brown, "Brief on Household Employment in Relation to Trade Union Organization" (1938), 9, prepared for the Leadership Division, National Board, YWCA, typescript, YWCA National Board MSS, Reel 98.5, "Unions, 1934–1938." "The Joint Job in the Home: Reports from Y.W.C.A.'s on Household Employment," *Woman's Press* 28 (May 1934): 252–53, gives accounts of projects in Denver, Tulsa, Chicago, Buffalo, Madison, Detroit, Seattle, Minneapolis, and Houston. Madge P. Pennel, "Richmond's Household Experiment," *Woman's Press* 28 (March 1934): 130–31, describes Richmond's efforts to draw up and establish codes. "Building of Public Opinion for Creating Better Standards in Household Employment," NCHE *Bulletin* (December 1934), NCHE MSS, Box 5.

47.   Emily L. Warrick, Richmond, to "Dear Association Workers," November 21, 1933, YWCA MSS, Box 45, Sophia Smith Collection.

48.   Alice Henry, Athens, Georgia, to E. Christman, NWTUL, August 23, 1927. In a letter headed "Southern Impressions," organizer Henry reported, "The first thing that impresses the northern visitor, and the last thing is that he is living in another country, a resident of another nation. . . . I am wondering how far you have progressed with your preparatory work in the South. The color question you will not be touching at present" (NWTUL MSS, Box 2, Folder 10, Schlesinger Archives).

49.   "The Joint Job in the Home," 253.

50.   Jesse Daniel Ames, Atlanta, Georgia, to Mary Anderson, November 21, 1933, NA RG 86, Box 927.

51.   Mrs. Kendall Emerson to the Presidents of Local Associations, October 23, 1933, YWCA MSS, Box 43, Sophia Smith Collection.

52.   *Household Employment Problems: A Handbook for Round-Table Discussions Among Household Employers*, issued by U.S. Department of the Interior, Office of Education, Vocational Division (September 1937), 12.

53.   Chicago Committee on Household Employment, "Fair and Clear in the Home," *Woman's Press* 29 (April 1935): 173.

54.   Numerous requests for model domestic work contracts are in NCHE MSS, Box 1, File 29. These were written to the NCHE in response to an article by Dorothy Wells, "Raising Standards of Household Employment," *Employment Service News* 1 (August 1935).

55.   "A Voluntary Agreement in Household Employment," proposed by the National Council on Household Employment, Chicago Affiliate, Committee on Household Employment of the Young Women's Christian Association, n.d., NA RG 86, Box 923.

56.   "Wages, Hours and Working Conditions of Domestic Employees in Connecticut," *Monthly Labor Review* 43 (December 1936): 1509–13.

57.   Lorna May Tuttle, Industrial Secretary, Minneapolis, to Dorothy L. Hubbard, March 7, 1934, National Board YWCA MSS, Reel 97.

58.   *Household Employment Problems*, 36, 44–45.

59.   Quoted on cover, NCHE *Bulletin* 2 (February 1935), in NAACP MSS, Box C322, "Labor-General, 3/3–4/22, 1935," LC.

60.   "The Perfect Treasure," *Junior League Magazine* 20 (February 1934): 85.

61.   Katherine R. Van Slyck to Emma H. Gunther, May 7, 1937, NCHE MSS, Box 1, Folder 32; Alice MacDonald, "Housework, the Feudal Occupation" (March 1941):

38–39; "Do You Know Your Place?" (April 1941): 28, 62; "Where Do We Go from Here?" (May 1941): 50, 70, all in *Junior League Magazine* 27. In anticipation of the approaching war, MacDonald warned that housewives must treat domestic workers fairly: "It is the only basis on which citizens of a free democracy should wish to run their homes" (April 1941): 62.

62.   "Proposals for Organization of Household Workers Union," prepared by Dorothy L. Hubbard, January 1935, NWTUL MSS, Box 3, Folder 25, Schlesinger Archives; Brown, "Brief on Household Employment," 3.

63.   "Discussion of Voluntary Agreement," led by Selma Armenheimer, National Convention, YWCA, n.d., NA RG 86, Box 926.

64.   Heywood Broun, "Like One of the Family," *Nation*, May 29, 1935, p. 631.

65.   "The Need of Organization Among Household Employees," Negro Workers' Council [of the National Urban League], Workers' Council Bulletin 16 (May 28, 1937), 4, 5, 7; Resolution passed at Chicago meeting, National Negro Congress, February 1936, YWCA MSS, Box 40, Sophia Smith Collection.

66.   Gene Nicholson, Organizer President, Domestic Employees Club, to Benjamin R. Andrews, Acting Chairman, NCHE, October 15, 1934, NWTUL MSS, Box 2, Folder 24. Nicholson pointed out that domestics were discouraged from attending union meetings by their employers' prejudices and that "union" was equated with "strike," which was not feasible and "repels the good type member, and attracts the less stable, who merely want to get even."

67.   Mary Ford, Local 139 President, to Julia Brown, YWCA, June 18, 1936, YWCA National Board MSS, Reel 98.5.

68.   "Brief on Household Employment in Relation to Trade Union Organization," 13–15, typescripts, prepared by Jean Brown for the Leadership Division, National Board, YWCA, 1938, NWTUL MSS, Box 3, Folder 25; "Household Occupation in the District of Columbia," 8, typescript, circulated by the Washington League of Women Shoppers [1940–1941], NCHE MSS, Box 6.

69.   Jean Collier Brown, *Program with Household Workers in the Y.W.C.A.* (New York: Woman's Press, 1941), 138. Brown did not name the union leader.

70.   "Proposals for Organization of Household Workers Union," 1.

71.   Gene Nicholson to Benjamin R. Andrews, October 15, 1934, NWTUL MSS, Box 2, Folder 24.

72.   Raymond C. Atkinson, Louise C. Odencrantz, and Ben Deming, *Public Employment Service in the United States* (Chicago: Public Administration Service for the Committee on Public Administration of the Social Science Research Council, 1940), v.

73.   Ibid., 34–35. Table 5, "Industrial Analysis of Private Placements Made by State Employment Services and the National Reemployment Service, July 1, 1933, to June 30, 1937," shows that in 1933–1934, of 1,305,873 jobs filled in private, nongovernmental employment by the Services, 342,213 (the largest number and 26.2 percent of placements) were in domestic and personal service. In 1936–1937, of 2,100,606 placements, 740,762 (35.3 percent) were in domestic and personal service jobs, down from 40.3 percent of placements in 1935–1936.

74.   Karen Anderson, *Wartime Women: Sex Roles, Family Relations, and the Status of Women During World War II*, Contributions in Women's Studies, 20 (Westport, Conn.: Greenwood Press, 1981), 34.

75.   "The Joint Job in the Home," 253; NCHE *Bulletin* (December 1934): 2, NCHE MSS, Box 5.

76. "Proposed Federal Legislation of Concern to Household Employees," 1935, lists hours and wages legislation for women pending in California, Connecticut, the District of Columbia, Illinois, Maryland, Massachusetts, Montana, New Hampshire, North Dakota, Pennsylania, Washington, and West Virginia. Only in California, Pennsylvania, and Washington did the legislative language not exclude domestic service in private homes (YWCA MSS, Box 43, Sophia Smith Collection).
77. Anna Roosevelt Boettiger, "Setting the Kitchen Clock Right," *Woman's Press* 32 (November 1938): 480–81; "Household Employment—A Study Outline," 57, typescript, NA RG 86, Box 561, later printed as *Household Employment: An Outline for Study Groups* (Washington, D.C.: Women's Bureau, 1940).
78. "Household Employment—A Study Outline," 52–54.
79. Cara Cook, *Help Wanted* (New York: New York Women's Trade Union League, 1939); "Household Employment—A Study Outline," 58–62.
80. Brown, *Concerns of Household Workers*, 97; Alice Keliher, *Household Workers* (New York: Harper & Brothers, 1941), 56.
81. Walter White, NAACP, Postal Telegraph to Hon. Franklin D. Roosevelt, February 6, 1935, NAACP MSS, Box C-406, File Soc. Sec., 1/17–2/20, 1935, "Board of Director Minutes," 2/11/35, Box C-2.
82. Henry Morgenthau, Jr., to Walter White, February 13, 1935, NAACP MSS, Box C-406, File Soc. Sec., 1/17–2/20, 1935.
83. "Memorandum on Discriminations Under the Federal Social Security Act," October 22, 1937, NAACP MSS, Box C-406, Soc. Sec. 6/5–11/17, 1937.
84. Erna Magnus, "Coverage of Domestic Workers by Social Insurance, 1939," NCHE MSS, Box 6. Magnus found that 30 percent of Georgia Old Age Assistance recipients in 1938 were former domestics; in California 39 percent of the total and 80 percent of the female recipients were in that category. Black recipients were heavily concentrated in Alabama, Florida, Georgia, Louisiana, Maryland, Mississippi, and South Carolina, and Magnus assumed that 50 percent of these were women, most of whom had worked as domestics. She concluded that blacks were overrepresented and that there was a "large over-representation of [domestics] among all old age assistance recipients" (pp. 20–22).
85. Jerry A. Cates, *Insuring Inequality: Administrative Leadership in Social Security, 1934–54* (Ann Arbor: University of Michigan Press, 1983), provides a lucid account of the ideologies of leading bureaucrats who designed the Social Security system and especially the commitment to holding down the size of a needs-based assistance program in favor of a job-linked entitlement. Using the metaphor of insurance enabled the planners to popularize the idea that Social Security retirement income recompensed a lifetime of work whereas Old Age Assistance charitably assisted those who had not worked enough or in the right job to accumulate benefits.
86. U.S. Congress, House of Representatives, Committee on Ways and Means, *Hearings Relative to the Social Security Act Amendments of 1939*, rev. print, 67th Cong., 1st sess., 1: rev. 5–6.
87. "Statement of William Hodson, Commissioner of Welfare, New York City," and "Statement of Mrs. Harris T. Baldwin, First Vice President, National League of Women Voters," ibid., 2:1319, 1377. Though states could budget as much as $30 per old person, many states did not. "In November 1938, 34 states had old-age assistance grants of $20 a month or less and 8 of these had grants averaging less than $10 a month," according to John P. Davis, National Negro Congress, ibid., 1545.

88.   Ibid., 1:5.

89.   Ibid., 7, 11.

90.   Statement of John P. Davis, National Negro Congress, ibid., 2:1543; Sylvia A. Law, "Women, Work, Welfare, and the Preservation of Patriarchy," *Pennsylvania Law Review* 131 (May 1983): 1249–1339, esp. 1254–61. Law cites *Anderson* v. *Burson*, 300 F. Supp. 401 (N.D. Ga., 1968), which held that "a presumption that field work was available for all 'appropriate,' that is to say black women, during cotton-chopping season was . . . unconstitutional." She cites a Report of the Mississippi State Advisory Committee to the U.S. Commission on Civil Rights, *Welfare in Mississippi* (n.p., February 1969), 31, which reported "case worker assertions that 'negro mothers always had farmed out their children to neighbors and relatives. . . . Therefore, . . . child care plans were not . . . a problem'" (p. 1258). These examples are from the 1960s and are taken by Law to represent practices that had persisted since the late 1930s.

91.   Julia Kirk Blackwelder, *Women of the Depression: Caste and Culture in San Antonio, 1929–1939* (College Station: Texas A&M University Press, 1984), 68–69.

92.   Only representatives from the YWCA and the National Negro Congress actually testified during the hearings, but the National League of Women Shoppers lobbied the committee and, along with the National Consumers League, the Women's Trade Union League, the Philadelphia Institute of Household Occupations, and the Newark Domestic Workers Union, requested time to testify. Nina P. Collier, National Legislative Chairman, League of Women Shoppers, to Honorable Robert L. Doughton, Chairman, House Ways and Means Committee, March 16, 1939, NWTUL MSS, Box 3, Folder 26.

93.   *Washington Post*, March 18, 21, 1939; U.S. Congress, *Hearings Relative to the Social Security Act Amendments of 1939*, rev. print, 1:1489, 1509–11; "Statement of Dr. Edwin E. Witte, Formerly Executive Director, President's Committee on Economic Security," Saturday, March 18, 1939, ibid., 2:1773–74.

94.   Erna Magnus, "Negro Domestic Workers in Private Homes in Baltimore," *Social Security Bulletin* 4 (October 1941): 3.

95.   Jean Collier Brown, "S.O.S. for Social Security," Division of Community Y.W.C.A.'s, National Board YWCA, 1941, YWCA MSS, Box 43, Sophia Smith Collection.

96.   "Committee on Workmen's Compensation for Household Employees," letterhead and correspondence in NCHE MSS, Box 1, Folder 43.

Seven

1.   Papers from the 1982 Barnard Scholar and the Feminist Conference, "Towards a Politics of Sexuality," ed. Carole S. Vance, in *Pleasure and Danger: Exploring Female Sexuality* (London: Routledge & Kegan Paul, 1984), have an implicit theme of what sex is acceptable to feminists. The problem that women feel "bad" because of their sexual proclivities is addressed explicitly in Muriel Dimen's "Politically Correct? Politically Incorrect?" and Dorothy Allison's "Public Silence, Private Terror."

2.   Mary Douglas's classic *Purity and Danger: An Analysis of Concepts of Pollution and Taboo* (London: Routledge & Kegan Paul, 1966) argues "that our ideas of dirt . . . express symbolic systems" and are not simply the consequence of hygienic

discoveries by science. Certainly historians can record changing notions of dirt, but Douglas adds that these notions reflect social arrangements of power and subordination and of goodness and badness and not simply progressive improvements in sanitation and scientific knowledge. Indeed, the current level of destructive world pollution should banish residual Enlightenment faith that science inevitably cleanses and heals.

3. Richard L. Bushman and Claudia L. Bushman, "The Early History of Cleanliness in America," *Journal of American History* 74 (March 1988): 1213–38, begins to tackle such issues, mainly through looking at bathing practices and the growth of soap manufacture during the nineteenth century. Cleanliness as a problem of sanitation has received some study, notably in Martin V. Melosi's excellent collection, *Pollution and Reform in American Cities, 1870–1930* (Austin: University of Texas Press, 1980). These pieces provide fascinating data about changing cleanliness practices but generally give a progressive interpretation of what these innovations mean.

4. Winthrop D. Jordan, *White Over Black: American Attitudes Toward the Negro, 1550–1812* (1968; rpt. Baltimore: Penguin Books, 1969), esp. chap. 4, "Fruits of Passion: The Dynamics of Interracial Sex," and chap. 11, "Thomas Jefferson: Self and Society."

5. Sigmund Freud, *New Introductory Lectures on Psychoanalysis,* trans. James Strachey (New York: Norton, 1965), 101; Sigmund Freud, *Civilization and Its Discontents,* trans. James Strachey (New York: Norton, 1962), says, "The incitement to cleanliness originates in an urge to get rid of the excreta, which have become disagreeable to the sense perceptions. We know that in the nursery things are different. . . . [The excreta] seem valuable to [children] as being part of their own body which has come away from it" (p. 47). I applied the Freudian understanding of dirt to the study of Victorian gentleman Arthur J. Munby's fascination with working women and his marriage to a domestic servant in Phyllis Marynick Palmer, "Domesticity and Dirt," in Harvey J. Graff and Paul Monaco, eds., *Quantification and Psychology: Toward a 'New' History* (Washington, D.C.: University Press of America, 1980), 258–93.

6. Joel Kovel, *White Racism: A Psychohistory* (1970; rpt. New York: Vintage Books, 1971), upholds the universality of psychoanalytic principles of love and aggression but argues that these may take many different forms, of which the development of the Western psyche during the period of capitalist expansion was a notably harmful one. Chapter 7, "The Psycho-Historical Matrix," argues that increased detachment from the body and harshly rational superego control of the libidinous self were essential elements in the success of capitalism. People had to learn to control impulse, rationalize work, and produce obsessively. Simultaneously, they found satisfaction for repressed erotic impulses in acquiring money and consuming the goods produced by their enlarged ability to organize resources, labor, and commercial exchange. These trends have continued to intensify from the eighteenth to the twentieth centuries, so that now we must produce more efficiently, find our sensual satisfactions in consumption of the goods produced, and repress more firmly "disgusting aspects of the world," notably our infantile, sensual selves (p. 159). Kovel connects this splitting of self into rational producer and deprived sensualist with the peculiarly harsh form of Western slavery, a system built on racism heightened by shame and fear of the repressed physical self and its identification with dark skins and people of color.

7.   Freud, *Civilization and Its Discontents*, states, "Women represent the interests of the family and of sexual life. The work of civilization has become increasingly
the business of men, it confronts them with ever more difficult tasks and compels
them to carry out instinctual sublimations of which women are little capable. Since a
man does not have unlimited quantities of physical energy at his disposal, he has to
accomplish his tasks by making an expedient distribution of his libido. What he em-
ploys for cultural aims he to a great extent withdraws from women and sexual life. His
constant association with men, and his dependence on his relations with them, even
estrange him from his duties as a husband and father. Thus the woman finds herself
forced into the background by the claims of civilization and she adopts a hostile attitude towards it" (pp. 50–51). Freud's equation of sexual temptation and the work of
the home is notable. In "Some Physical Consequences of the Anatomical Distinction
Between the Sexes," in *The Standard Edition of the Complete Psychological Works
of Sigmund Freud*, ed. James Strachey (London: Hogarth Press and the Institute of
Psycho-Analysis, 1961), 19:257, Freud concludes that "[women's] super-ego is never
so inexorable, so impersonal, so independent of its emotional origins as we require it
to be in men."

8.   Dorothy Dinnerstein, *The Mermaid and the Minotaur: Sexual Arrangements
and Human Malaise* (New York: Harper Colophon Books, 1976), posits that all
women are unconsciously experienced as connected with bodies and infancy because
women, and not men, provide the caretaking for small children. Nancy Chodorow,
The Reproduction of Mothering: Psychoanalysis and the Sociology of Gender (Berkeley and Los Angeles: University of California Press, 1978), explains how mothers
transmit attitudes of physical and emotional connectedness in relations with daughters. Jane Flax, "The Conflict Between Nurturance and Autonomy in Mother-
Daughter Relationships and Within Feminism," *Feminist Studies* 4 (Summer 1978):
171–89, usefully shows how the tensions over connectedness and autonomy persist
in adult women's relationships.

9.   Lillian Smith, *Killers of the Dream* (1961; rpt. New York: Norton, 1978), describes how children in the American South learned in racial terms the lesson of splitting mother from servant: "Before the ego has gained strength, just as he is reaching
out to make his first ties with the human family, this small white child learns to love
both mother and nurse; he is never certain whom he loves better. . . . Yet before he
knows words, he dimly perceives that his white mother has priority over his colored
mother, that somehow he 'belongs' more to her. . . . [H]is conscience, as it grows in
him, ties its allegiance to [his white mother] and to the white culture and authority
which she and his father represent. But to the colored mother, persuasive in her re-
laxed attitude toward 'sin,' easy and warm in her physical ministrations, generous
with her petting, he ties his pleasure feelings. . . . He accords his mother the esteem
and respect that are hers; he feels more and more a pulling obligation to her, . . . and
after a time, he feels that he 'owes' her so much that he steals the adoration which he
had conferred upon his colored mother long ago, and returns it to his white mother as
rightfully hers" (pp. 131–33).

10.   Clara M. Thompson, "Some Effects of the Derogatory Attitude Toward Female
Sexuality," in *On Women*, ed. Maurice R. Green (New York: New American Library,
Meridian Book, 1986), 151.

11.   Jane Flax, "Remembering the Self: Is the Repressed Gendered?" *Michigan
Quarterly Review* 26 (Winter 1987): 92–110, movingly analyzes the effects of these

splits and ambivalences about power and dependency within each woman's psyche. Women experience feelings of autonomy, the development of autonomous selves, as guilt-provoking and repress impulses to power and desire. I would add that these are felt as "dirty" impulses.

12.   John D'Emilio and Estelle B. Freedman, *Intimate Matters: A History of Sexuality in America* (New York: Harper & Row, 1988), conclude, "In contrast to the exaggerated protection of white women's virtue and the containment of female sexuality within marital, reproductive relations, southern white men of the planter class enjoyed extreme sexual privilege [so long as they gratified lust] discreetly with poor white or black women" (p. 95). See also Milton Rugoff, *Prudery & Passion: Sexuality in Victorian America* (London: Rupert Hart-Davis, 1971).

13.   Steven Marcus, *The Other Victorians: A Study of Sexuality and Pornography in Mid-Nineteenth Century England* (London: Weidenfeld and Nicolson, 1966), 129.

14.   Jacquelyn Dowd Hall, "'The Mind That Burns in Each Body': Women, Rape, and Racial Violence," and Barbara Omolade, "Hearts of Darkness," in Ann Snitow, Christine Stansell, and Sharon Thompson, eds., *Powers of Desire: The Politics of Sexuality* (New York: Monthly Review Press, 1983), 328–49, 350–67. Hall and Omolade point out that the system of sexual dualism harmed both white women and black; white women because they had to restrain themselves to appear unaware of erotic feeling and black women because they experienced their sexuality in relations of domination and threat. Peter T. Cominos, "Innocent Femina Sensualis in Unconscious Conflict," in Martha Vicinus, ed., *Suffer and Be Still: Women in the Victorian Age* (Bloomington: Indiana University Press, 1972), 155–72, points out that all women were believed to have latent depravity; only ignorance and inexperience kept the good woman from uncovering and acting on her base impulses. By the end of the century, ignorance was seen as inadequate; the good woman had to know her potential and consciously choose not to exercise it.

15.   Peter Gay, *The Bourgeois Experience, Victoria to Freud*, Vol. 1, *The Education of the Senses* (New York: Oxford University Press, 1984), says, "No century depicted woman as vampire, as castrator, as killer so consistently, so programmatically, and so nakedly as the nineteenth" (p. 207).

16.   Ben Barker-Benfield, "The Spermatic Economy: A Nineteenth-Century View of Sexuality," in Michael Gordon, ed., *The American Family in Social-Historical Perspective* (New York: St. Martin's Press, 1973), 336–72. Barker-Benfield notes American men's anxiety about "place" in a country with a fluid economy, politics, and statuses, and how this anxiety took the form of controlling nature, perceived as female, and women, perceived as natural and uncontrollable. Only by taming women could men save their energies from sexual temptation and exercise the discipline necessary to tame nature.

17.   Gay, *Bourgeois Experience*, chap. 6, p. 3, "The Democratization of Comfort."

18.   Nancy F. Cott, "Passionlessness: An Interpretation of Victorian Sexual Ideology, 1790–1850," in Nancy F. Cott and Elizabeth H. Pleck, eds., *A Heritage of Her Own: Toward a New Social History of American Women* (New York: Simon and Schuster, 1979).

19.   Evelyn Fox Keller, *Reflections on Gender and Science* (New Haven: Yale University Press, 1985), describes in chap. 3, "Spirit and Reason at the Birth of Modern Science," how the development of modern science in the seventeenth century confirmed male potency and domination over the natural world and required and co-

incided with reducing nature to "its mechanical substrate" and woman "to her asexual virtue" (p. 64). For women, of course, the male–female dichotomy overlaid on the reason–emotion dichotomy raised the fear that they could never attain to the reason men possessed, the male-linked trait that became the measure of human virtue during the Enlightenment. Asexuality held out the hope that at least women could control themselves enough to enable their reason and humanity to develop.

20.   Clifford Edward Clark, Jr., *The American Family Home, 1800–1960* (Chapel Hill: University of North Carolina Press, 1986), chap. 2, "Dreams and Realities," 42.

21.   Leonore Davidoff, *The Best Circles: Society Etiquette and the Season* (London: Croom Helm, 1973), 115, n.9.

22.   Leonore Davidoff, "Class and Gender in Victorian England: The Diaries of Arthur J. Munby and Hannah Cullwick," *Feminist Studies* 5 (Spring 1979): 86–141, argues that "the sheltered lives that middle-class ladies were ideally supposed to lead depended directly on the labor or working-class girls and women, who through their services created the material conditions necessary to maintain a middle-class lifestyle for men and women alike" (p. 130).

23.   Dale T. Knobel, *Paddy and the Republic: Ethnicity and Nationality in Antebellum America* (Middletown, Conn.: Wesleyan University Press, 1986), in chap. 3, "An Irishman by Nature," documents the tendency to see "differences between ethnic groups as matters of 'race,' as immutable characteristics traceable to prehistory" (p. 89).

24.   Jordan, *White Over Black*, esp. chaps. 4 and 12.

25.   Dinnerstein, *The Mermaid and the Minotaur*, clarifies that women's being experienced in infancy as overpowering leads both men and women to equate the rational, the intellectual, and the self-controlled with men. See especially chap. 9, "Mama and the Mad Megamachine." Kovel's *White Racism* is a meditation on how denial of the body and despising dark races is the underside of calculation and capitalist expansion during the eighteenth and nineteenth centuries.

26.   Keller, *Reflections on Gender and Science*, points out the persistence of dualisms of "mind and nature, reason and feeling, masculine and feminine," though she warns that these are not "historically invariant" but change in different historical periods (p. 44). See also Sheila Ruth, "Bodies and Souls/Sex, Sin and the Senses in Patriarchy: A Study in Applied Dualism," *Hypatia* 2 (Winter 1987): 149–64.

27.   D'Emilio and Freedman, *Intimate Matters*, 262.

28.   Doris Davenport, "The Pathology of Racism: A Conversation with Third World Wimmin," in Cherríe Moraga and Gloria Anzaldua, eds., *This Bridge Called My Back: Writings by Radical Women of Color* (Watertown, Mass.: Persephone Press, 1981), 88.

29.   Sandra Lee Bartky, "Narcissism, Femininity and Alienation," *Social Theory and Practice* 8 (1982): 127–43, makes the point about women's narcissism as a form of alienation, since women internalize male and commercial viewpoints of beauty and learn to assess themselves constantly by this alien standard. Succeeding may be pleasurable, but it is also repressive because it ties women to systems of male and capitalistic domination of women's sense of self-worth. Kim Chernin's *The Obsession: Reflections on the Tyranny of Slenderness* (New York: Harper Colophon Books, 1982) is one of many feminist books about women's hating and abusing their bodies. Chernin notes that the abuse of slenderness is a particularly upper-middle-class phenomenon that is a problem of especially "good girls." She also implicitly recognizes the connec-

tions between abuse of the body through food and sex: "Is it possible," she asks, "that we today worry about eating and weight the way our foremothers and their doctors worried about women's sexuality?" (p. 94). I would say yes, and, moreover, it is the same worry about women's being physically powerful and flaunting their bodies instead of making them invisible.

30.   Ann Barr Snitow, "Mass Market Romance: Pornography for Women Is Different," in Snitow, Stansell, and Thompson, eds., *Powers of Desire*, 245–63; and Sharon Thompson, "Search for Tomorrow: On Feminism and the Reconstruction of Teen Romance," in Vance, ed., *Pleasure and Danger*, 350–84. That lesbian women suffer the same internal divisions and have turned them into political positions is made painfully clear in Dorothy Allison's "Public Silence, Private Terror," ibid., 103–14.

31.   "Women, Jobs, and Children: A New Generation Worries," *New York Times*, November 27, 1988, p. A30, reports on a meeting of a women's support group at the Stanford University Business School at which a married woman with a child told current students about her daily life. "'She mentioned that she had changed 16 diapers the day before,'" the group's leader said, "'and I thought everybody was going to run out and get their tubes tied.'"

Afterword

1.   Mrs. Shelby Cullom Davis, "Household Servants Are Gone Forever," *American Magazine*, March 1945, pp. 32–33, 89–92, and condensed in *Reader's Digest* 46 (April 1945): 76–78.

2.   "Information on Domestic Service," 1, typescript, prepared for discussion purposes by staff members, Women's Bureau, November 1944, in Hattie Hyland Smith MSS, Box 4, Folder 22, Schlesinger Archives; Ethel Josephine Payne, *Community Household Employment Programs*, Bulletin 221 (Washington, D.C.: U.S. Women's Bureau, 1948), 9.

3.   *Household Employment: A Digest of Current Information* (Washington, D.C.: U.S. Women's Bureau, 1946), 46–51, lists eighty-eight courses nationwide (in Alabama, Arkansas, California, Georgia, Indiana, Kansas, Kentucky, Michigan, Mississippi, Missouri, New York, North Carolina, Ohio, Oklahoma, Tennessee, Texas, and Virginia), of which twelve were for white students.

4.   "St. Louis 'Calls Back' the Domestic," "Akron's Plan," and "Household Employment in Detroit," *Employment Service Review* 13 (November 1946): 8–13.

5.   Frieda S. Miller, Director, Women's Bureau, "New Approaches to Old Problems of Domestic Service or Servicing the Home," typescript of article for *New York Times*, July 1, 1946, p. 9, Frieda Segelke Miller MSS, Box 13, Folder 270, Schlesinger Archives. Miller quoted from the Presbyterian church women's pamphlet, "Martha in the Modern Age" (Philadelphia: Presbyterian Church—U.S.A., 1945).

6.   Vera Woods, "Bulletin on Household Employment," September 16, 1946, p. 8, typescript, YWCA National Board MSS, Reel 98.5; "Akron's Plan," *Employment Service Review* 13 (November 1946): 12.

7.   U.S. Congress, Senate, Committee on Finance, *Social Security Act Amendments of 1950: Report to Accompany H.R. 6000*, 81st Cong., 2d sess., 6. As of January 1955, the 24-days-of-work restriction was dropped. Emphasis on covering only

full-time or regular part-time workers meant that many domestic day workers would continue to be ineligible for Social Security coverage in their housework jobs, even though they might have to pay taxes as they revolved into covered jobs in commercial cleaning or restaurant work. The fact that many domestics had paid (and do pay) Social Security taxes in commercial jobs without working in those jobs long enough to get vested in the system may explain their reluctance to pay those taxes. It is a protection that seems elusive, even when one has made contributions.

8.   *Unemployment Insurance Coverage of Household Workers in New York State,* Research Bulletin 1969, No. 10 (Albany: New York State Department of Labor, Division of Employment, September 1969), 3; U.S. Congress, Senate Committee on Finance, *Unemployment Compensation Amendments of 1976, Hearings on H.R. 10210,* September 8 and 9, 1976, 94th Cong. 2nd sess. (Washington, D.C.: U.S. Government Printing Office, 1976), 213, 225.

9.   Miller, "New Approaches to Old Problems of Domestic Service," 3.

10.   Barbara Haber, "Is Personal Life Still a Political Issue?" *Feminist Studies* 5 (Fall 1979): 417–31, asks what happened to women's liberation demands for sharing housework and childrearing and looks at the failure of collective solutions and the retreat to heterosexual, coupled households.

11.   Zillah Eisenstein, "Anti-Feminism in the Politics and Election of 1980," *Feminist Studies* 7 (Summer 1981): 187–205; Rosalind Pollack Petchesky, "Antiabortion, Antifeminism, and the Rise of the New Right," *Feminist Studies* 7 (Summer 1981): 206–46.

12.   Elliott Currie, Robert Dunn, and David Fogarty, "The New Immiseration: Stagflation, Inequality, and the Working Class," *Socialist Review* 59 (November–December 1980): 7–31, and Washington Area Marxist–Feminist Theory Study Group, "None Dare Call It Patriarchy: A Critique of 'The New Immiseration,'" *Socialist Review* 61 (January–February 1982): 105–12, the former an example of the Left's appeal to family values and the latter a feminist critique of upholding images of family that ignore women's situation as housekeepers and low-wage workers.

13.   Mary Romero, "Domestic Service in the Transition from Rural to Urban Life: The Case of La Chicana," *Women's Studies* 13 (1987): 199–222; Mary Romero, "Day Work in Suburbs: The Work Experience of Chicana Private Housekeepers," in Anne Statham, Eleanor M. Miller, and Hans O. Mauksche, eds., *The Worth of Women's Work: A Qualitative Synthesis* (Albany: State University of New York Press, 1987); Mary Romero, "Chicanas Modernize Domestic Service," 1987, typescript. I am deeply grateful to Mary Romero, Evelyn Glenn, Shellee Colen, Joan Anderson, and Judith Rollins, my co-panelists, for a memorable presentation, "The Intersection of Class, Gender, and Race: North American Women of Color in Domestic Service," at the National Women's Studies Association Annual Meeting, Spelman College, Atlanta, June 1987.

14.   Judith Stacey, "The New Conservative Feminism," *Feminist Studies* 9 (Fall 1983): 559–84, analyzes the crisis of consciousness even among feminists, who fear the loss of caring values when women adopt men's professions and life paths.

15.   *Washington Post Food,* June 1, 1988, pp. E1, 12

Index

Adkins v. *Children's Hospital,* 115
Afro-American women: in domestic service, 6, 12–13, 67–68, 69, 86, 182 n.4; in domestic worker unions, 126; employer attitudes toward, as domestics, 61, 74, 84; families of, as domestic workers, 12–13, 70, 183 n.8; and New Deal, 100, 104, 108, 109, 119–21; as sexual objects, 203 nn.12,14; and training in home economics, 94–95, 97, 98–99, 101; and treatment under Social Security Act, 131, 132–33, 199 n.84, 200 n.90; in YWCA, 120, 123
Aging. *See* Beauty
Allen, Ida Bailey, 17–18, 23
Altmeyer, Arthur, 131
Ambrose Holt and Family (Susan Glaspell), 34–35
American Association of University Women (AAUW): and members as domestic service employers, 8, 180 n.61; and work to improve domestic service, 125
American Federation of Labor (AFL). *See* Labor unions
"American girl," 21
American Home Economics Association (AHEA), 90, 116, 132; and adoption of vocational education laws, 92–93

American Indian women: in domestic service, 6, 12, 67, 68, 70, 182 n.3; and home economics, 97
Ames, Jessie Daniel, 123–24
Anderson, Mary, 77, 80, 116, 117, 120, 123–24
Andrews, Benjamin, 52, 116, 122
Andrews, Dana, 31, 38
Another Thin Man, 19, 31, 37
Armstrong, Samuel Chapman, 94
Asian-American. *See* Chinese-American domestics; Japanese-American domestics
Atlanta, Ga., 72, 84, 124, 126

Bailey, Beth L., 38
Baltimore, Md., 83, 86, 108, 115, 120, 126, 129, 133, 134, 181 n.71, 183 n.8
Barberry Bush (Kathleen Norris), 23–24
Baylor, Adelaide, 95
Beauty, 137; denial of aging and, 149–50; and exercise, 33; as female obsession, 204 n.29; of home, 27; as requirement for wives, 23, 33, 56, 137, 148, 150; of wife, and cosmetics, 36
Beavers, Louise, 40
Berlin, Mrs. Irving, 134
Bernstein, Irving, 119
Bethune, Mary McLeod, 108